M

Authorizing Words

Authorizing Words

Speech, Writing, and Print in the English Renaissance

MARTIN ELSKY

Cornell University Press

ITHACA AND LONDON

Publication of this book was supported in part by a grant from the
CUNY Research Foundation.

First published 1989 by Cornell University Press.

International Standard Book Number 0-8014-2173-X
Library of Congress Catalog Card Number 89-42875
Printed in the United States of America
Librarians: Library of Congress cataloging information
appears on the last page of the book.

⊗ The paper used in this publication meets the minimum requirements of
the American National Standard for Permanence of Paper for Printed
Library Materials Z39.48–1984.

To the memory of my parents
and to Harriet, Stephanie,
Julia, and Elaine

Contents

Acknowledgments

My thanks for the guidance and friendship of my teachers and colleagues Edward W. Tayler, James V. Mirollo, and Lawrence V. Hyman are greater than can be expressed here. To Joseph A. Mazzeo I am indebted for my interest in Bacon. I would not have been able to write this book without the support of my colleagues Neil Schaeffer and Thomas Mermall. I owe special thanks to Ernest Gilman for his invaluable advice, especially on matters related to Renaissance hieroglyphics. Many important suggestions were made by those who read this work, either in whole or in part, while it was still in manuscript, including Cathy Eden, Stanley Fish, Sid Leiman, Timothy Murray, Ted-Larry Pebworth, John Shawcross, and Claude Summers. I thank Martin Dodsworth and Nicholaus Kiessling for generously opening their research on Robert Burton to me during a memorable stay in Oxford. I am also grateful to the Research Foundation of the City University of New York for its continuing and unstinting support of this project from its inception, and to the National Endowment for the Humanities for a Summer Stipend that helped me complete my work on Bacon. For their encouragement during this labor I thank Jerry Mermel, Virginia Hyman, and Roberta Chapey, and for her indefatigable help on the manuscript, I thank Martha Linke of Cornell University Press. Most of all I thank my family, Harriet, Stephanie, Julia, and Elaine.

Earlier drafts of several chapters of this book have already appeared in print. Chapter 3 is a revised and expanded version of "Words, Things, and Names: Jonson's Poetry and Philosophical Grammar," in *Classic and Cavalier: Essays on Jonson and the Sons of Ben,* ed. Claude J. Summers and Ted-Larry Pebworth (Pittsburgh: University of Pittsburgh Press, 1982), pp. 91–104. Chapter 6 draws on "George Herbert's Pattern Poems and the Materiality of Language: A New Approach to Renaissance Hieroglyphics," *ELH,* 50, no. 2 (1983), 245–60; and "Bacon's Hieroglyphs and the Separation of Words and Things," *Philological Quarterly,* 63, no. 4 (1984), 449–60. I am grateful to the journal editors and to the University of Pittsburgh Press for their kind permission to use this material. I am also grateful to the Pierpont Morgan Library and the British Library for their kind permission to reproduce photographs from, respectively, Aristotle, *Opera* (Venice, 1483), and Augustine, *Explanatio Psalmorum* (Naples, 1480).

MARTIN ELSKY

Brooklyn College, CUNY

Authorizing Words

Introduction

THE main subject of this book is the interplay of spoken and written language in Renaissance linguistic theory and in various Renaissance literary and nonliterary English texts, mostly of the early seventeenth century. By examining these works in different historical contexts, I attempt to apply the theoretical and practical insights of those critics and historians who see broad cultural implications in the ways speech and writing can be appropriated in a text. My analysis draws on materials from a wide variety of sources: logic manuals, grammar textbooks, treatises on language and philosophy, poetry, scientific prose, and personal correspondence.

I conceived of this project after reading Jacques Derrida's essay "Edmond Jabès and the Question of the Book," which provided a point of departure for examining the activity of writing as a determinant as much as a determinate of thought, though in the end I was unconverted to a more philological manner of proceeding.[1] Derrida of course presents one of the more celebrated contemporary accounts of the relationship between speech and writing. His deconstructive approach and its semiotic background are by now well known, and his influence appears to have reached its peak and perhaps even declined. I rehearse his notion of writing here only to distinguish it from

---

[1]Jacques Derrida, "Edmond Jabès and the Question of the Book," in *Writing and Difference*, tr. Alan Bass (Chicago: University of Chicago Press, 1978), pp. 64–78.

my own.[2] The philosophical context of Derrida's idea of writing is his attack on the autonomous subject and a metaphysically objective reality. He challenges these fundamental concepts by questioning the apparently innocent, commonsense notion that the mind's engagement with reality produces speech, and speech can be imitated by writing. Speech, according to this view, is the authentic reaction to reality, whereas writing is a weaker copy of speech, its decayed trace remaining in the absence of the speaker and thus having a more uncertain access to truths communicated *viva voce*. This relationship between speech and writing Derrida regards as the most pervasive perpetuator of the belief in the autonomous subject and objective reality.

Derrida replaces this view of speech and writing with a semiotic concept of language which undermines the primacy of speech over writing.[3] The consequences of this view of writing which have made the strongest impact on literary studies are that all language acts are contingent, resistant to closure, and lack an authorizing origin. There is, in short, no ultimate ground upon which to authorize the meaning of words. The view that language as writing can never achieve closure appears to be the most influential deconstructive idea in explaining Renaissance literary texts as well.[4]

Though such applications of the Derridean notion of writing have done much to transform Renaissance studies by arguing against a linear, univocal logic in the discourse of the period, the Derridean notion of writing does not tell us anything about the cultural relation-

[2]My account of Derrida's concept of writing is based primarily on *Of Grammatology*, tr. Gayatri Chakravorty Spivak (Baltimore: Johns Hopkins University Press, 1976). I am indebted to Jonathan Culler's introduction to the subject in *On Deconstruction: Theory and Criticism after Structuralism* (Ithaca: Cornell University Press, 1982), pp. 87–110.

[3]For the details of Derrida's use of Saussurean semiotics, see Culler, *On Deconstruction*, p. 96.

[4]See, e.g., David Quint, *Origin and Originality in Renaissance Literature: Versions of the Source* (New Haven: Yale University Press, 1983); Jonathan Goldberg, *Endlesse Worke: Spenser and the Structure of Discourse* (Baltimore: Johns Hopkins University Press, 1981); Patricia Parker, *Inescapable Romance: Studies in the Poetics of a Mode* (Princeton: Princeton University Press, 1979), and "Deferral, Dilation, Difference: Shakespeare, Cervantes, Jonson," in *Literary Theory/Renaissance Texts*, ed. Patricia Parker and David Quint (Baltimore: Johns Hopkins University Press, 1986), pp. 182–209; Gary F. Waller, "The Rewriting of Petrarch: Sidney and the Languages of Sixteenth-Century Poetry," in *Sir Philip Sidney and the Interpretation of Renaissance Culture: The Poet in His Time and Ours*, ed. Gary F. Waller and Michael D. Moore (Totowa, N.J.: Barnes & Noble, 1984), pp. 69–83.

ship of speech and writing as actual activities. Terence Cave, however, applies Derrida's semiotic notion of writing to Renaissance rhetorical theory and practice.[5] Some of his conclusions appear to me to be an inescapable consequence of the deconstructive critique of speech. He argues that Renaissance rhetoricians, in assuming that speech and language can be separated, were incapable of articulating a coherent theory of language. They were unable "to produce a coherent account of the relationship of language to 'world,' 'thought,' 'truth,'" and this inability, Cave continues, is indicative of humanism's historical crisis, "the fragmentation of the logos."[6] This crisis, however, is only a particularly poignant example of a transhistorical condition: Cave's approach denies the possibility of producing a coherent account of language altogether, at any time.

Although I agree with Cave that the humanists' elevation of speech depended on the dissemination of language in writing, I am especially opposed to the Derridean notions that language is at root incoherent and that the distinction between speech and writing is a duplicitous attempt to justify the autonomous subject and the objective world. Granted that theoretical formulations of any period, the Renaissance included, are contingent and bound to be replaced in succeeding epochs, the deconstructive certification that Renaissance language theory is incoherent and its attendant claim that speech is reducible to writing and writing to speech glosses over phenomena of major importance in the history of language and literature. The various explanations articulated in the Middle Ages and Renaissance of how language is authorized to mean—claims that language must be valorized by sheer thought or by speech or by writing—have significant consequences for literary culture, indeed for the very definition of a literary text itself. The deconstructive attempt to bury these distinctions beneath assertions of incoherence would render invisible concepts of great historical—and current—interest.

While deconstruction has been a powerful force highlighting the larger implications of focusing on the role of writing in thought, it has of course not been alone in emphasizing this issue. One approach that has been a direct influence on this book is the historical distinction

---

[5]Terence Cave, *The Cornucopian Text: Problems of Writing in the French Renaissance* (Oxford: Clarendon Press, 1979), pp. 132–56.

[6]Ibid., p. 157.

between speech and writing in the Renaissance "prose of the world" and seventeenth-century "classical" discourse, a distinction that Michel Foucault makes in *The Order of Things* and that Timothy J. Reiss skillfully adapts to literary study in *The Discourse of Modernism*.[7] The core conceptual framework of my approach is in many ways derived from Foucault's analysis of two historical models of language: written language on the one hand, spoken language on the other. Written language, though itself part of the world, is divinely ordained as a series of signs inherently connected to their referents; these written signs are the source of human speech, which must imitate them to be meaningful. Spoken language, uttered as the result of the contact of the mind with the world (Derrida's "presence"), expresses itself in sounds conventionally related to their referents and imitated in writing.

Although the distinction between these two ways of formulating the nature of language is central to my approach, I depart from Foucault on some key points. As many of his critics have objected, his concept of an *episteme*, the concept that all elements of knowledge are integrally interrelated in a given culture at a given time, is less than helpful. His argument that different *epistemes*, because they are total, are mutually exclusive, cannot be supported by historical evidence in the case of the language models he proposes. Specifically, we cannot show that within the Renaissance and the classical period of the seventeenth century the written model preceded the spoken model, nor can we say that the spoken model simply replaced the written model. Only by ignoring an intellectual movement as important as humanism can one argue that writing and not speech provided the theoretical basis for understanding language in the Renaissance. Indeed, as Murray Cohen has shown, both written and spoken models of language coexisted in the seventeenth century, as they did in the sixteenth.[8] The spoken model, in fact, by far predominated in language teaching in the educational system as it was reshaped by the humanists, who, as perhaps the most articulate producers of linguis-

[7]Michel Foucault, *The Order of Things: An Archaeology of the Human Sciences* (New York: Random House, 1970); Timothy J. Reiss, *The Discourse of Modernism* (Ithaca: Cornell University Press, 1982).

[8]Murray Cohen, *Linguistic Practice in England, 1640–1785* (Baltimore: Johns Hopkins University Press, 1977), pp. 1–42.

tic theory, are left unexplained by Foucault. Moreover, the very criterion Foucault uses to describe "classical" discourse, what Reiss has called "analytico-referential discourse," is as conspicuous in scholastic grammar and the logic of the later Middle Ages as it is in Bacon's *Novum Organon*. That is, to explain relationships between speech and writing in the period I deal with here, the idea of an *episteme* marked off by abrupt and severe ruptures is less satisfactory than the concept, however fustier, of a tradition, slowly evolving, cutting across periods, whose discontinuities are balanced by significant continuities.[9] And as students of Foucault would be quick to recognize, my recourse to the notion of tradition is not unrelated to my intervention in the literary text at the level of the subject.

In the end, however, I have found my greatest intellectual affinities in the media-history of Walter J. Ong.[10] Simply stated, Ong's position is that a culture is profoundly affected by the medium it uses to organize, store, and communicate its experience. Ong particularly highlights the difference between those cultures which depend primarily on the oral-aural sensorium of speech and those which depend on the visual sensorium of writing and print. Other scholars, Brian Stock, for example, and even Ong himself, have fine-tuned this basic scheme that opposes the oral to the visual to include cultures, such as the medieval, whose dependence on scribes and orally delivered manuscripts reveals a complex interdependence of the oral and the visual.[11] Just as important, Ong, along with Stock and Cohen, has also provided exemplary models of how this theoretical position can produce fruitful historical research. I am also indebted to the work of M. T. Clanchy, Elizabeth Eisenstein, Jack Goody, and Ian Watt. Through their own disciplines, each of these scholars points to the role of writing technologies in the social and intellectual attitudes

[9] For Foucault's argument against the idea of a tradition, see his essay "Nietzsche, Genealogy, History," in *Language, Counter-Memory, Practice,* tr. Donald F. Bouchard and Sherry Simon, ed. Donald F. Bouchard (Ithaca: Cornell University Press, 1977), pp. 139–64.

[10] The works of Walter J. Ong which I found most helpful were *Ramus, Method, and the Decay of Dialogue: From the Art of Discourse to the Art of Reason* (Cambridge: Harvard University Press, 1958); *Rhetoric, Romance, and Technology: Studies in the Interaction of Expression and Culture* (Ithaca: Cornell University Press, 1971); and *Orality and Literacy: Technologizing the Word* (London: Methuen, 1982).

[11] Brian Stock, *The Implications of Literacy: Written Language and Models of Interpretation in the Eleventh and Twelfth Centuries* (Princeton: Princeton University Press, 1983).

of historical cultures;[12] each provides ways to evaluate the relative weight with which speech and writing, including print, were conceived to have authorized words.

The first three chapters of this book focus on speech-dominated views of language. My actual conceptual starting point is the insistence of Renaissance humanists that language is primarily speech, historically and culturally determined, embodying the consensus of the social community from which it arises and expressing the community's ability to represent reality with moral astuteness (Chapter 2). I present the humanist position primarily in the theory and practice of grammar. To highlight the humanists' point of view, however, I begin with my exposition not with the humanists' position itself but with the medieval theories they rejected, particularly those of scholastic logicians who sought in mental discourse an ideal transparent, representational language, even while they were aware that such a language is subverted by the natural languages of speech in which it must of necessity be trapped (Chapter 1). The medieval theorists, in other words, were repelled by the idea that speech is culturally determined by convention; for them culture is ultimately the enemy of language and meaning. This position the humanists of course found abhorrent.

The humanists, nonetheless, were aware of the problems inherent in their own theory of speech, and in Chapter 3 I examine some of their concerns, first in a philosophical work by Thomas Elyot and a historical work by Roger Ascham but primarily in the poetry of Ben Jonson. Jonson provides an intriguingly complex response to the social authority of speech, for, in the absence of a social consensus that should constitute language, he yet takes a stance as the proclaimer of moral norms. In the process, he declaims his own role as author, which he cannot comfortably situate at the center of society. Jonson remains a practitioner of the humanist theory of speech despite his intuition that it does not quite work. His authorship is constituted by that perception.

In the next three chapters I discuss writing-dominated views of

[12]M. T. Clanchy, *From Memory to Written Record: England, 1066–1307* (Cambridge: Harvard University Press, 1978); Elizabeth Eisenstein, *The Printing Press as an Agent of Change* (Cambridge: Cambridge University Press, 1979); Jack Goody and Ian Watt, "The Consequences of Literacy," in *Literacy in Traditional Societies*, ed. Jack Goody (Cambridge: Cambridge University Press, 1968), pp. 27–68.

language, beginning with the spatialization of speech in the printed Renaissance book and its coincidence with Renaissance views—Hebraicist and Cabalist—that give writing logical and historical primacy over speech, particularly in the belief that God created writing before man pronounced the written letters of God's alphabet (Chapter 4). I then argue that George Herbert's hieroglyphic poems, which project themselves both aurally and visually, occupy a textual space made possible by print and Renaissance Hebraicism, a space in which the human voice and divine writing intersect and vie with each other. I contrast this tension between speech and writing in Herbert to Bacon's articulation of the artificial written sign to be used in scientific communication; Bacon's artificial language would consist of signs divorced both from the humanist touchstone of social consensus and from the Hebraicist totem of divine writing (Chapter 5). Yet Bacon's interest in an artificial scientific language was not determined by linguistic philosophy alone; it was related to his adoption of the printed book as the principal means of transmitting scientific knowledge (Chapter 6). Bacon's attraction to the printed book is tied to his interest in the social organization of scientific investigation, which for him best defines the scientist as, among other things, an author. The issue is generated for Bacon by his own failure to situate himself in the social position he felt was his by right of birth.

To conclude, I turn to Burton's *Anatomy of Melancholy.* If medieval logic and Scholastic philosophical grammar, humanist grammar, Cabalist and Baconian hieroglyphics all represent different ways of finding authority for language, Burton's *Anatomy* represents a skeptical reaction against such authority. Fashioning a style that imitates spoken discourse, and exploiting the possibilities of the revised printed edition, Burton subverts the technology of movable type to deny the attribute it lent to both speech and writing, an attribute most valued by many of the champions of the printed book—fixity. Burton's *Anatomy* is the locus of an eccentric commingling of philosophical skepticism and a new technology of the written word. In a loose sense, then, there is a kind of historical narrative implied in the progression of topics in this book. It moves from various attempts, in spite of recognized difficulties, to justify first speech, then writing as the basis of a representational language and ends on a note of willful subversion of the doctrines of both speech and writing.

1 /

Scholastic Logic and Grammar:

The Inescapability of Speech

STUDENTS of the Renaissance have long accepted a strict dichotomy between the Scholastic and humanist views of language. This perception has been reinforced by the customary practice of analyzing the humanist approach to language from the perspective of Renaissance rhetoric itself. From this perspective, Renaissance rhetoricians appear to have dismissed the assumptions that were the very basis of the scholastic theory, substituting a theory of language based on the conventions of actual speech for the Scholastics' semiological theory of verbal reference.[1] The

[1] Explanations for the humanists' purported rejection of a semiological view of reference include their incipient proclivity toward philosophical skepticism, their antipathy toward a scientific understanding of truth, and their playful attitude toward the representation of self. For humanist rhetoric and philosophical skepticism, see Jerrold E. Seigel, *Rhetoric and Philosophy in Renaissance Humanism: The Union of Eloquence and Wisdom, Petrarch to Valla* (Princeton: Princeton University Press, 1968), pp. 57–58, 74–75; Victoria Kahn, *Rhetoric, Prudence, and Skepticism in the Renaissance* (Ithaca: Cornell University Press, 1985); Robert M. Strozier, "Theory and Structure in Roger Ascham's *The Schoolmaster*," *Neuphilologische Mitteilungen*, 74 (1973), 144–62; Lisa Jardine, "Lorenzo Valla and the Intellectual Origins of Humanist Dialectic," *Journal of the History of Philosophy*, 15 (1977), 143–64; Nancy S. Struever, *The Language of History in the Renaissance: Rhetoric and Historical Consciousness in Florentine Humanism* (Princeton: Princeton University Press, 1970), pp. 5–39. For the distinction between humanistic and scientific, philosophical attitudes toward knowledge, see Paul Oskar Kristeller, "Humanism and Scholasticism in the Italian Renaissance," in *Renaissance Thought* (New York: Harper & Row, 1961), pp. 92–119; Hanna H. Gray, "Renaissance Humanism: The Pursuit of Eloquence," *Journal of the History of Ideas*, 24 (1963), 497–514; Joseph Anthony Mazzeo, *Renaissance and Revolution: The Remaking of European Thought* (New York: Random House, 1965), pp. 23–35; and Charles Trinkaus, *The Scope of Renais-*

dichotomy between the Scholastic and humanist theories of language has acquired the status of fact for another reason as well. Both theories seem to bear out the traditional distinction between Scholasticism and humanism based on the particular branch of the curriculum each movement emphasized: philosophy (or, more accurately, logic) for the Scholastic, rhetoric for the humanist.[2] Scholarly convention has further institutionalized the dichotomy between Scholasticism and humanism by associating each of these movements with one of two opposing figures from antiquity: Aristotle is seen as the presiding spirit of the Scholastics, Cicero (or, equally important, Quintilian) that of the humanists.

The dichotomy between the Scholastic and humanist conceptions of language is not absolute, however, and I will argue that both Scholastic and humanist conceptions of language depend on a semiological theory first formulated by Aristotle. Both Scholastic logicians and humanist rhetoricians elaborate, with significantly different modifications, Aristotle's concept of the relationships between reality, thought, speech, and writing.[3] Although I do not attempt to trace

---

sance Humanism (Ann Arbor: University of Michigan Press, 1983), pp. 169–91, 437–49. For rhetoric and self-shaping, see Richard Alan Lanham, *The Motives of Eloquence: Literary Rhetoric in the Renaissance* (New Haven: Yale University Press, 1976).

[2] Modern commentators on this dichotomy often perpetuate the controversy by choosing to study language under the rubric of either philosophy or literature. For two divergent evaluations of grammar under the control of logic in the Scholastic Middle Ages, see Paul Abelson, *The Seven Liberal Arts: A Study in Medieval Culture* (New York: Teacher's College, Columbia University, 1906), pp. 11, 33–34, and I. M. Bochenski, *A History of Formal Logic*, tr. and ed. Ivo Thomas (Notre Dame: University of Notre Dame Press, 1961), p. 12. Similarly, G. A. Padley champions the philosophical, logical attitude toward language of Bacon and his followers, as opposed to the humanists' interest in the "vagaries . . . of usage" (*Grammatical Theory in Western Europe, 1500–1700: The Latin Tradition* [Cambridge: Cambridge University Press, 1976], p. 75). Like so many contemporary historians of linguistics, Padley is decidedly influenced by Noam Chomsky, and tends to evaluate linguistic theories of the past according to the extent to which they resemble Chomsky's distinction between deep and surface structure. Chomsky himself applied this distinction to the history of linguistic ideas in perhaps the most influential work on the history of linguistics, *Cartesian Linguistics: A Chapter in the History of Rationalist Thought* (New York: Harper & Row, 1966). The connection between Chomsky's linguistic categories and Scholastic grammar is made explicit in John A. Trentman, "Speculative Grammar and Transformational Grammar: A Comparison of Philosophical Presuppositions," in *The History of Linguistic Thought and Contemporary Linguistics*, ed. Herman Parret (Berlin: De Gruyter, 1976), pp. 279–301; and W. Keith Percival, "Deep and Surface Structure Concepts in Renaissance and Medieval Syntactic Theory," in Parret, *History of Linguistic Thought*, pp. 238–53.

[3] For the full range of Aristotle's thoughts on language, see Richard McKeon, "Aris-

systematically the transmission of influence from Aristotle to the sixteenth-century English humanists, I argue that the humanists add the cultural dimension of language to their theory of verbal reference, a dimension of little interest to Scholastic analysts of language. Far from rejecting a referential, philosophical understanding of language, the humanists incorporate this understanding into a cultural explanation of language as a social artifact transmitted through conventions. In this sense the humanists synthesize the premises of Scholastic linguistic analysis—Aristotle's theories—with a cultural definition of language implied by Aristotle but most fully developed by Cicero, Quintilian, and the Stoics. This synthesis, however, was to come under attack in the seventeenth century when Bacon questioned the contribution of social context to the linguistic representation of thought and reality.

Renaissance scholars have just begun to look at the humanist attitude toward language from the perspective of its emphasis on grammar as opposed to rhetoric. A look at humanist grammatical theory might lead us to modify some conventional notions about humanist views of literary language.

In its opening address "To the Reader," John Colet and William Lily's *Shorte Introduction of Grammar* (generally known as Lily's *Grammar*), the standard grammar text of the English Renaissance, emphasizes the importance of Latin grammar as the introduction to all studies by invoking an architectural metaphor: a student's education is like a "buyldynge," which cannot "bee perfect, when as the foundacion and grounde worke is readye to fall, and vnable to vpholde the burthen of the frame." The edifice of learning is founded on the study of grammar, itself the art that teaches how to compose linguistic structures from the human voice or from the constituent building blocks of language, letters, syllables, and words. In his treatise on spelling, Thomas Smith called the process of putting words together

---

totle's Conception of Language and the Arts of Language," *Classical Philology*, 41 (1946), 193–206, and 42 (1947), 21–50. I base my argument on only one area of Aristotle's linguistic ideas, his semantic theory explaining the relationship of mind, reality, and language, as explained by McKeon in the first of these two articles. See also Miriam Therese Larkin, *Language in the Philosophy of Aristotle* (The Hague: Mouton, 1971).

from letters an *exaedificare*, literally a "building out of."[4] The six-teenth-century grammar school student learned how to put the con-stituent elements of words together in the course of studying how to read Latin literature and speak and write Latin with literary elegance.

English humanists used the teaching of Latin grammar to express their linguistic theory: in their practical instruction on how to teach and learn Latin they retained some linguistic assumptions of Aristo-telian logic while rejecting the elaborate philosophical apparatus im-posed on it by the scholastics. We can observe the difference between the scholastic and humanist approaches to verbal reference, first, by examining Aristotle's formulation, in his logic, of the connections between things, thought, speech, and writing, and then by examining the widely different ways in which Scholastics and humanists refor-mulated Aristotle to shape the frame (to recast Lily's metaphor) of the discourse each school thought could support truth.

Walter J. Ong has argued that Aristotle's logic does not simply sup-ply a classification of things or ideas; it also offers ways of saying something about something. Aristotle's logical classifications are "'outcries' in the market place or assembly, *categoriae,* transformed into Latin as *praedicamenta*, things spoken out." Though Aristotle may not always say so explicitly, his "categories are at root . . . conceived as parts of enunciations. Human knowledge for Aristotle exists in the full sense only in the enunciation . . . ; the *saying* of something about something, the *uttering* of a statement, the expression of a *judg-ment* . . . , or . . . a union of subject and predicate (*praedicatum* = the thing *said*)."[5] In the first extensive, systematic attempt at formulating logical principles as an instrument of knowledge, Aristotle thus inex-tricably intertwines knowledge and language in logic.

A key source for both humanists and Scholastics on language is the opening of Aristotle's *De interpretatione,* though their differing inter-pretations of Aristotle account for many of the more general differ-

[4]William Lily [et al.], *A Shorte Introduction of Grammar* (London, 1567; facs. rpt. New York: Scholars' Facsimiles and Reprints, 1945), sig. Aiir; Thomas Smith, *De recta et emendata linguae Anglicae scriptione, dialogus* (London, 1568; rpt. Menston: Scolar Press, 1968), sig. Civ.

[5]Walter J. Ong, *Ramus, Method, and the Decay of Dialogue: From the Art of Discourse to the Art of Reason* (Cambridge: Harvard University Press, 1958), pp. 106, 108.

ences between them. Aristotle tries to explain how a fundamental problem of expression is overcome, namely, how language, which is by nature conventional, can represent thought, which (for Aristotle) is by nature universal:

> Now spoken sounds are symbols of affections in the soul, and written marks symbols of spoken sounds. And just as written marks are not the same for all men, neither are spoken sounds. But what these are in the first place signs of—affections of the soul—are the same for all; and what these affections are likenesses of—actual things—are also the same.[6]

Metaphysically, Aristotle's view presupposes an objective range of existents—of Being—which is the same for all people, just as the perception of this Being—"affections of the soul"—forms a "likeness" of it which is also the same for all people. The expression of these ideas, however, is manifested in speech, whose meaningful sounds are not the same for all but differ according to one's natural language, whose elements are determined by convention. Writing, finally, is the use of written marks that record the conventional sounds of speech, and its elements too are conventional.[7]

Richard McKeon has suggested that Aristotle's semantic theory implies two levels of language: on the one hand, an inner discourse, the "discourse of the soul," or the level of language almost identical with ideas in the mind reflecting an extramental reality, the language of thought common to all people prior to utterance in a natural language; on the other hand, an "outer discourse," or the *expression* of the universal language of thought in the utterances of natural language, which can be recorded in writing as well. Aristotle clearly distinguishes between inner discourse as natural, almost physiological, and outer discourse as conventional. Mental discourse is a natural occurrence in an organism responding to stimuli and is thus universal. Outer discourse, the actual spoken language that expresses men-

---

[6]Aristotle, *Categories and De interpretatione*, tr. J. L. Ackrill (Oxford: Clarendon Press, 1963), p. 43.

[7]Cf. Jacques Derrida's keen awareness of the metaphysical foundations of Aristotle's "speech," and his hostility to it in its more recent appearance in Saussure and Husserl, in *Of Grammatology*, tr. Gayatri Chakravorty Spivak (Baltimore: Johns Hopkins University Press, 1976), chap. 1.

tal discourse, is shaped by usage and convention and differs from nation to nation.[8]

Mental and spoken discourse—*ratio* and *oratio*—are nevertheless closely related as *logos*. In McKeon's words: "The discourse of the soul and verbal discourse are in a sense the same discourse, since words are symbolic directly only of thoughts, and therefore discourse—logos— may signify speech or thought, and there is no sharp line to separate the [verbal] formula expressive of meaning from the meaning expressed in the formula." McKeon explains that the "achievement of truth" in Aristotle depends both on the knowledge of things and on a knowledge of the properties of language which makes it possible to replicate the truth of things in words. Whereas strictly speaking the discourse of scientific proof is expressed only in the inner discourse of the mind, *logos* is intimately connected to meaning expressed in significant sound, the articulated human voice that utters outer discourse.[9] McKeon makes it clear, however, that for Aristotle outer discourse borrows "a kind of natural status" because it is grounded in mental discourse, which is grounded in things themselves. Accordingly, McKeon further argues, not only is the discourse of the mind based on things; so too are the scientific, practical (i.e., social), and artistic uses of language, which are therefore mimetic and representational.

This interrelationship between mental and spoken discourse is also apparent in Aristotle's discussion of the constituents of statements that can be judged true or false, that is, in propositions that are the material of the language of logic.[10] Such propositions, which Aristotle calls *logoi* (usually translated as *sentences*), are composed of a "name" and a "verb." Aristotle explicitly defines a "name," and implicitly a "verb," as "spoken sound made significant by convention."[11] He does not explain exactly what he means by convention, nor does he explain just what role convention plays in logic, but he does define *logoi,* the constituents of the logical discourse of the soul, so that they are inseparable from the conventions of the significant sounds that make up spoken utterance in Greek. Aristotle thus locates the logical

[8]McKeon, "Aristotle's Conception of Language," pp. 202–3.
[9]The following discussion draws on ibid., pp. 201–3.
[10]See Aristotle, *Categories*, pp. 45–46.
[11]Ibid., p. 43.

basis of grammatical categories, the parts of speech, in nature, but in such a way that those categories overlap with the conventions of speech.

Generally, the difference between the Scholastic and the humanist approaches to language resides in the way each treats this connection between mental and spoken discourse, a connection they both accept. Aristotle's own treatment of the issue emphasizes mental discourse over conventional speech, and in describing the philosophical foundations of the parts of speech, he makes grammar an adjunct to logic. Scholastic logicians inherited this emphasis and developed it further in an elaborate system of logic that was also the basis of a linguistic science. This science, they reluctantly admitted, was connected, however tenuously, to external, spoken discourse. Humanists, on the other hand, while accepting the logical basis of external discourse in things and in inner discourse, emphasized the role of convention in language and so were primarily interested in speech, which connects language to its cultural milieu, its social, political, moral, religious, and historical environment. Humanists embodied this linguistic approach in their grammatical theory, which they saw as an adjunct to literary studies rather than to logic. The controversy between Scholastics and humanists, when seen in relation to their respective approaches to language, becomes a debate not between rhetoric and philosophy but between grammar and logic.

"Language," however, is too general a word to provide an accurate picture of the differences between Scholastic and humanist approaches to Aristotle. Whereas Aristotle tended to see a basic concordance among thought, speech, and writing, medieval and Renaissance thinkers often gave vastly different, and sometimes competing, emphases to one of these three levels of language. And different emphases of course yield different views of language, varying with the particular discourse one privileges, whether it be mental discourse (as in Scholastic logic), spoken (as in humanist grammar), or written (as in Cabalist hieroglyphics). For the humanists, literature is a privileged discipline of thought because it best embodies external discourse, or speech, which places language at the intersection of things, mind, and—the element missing in the Scholastic scheme—culture. The Scholastics, in contrast, assigned external discourse only a secondary role in their construction of language, consistent with their low estimation of the literary arts. Although the relationship between speech and thought is an articulated concern for Scholastics, they often regard speech and thought to be at odds with each other in a way that Aristotle did not. The positions of individual Scholastics vary greatly, however, and an examination of these various attitudes toward externalized speech can provide a backdrop against which the humanist view of speech and natural, spoken language may come into clearer focus.

Ong has aptly described medieval logic as "a study of the reflection of [the] material world . . . in the structures of the mind"; this representation of things in thought, as he says of Aristotle's logic, naturally issues predication, a saying about.[12] Most modern students of Scholastic logic have taken modern mathematical formal logic as their vantage point, usually lamenting two major differences between it and its medieval predecessor. For one thing, unlike purely abstract modern formal logic, Scholastic logic is ultimately based in things, in existents, even though logicians in the period tried to keep logic separate from metaphysics, and even though Scholastic logic may tend toward the abstraction of modern logic in its doctrines of the syllogism and logical consequences.[13] Second, Scholastic logic is expressed in a natural language, Latin, rather than in the artificial logical language of symbols used in modern logic. Historians of logic are keenly aware of the Scholastic logician's dependence on natural language and are accordingly attentive to the semantic theory that is so much a part of it.[14] Scholastic logicians generally use the concept of *vox*, voice made significant by convention or the uttered sounds of natural language, what McKeon calls outer discourse. They usually try to formulate some relationship between spoken sounds (of which

[12]Ong, *Ramus,* p. 74.

[13]Philotheus Boehner finds Scholastic logic immature for this reason (*Medieval Logic: An Outline of Its Development from 1250 to c. 1400* [Chicago: University of Chicago Press, 1952], pp. 36, 45, 59). Bochenski, *History of Formal Logic,* pp. 3–4, regards formal logic as the center of the history of logic, though he assigns an important, but secondary, role to semantics.

[14]Modern logicians sometimes regard some of the issues of Scholastic logic to be the spurious results of the lack of a definite article in Latin, rather than the result of genuinely logical considerations; see William and Martha Kneale, *The Development of Logic* (Oxford: Clarendon Press, 1962), p. 274. Boehner alternately regrets that Scholastic logic is "bogged down" by Latin and laments that modern formal logic is separated from natural language (*Medieval Logic,* pp. 29, 51).

writing is just a secondary visual image) and the mental propositions of logic, but they often do so with evident discomfort.[15]

Working with a natural language, Latin, Scholastics define language in purely referential terms. Like their seventeenth-century counterparts in the Royal Society, they seek a totally neutral scientific language, capable of purely transparent representation. They assume that it is possible to stand outside society, which otherwise shapes the conventions of natural language, and outside history, which generates changes that alter those conventions. In effect, Scholastic logicians attempt to deculturate language. Nevertheless, they are often aware of the inescapability of natural language, their attitude toward which is evident in their treatment of the *vox* of utterance. The often troubled relationship in Scholastic logic between mental discourse and speech is further complicated by the fact that none of the logicians considered here spoke Latin as his natural language. Unlike Aristotle, who was explaining the logical properties of the same language he used both to order his dinner and to describe the nature of being, Scholastic logicians use a language that is not their own, a once quotidian Latin, as the voice of a mental language that is supposed to be divorced from the conventions of speech. This basic problem appears in a variety of representative thinkers.

For Aquinas, a realist who regards logic as a *scientia rationis,* the subject matter of logic is the mind's operation on things.[16] Aquinas constructs a theory to show how language can express mind, but ultimately he believes that language contributes little to meaning. He distinguishes between "being in things" (*ens in rebus*) and "being in the mind" (*ens in intellectu*) (*Summa,* I, q. 16, a. 3) and defines logic as the

[15]Because Scholastic logicians follow the Aristotelian paradigm according to which writing is a record of speech, they are dealing with speech—from a theoretical point of view—even when they are working in writing. From this point of view, writing is a special form of utterance in the *vox* of natural language.

[16]I follow E. J. Ashworth's division between, on the one hand, realists, who consider logic a rational science as opposed to a verbal science and, on the other, nominalists, who generally consider it a verbal science (*Language and Logic in the Post-Medieval Period* [Dordrecht: Reidel, 1974], p. 32). What follows is not meant to cover all the positions of the major Scholastic logicians but only a representative range. Though Scholastic logicians tried to keep logic separate from metaphysics, their attitude toward universals could not help but affect their logical position. Nevertheless, ontological considerations are not pertinent to my discussion of the place of *vox* in Scholastic logic.

discipline that deals with the latter.[17] In his commentary on Aristotle's *De interpretatione,* Aquinas explicitly states that language is important in logic only insofar as language "interpret[s] what is in the intellect," that is, expresses statements that are true or false.[18] Yet, even in this subordinate position, language must still be accounted for, as Aquinas's discussion of truth in the *Summa* (I, q. 16) makes clear. There Aquinas opens the discussion in the first question by referring to Aristotle's dictum that truth is not in things but only in the mind's perception of things, that is, in the accurate correspondence of mental concepts to things.[19] Like Aristotle, he includes language in the relationship between things and the intellect: "words are said to be true so far as they are signs of truth in the intellect" (*dicitur oratio vera, in quantum est signum intellectus veri*).[20] Similarly, the discussion in the first half of Book I of the commentary on *De interpretatione* is devoted to logical language defined as the product of reason and opposed to poetry and rhetoric, whose only purpose is to facilitate expression and communication. Language as the transparent, lucid reflection of mental concepts, *oratio,* is for Aquinas the only level of language useful in philosophical and logical study, and in this sense logical discourse is as close as possible to what McKeon calls inner discourse.

Nevertheless, Aquinas does not exclude spoken, natural language (*vox*) from his consideration of logical language. Though he treats *vox* as completely separate from *oratio, vox* can still transmit *oratio. Vox* is superadded to mental discourse, however, not because it has an in-

[17]See Bochenski, *History of Formal Logic,* pp. 154–56, who also observes a similar view in logicians as different as Albert of Saxony and Ockham.

[18]*Aristotle: On Interpretation. Commentary by St. Thomas and Cajetan,* tr. Jean T. Oesterle (Milwaukee: Marquette University Press, 1962), p. 18. All references are from this edition (hereafter cited as Oesterle). Where appropriate, I also supply the Latin text from Thomas Aquinas, *Opera Omnia,* vol. 18, *In Aristotelis Stagiritae Nonnullos Libros Commentaria* (Parma: Fiaccadoro, 1865; rpt. New York: Musurgia, 1949). This volume is hereafter cited as Fiaccadoro.

[19]Boehner sees this issue as the starting point of logic as a science of signs, including language signs, and he traces the idea through Alexander of Hales, Bonaventure, Aquinas, Scotus, and Ockham ("Ockham's Theory of Truth," in *Collected Articles on Ockham,* ed. Eligius M. Buytaert [St. Bonaventure, N.Y.: Franciscan Institute, 1958], pp. 174–200).

[20]Thomas Aquinas, *Summa Theologica,* tr. Fathers of the English Dominican Province (New York: Benziger, 1947), I, 90; *Opera Omnia,* I, 73.

trinsic connection to mental discourse, but because of the social nature of man: societies are held together by communication through
spoken, natural language, through significant vocal sounds (*voces
significativae*), which are different in different societies, whose members speak different languages (*diversae linguae*) (Oesterle, p. 24; Fiaccadoro, p. 3). Aquinas thus maintains the detachment of spoken
utterance, *vox*, from the underlying logical structure of thought and
oratio. Only "the signification of vocal sound," not vocal sound itself,
"is immediate to the conceptions of the intellect" (*significatio vocum . . .
est immediata ipsis conceptionibus intellectus*) (Oesterle, p. 24; Fiaccadoro,
p. 5). Internal discourse may be only secondarily expressed in the
voces of speech, which lie somewhere between mental concepts and
oratio, on the one hand, and the purely physical vibration of sound, on
the other. William and Martha Kneale observe that Aquinas does
sometimes move easily back and forth between terms that refer both
to thought and to language, almost as if he equates them.[21] Even so,
vox is linguistically meaningful only insofar as it is the materialization
of the mental concepts of *oratio*. The conventionality of natural language plays no role in meaning and so Aquinas largely ignores it. He
defines the mental apprehension of a thing as the "cause" (*causa*) of
vox which "imitates" (*imitatur*) it as an "effect" (*effectus*) (Oesterle,
pp. 30–31; Fiaccadoro, p. 5), but otherwise *vox* is extraneous to his
explanation of how real discourse works.

The *oratio* of logic, however, is not the only form of expression.
Aquinas explains that reason functions not only to perceive the truth
of things but also "to direct and order others in accordance with what
it conceives" (Oesterle, p. 61; Fiaccadoro, p. 15). Among the four
other kinds of expression—Aquinas uses the term *oratio* for them
too—are rhetoric and poetry, which "move their auditors by arousing
certain passions in them"; thus, according to Aquinas, "this kind of
speech . . . is concerned with the ordination of a hearer towards
something." Aquinas here refers to a social concept of language; the
grammarian supplies the suitable construction of spoken utterances
(*voces*) for this purpose (Oesterle, pp. 61–62; Fiaccadoro, p. 15).
Aquinas, then, envisions a grammar attached to literary—that is,

---

[21]W. Kneale and M. Kneale, *Development of Logic*, p. 240. The Kneales refer to such
words as *enuntiabile*, *oratio*, and *propositio*.

rhetorical and poetic—study, which he regards as the study of social utterance, as distinct from a grammar based on logical categories inherent in the mind's perception of reality. These two kinds of grammar are the vehicles for two kinds of *oratio,* one concerned with the relationship of language to thought and things (the scientific disciplines of logic and philosophy), the other concerned with the relationship of language to the disposition of an auditor (the literary arts of rhetoric and poetry).[22] Aquinas sees little connection between a socially uttered *vox* and a *vox* expressing things. Actual speech as a cultural phenomenon is for Aquinas philosophically insignificant.

A different approach to the relationship between natural language and mental concepts was presented early in the Scholastic Middle Ages by Abelard, a realist who, unlike Aquinas, considered logic a *scientia sermocinalis,* a verbal science. In general, those who looked at logic in this way were more likely to see a closer connection between *oratio* and *vox* than Aquinas did (and were also more likely to have been known, and derided, by Renaissance humanists, though not for that reason). In the *Dialectica,* Abelard distinguishes between logic and physics: logic studies how linguistic conventions (*voces*) convey meaning through words, and physics investigates whether things have the properties ascribed to them in verbal statements (*enuntiationes*). Abelard further explains that in order to understand what words mean and to use them in meaningful conventions of speech (*pro vocum impositione*), one must first understand the nature of things: "When the nature of things has been investigated, the meaning of [conventional, spoken] words [*significatio vocum*] must be established according to the properties of things, first in individual words [*in singulis dictionibus*], and then in discourse [*oratio*]."[23] *Vox,* then, is much more central to Abelard's view of *oratio* than it is to Aquinas's; for Abelard logic is in a real sense an art of language. The Kneales in fact suggest that Abelard may be recommending a way to improve and regularize language so that the proper study of language would enable one to become "a master of all science."

---

[22]See Ong, *Ramus,* p. 101, on logic as probable and demonstrable science in Aquinas.

[23]This discussion of Abelard is based on a passage quoted in W. Kneale and M. Kneale, *Development of Logic,* p. 219. For a similar view in Boethius, see ibid., p. 194. The idea also appears in William of Sherwood, *Introduction to Logic,* tr. Norman Kretzmann (Minneapolis: University of Minnesota Press, 1966), p. 21.

Abelard's position in this debate seems similar to that of Hugh of St. Victor, who, very early in the development of Scholastic logic, argued that language ruled only by usage existed before logic, whose rules were formulated to regularize the vagaries of usage.[24] For both Hugh and Abelard, logic corrects linguistic convention to keep *vox* in line with *oratio,* or in other words, to keep outer discourse in line with inner discourse. Both recognize that logical propositions are inescapably couched in the linguistic conventions of natural language. If natural language is to be meaningful, it must then be made to conform to mental discourse about things.

The classic account of the interrelationship of *vox* and *oratio* in logic appears in the opening of Peter of Spain's thirteenth-century *Summulae Logicales,* perhaps the most widely used logic textbook of the Scholastic era. Well-known to Renaissance humanists, this work was also the particular object of their scorn. Peter begins by describing the elements from which the basic unit of logical discourse, the proposition, is constructed.[25] He points out that the word *dialectic* is derived from Greek words that mean speech (*sermo*) and reason (*ratio*); dialectic, that is, logic, is thus the expression of reason in words. This definition is related to the function of logic in disputation, as oral performance, must be conveyed by speech (*mediante sermone*), which in turn requires utterance and sound (*vox* and *sonus*). Peter's definition closely follows the opening of William of Sherwood's earlier, thirteenth-century *Introduction to Logic,* which explicitly asserts that logic teaches to speak truly (*[logica] docet vere loqui*).[26] For Peter, as for William, the *oratio* of logic is firmly set in the physical apparatus of the voice, and its principles cannot be detached from expression in speech or in sounds made significant by convention. Logic cannot escape language.

[24]For Abelard, see W. Kneale and M. Kneale, *Development of Logic,* p. 219. Hugh of St. Victor's position is stated in *Didascalion* I, 11, as quoted in Ernest Addison Moody, *Truth and Consequence in Medieval Logic* (Amsterdam: North-Holland, 1953), pp. 13–14. For the original Latin, see Hugo de Sancto Victore, *Didascalion. De Studio Legendi, A Critical Text,* ed. Charles Henry Buttimer (Washington, D.C.: Catholic University Press, 1939), p. 21.

[25]The passage I refer to appears in Peter of Spain, *Tractatus, Called Afterwards Summule Logicales,* ed. Lambertus Mariede de Rijk (Assen: Van Gorcum, 1972), pp. 1–3.

[26]Sherwood, *Introduction to Logic,* p. 21; *Die Introductiones in logicam des Wilhelm von Shyrewood,* ed. Martin Grabmann, Philologische-historische Abteilung, vol. 10 (Munich: Bayerischen Akademie der Wissenschaften, 1937), p. 30. All quotations from the Latin are from this edition.

This intermingling of *oratio* and *vox*, thought about things and speech about things, is evident in a major original contribution of Scholastic logic, the doctrine of the properties of terms. This doctrine was first fully enunciated by William of Sherwood, though evidence suggests that this branch of Scholastic logic actually developed earlier.[27] William maintained that the principal concern of logic is the syllogism, which can be reduced to its constituent verbal units in decreasing order of complexity: syllogisms are constructed out of propositions, which are constructed out of *terms*, or words used in propositions to refer to things.[28] We can understand the ultimate aim of logic, the construction of syllogisms, only if we understand how words—terms—function by referring to reality in propositions.

Terms have several kinds of properties, but the kind most concerned with the relationship of language and reality is supposition. In a widely disseminated formulation of the issue, Peter of Spain defines supposition as "the acceptance of a substantive term [*terminus substantivus*] for something [*pro aliquo*]."[29] The theory of *suppositio* (from *supponere*, "*to stand in place of*," or "*to substitute for*") is the elaborate Scholastic logical apparatus that describes how certain kinds of words—terms—function in relation to the reality they name when used in logical propositions. Supposition theory is a referential explanation of language. Suppositing terms are, strictly speaking, categorematic words (usually coincident with the declinable parts of speech). As Joseph Mullally points out, through supposition theory, Peter's logic becomes an adjunct of metaphysics, explaining the possibility of meaning in language through its anchorage in the categories of reality.[30]

---

[27]See Boehner, *Medieval Logic*, p. 17, for the derivation of properties of terms from the first book of Aristotle's *De interpretatione;* see Boehner, "Ockham's Theory of Truth," pp. 182–83, for prototypes of properties of terms in Anselm; W. Kneale and M. Kneale, *Development of Logic*, p. 209, for prototypes in Abelard.

[28]See Sherwood, *Introduction to Logic*, p. 21. For a general treatment of properties of terms, see Alan R. Perreiah, "Approaches to Supposition-Theory," *The New Scholasticism*, 45 (1971), 381–408; W. Kneale and M. Kneale, *Development of Logic*, pp. 246–74; Boehner, *Medieval Logic*, pp. 27–51; Moody, *Truth and Consequence*, pp. 18–25.

[29]Peter of Spain, *Summulae Logicales*, ed. and tr. Joseph P. Mullally (Notre Dame: University of Notre Dame Press, 1945), pp. 2, 3 (hereafter cited as Mullally). Mullally provides only Tract VII on the properties of terms, and includes the Latin text (even numbered pages). All quotations are from this edition.

[30]For the relationship of Peter's realism and his supposition theory, see Mullally, pp. xxxi–xxxii.

Just how conventions of language come to embody the order of reality speakable in propositions is apparent in the terminist logician's distinction between signification and supposition. Signification is the process by which meaning is conventionally imposed on sound (*vox*) to create words that name things. Signification, Peter of Spain explains, is "the representation [*representatio*], established by convention [*secundum placitum*], of a thing [*res*] by an utterance [*vox*]" (pp. 2, 3). This definition, again, points to the interconnection between spoken, natural language—sounds made significant by convention—and the basic units of propositions. Peter, however, makes a strong distinction between signification and supposition: whereas signification is accomplished through the imposition of a spoken word to signify a thing [*per impositionem vocis ad significandum rem*]," supposition "is the acceptance of a term already significant as denoting something [*acceptio termini iam significantis rem pro aliquo*]" (pp. 2–4, 3–5). Signification is the process by which a particular conventional, sounded word acquires its meaning in relation to a thing, but supposition is the property of a term, an already significant sound, which actually stands for a thing in a proposition. The distinction thus posits two stages in the construction of referential language as an instrument of thought about things. Signification establishes a vocal sign in a natural language to represent a thing; supposition is the use of a number of such signs to establish a relationship among them.[31] The elaborate structure of Scholastic terminist logic thus ultimately depends on human sounds that convention has made significant as meaningful signs representing thought about things.

The grounding of language in conventional sound, on the one hand, and the total subordination of language to things, on the other, give natural language and spoken utterance an elusively ambiguous status in scholastic logic. This ambiguity is evident in the way logicians place propositions in time. Scholastic logicians discuss whether the word *homo*, for example, when used in a proposition, applies to all men, past and future as well as present, the present of a proposition in which the word is used. Supposition theory, that is, considers the present tense of a proposition in relation to the moment of its utter-

---

[31]Mullally's explanation of the difference between *significatio* and *suppositio* (Mullally, p. xli) is helpful.

ance, but the abstract nature of its temporality excludes any kind of concrete social or cultural situations and any kind of rhetorical considerations. The scholastics, in sharp contrast to the humanists, believed the time of logical utterances has no coordinates in historical time, conceived as either social, political, or sacred.[32] Supposition recognizes the dependence of propositions on conventional *vox* but seeks to guard against and correct distortions resulting from idiomatic usage by continually clarifying the referential relationship of words to things. In this sense supposition theory abstracts conventional speech from the conditions of its utterance in places where people actually speak or construct utterances with cultural coordinates. As the Kneales put it, Scholastic logic strives for a "precise description of various idioms of natural language used for philosophizing."[33] In other words, recognizing the inextricability of *oratio* and *vox,* supposition theory prevents the conventions of *vox* from determining language norms and thus keeps language isolated from culture. And since the *voces* used in Scholastic logic are those of Latin, Scholastic logicians in effect transform the sounds of Latin as a natural language, sounds made significant by convention, into a metalanguage coincident with the structure of thought about things.

Under what conditions and in what context is meaning conventionally imposed on a sound to create a word? Scholastic logicians usually took *significatio* for granted, offering little explanation. But the logician's ally, the Scholastic grammarian, did provide fuller explanation. Twelfth-century Scholastic commentators on Priscian, the ancient source of most medieval grammar, posed the theory of the *causa inventionis,* a theory of the origin of language in the initial imposition of names on things, the logician's *significatio.*[34] The theory presupposed, in the manner of an etiological myth, a *primus inventor* or *impositor* who first created words; he was followed by successive

---

[32]See Boehner, *Medieval Logic,* pp. 10–12; and Ashworth, *Language and Logic,* pp. 82, 89–90. In an offshoot of the issue, Renaissance Scholastic logicians debated whether a word in a book has supposition when the book is closed.

[33]W. Kneale and M. Kneale, *Development of Logic,* pp. 273–74.

[34]For the theory of the *causa inventionis,* see R. W. Hunt, "Studies in Priscian in the Eleventh and Twelfth Century," *Medieval and Renaissance Studies,* 1 (1941–43), 211–13. For similar conclusions about philosophy as the genesis of language in Scholasticism, see Terence Heath, "Logical Grammar, Grammatical Logic, and Humanism in Three German Universities," *Studies in the Renaissance,* 18 (1971), 9–13.

inventores until language was perfected. The original *inventores* tagged each part of speech with distinguishing accidents of inflection to indicate its grammatical form, which corresponded to an ontological category in reality. Words, that is, were first constructed by philosophers. Accordingly, Scholastic logicians and grammarians did not accept the idea that conventional, natural language is in any way, logically or experientially, prior to the content of concepts. "Rather," as E. J. Ashworth argues, the logician and logical grammarian contended that "we must aquire concepts before we can aquire a language, for spoken [conventional] language is developed in order that we may express our concepts."[35]

The logical use of natural language as a vehicle for thought about reality had profound implications for the study of grammar in the Scholastic Middle Ages.[36] Many of the terms used in Scholastic logic are derived from Priscian's grammar; supposition theory itself seems to have its origins in grammar. Logic tends to treat the categories of reality as parallel to the categories of grammar. Similarly, syntactical structure parallels the logical structure of the mind. Some logicians went so far as to argue that the analogy of thought and language was so close that mental propositions could be regarded as having a grammar like that of spoken or written propositions.[37]

The correlation between grammatical and logical categories strongly influenced the development of a particularly Scholastic approach to grammar, commonly known as philosophical or speculative grammar. This approach treats the study of language as an adjunct of logic and explains in great detail how grammatical constructions are the reflection of the mind's perception of the logical and metaphysical order of things. Speculative grammar emerged with the rise of Scholasticism itself. The nature of grammatical study in medieval universities depended largely on which art of the trivium it was most closely

[35]Ashworth, *Language and Logic*, p. 42, makes the point about Scholastic logicians in the Renaissance, but it is also applicable to medieval Scholasticism. I therefore disagree with Michael McCanles's view that Scholastic logic defines knowledge by what can be put into linguistic structures. (McCanles, "Peter of Spain and William of Ockham: From Metaphysics to Grammar," *The Modern Schoolman*, 43 [1965–66], 133–41). The relationship, it seems to me, works in the other direction: linguistic structures are defined by the categories of knowledge.

[36]For the following observations about grammar and logic, see Mullally, introduction, esp. pp. xxxix–xliii, and Heath, "Logical Grammar," pp. 9–13.

[37]W. Kneale and M. Kneale, *Development of Logic*, p. 230.

allied to. Before the eleventh century, grammar was a propaedeutic to the study of classical Latin literature and was considered an *ars recte loquendi et scribendi*. This tradition of grammatical study prevailed in the twelfth- and thirteenth-century schools of Chartres and Orléans, though it survived in some form throughout the Middle Ages. In the eleventh century a grammatical school more closely allied to Scholastic logic and philosophy emerged, as grammar itself became a branch of speculative philosophy. As a result, both grammar and logic now came to share a common foundation in Aristotle's *De interpretatione*.[38]

The Scholastic approach to grammar is generally characterized by a search for the *causae*, or philosophical reasons, underlying grammatical constructions. The philosophizing of grammar is apparent early in the Scholastic tradition in Anselm, who, as Desmond Henry explains, distinguished between two ways of approaching grammar which correspond to two levels of language itself. On the one hand, there is the surface structure of utterances that are determined by usage. On the other hand, there is the underlying logical structure that makes utterance meaningful. From the logical point of view, as Henry points out, usage is "riddled with . . . improprieties and inexactitude of expression." Common usage can thus be at odds with accurate, logical expression. Contrasting *usus loquendi* to the logical basis of language, Anselm criticizes traditional authority in grammar, that is, the traditional grammarians who repeat each other from the time of Donatus and Priscian and whose ultimate authority is the *usus loquendi* of sanctioned authors, a criterion of language that was to be hallowed by Renaissance humanists.[39] For Scholastic grammarians,

[38]For surveys of the Scholastic study of grammar, including philosophical grammar, see Paul Abelson, *The Seven Liberal Arts: A Study in Medieval Culture* (New York: Teacher's College, Columbia University, 1906), pp. 11–51; Louis John Paetow, *The Arts Course at Medieval Universities with Special Reference to Grammar and Rhetoric* (Urbana-Champaign: University of Illinois Press, 1910), pp. 33–60; Richard McKeon, "Rhetoric in the Middle Ages," *Speculum*, 17 (1942), 1–32; Robert H. Robins, *Ancient and Medieval Grammatical Theory in Europe* (London: G. Bell & Sons, 1951); G. L. Bursill-Hall, *Speculative Grammars of the Middle Ages* (The Hague: Mouton, 1971); James Jerome Murphy, *Rhetoric in the Middle Ages: A History of Rhetorical Theory from St. Augustine to the Renaissance* (Berkeley: University of California Press, 1974), pp. 135–63. The recovery of Aristotle's *De interpretatione* and its effect on scholastic grammar are discussed in Marcia Colish, *The Mirror of Language: A Study in the Medieval Theory of Knowledge* (New Haven: Yale University Press, 1968), pp. 98–101.

[39]For Anselm on grammar, see Colish, *Mirror of Language*, pp. 82–160; and Desmond Paul Henry, "Two Medieval Critics of Traditional Grammar," *Historiographia Linguistica*, 7 (1980), 85–107.

good language is more likely to be distorted rather than enhanced by the mere fact of its having been spoken before; culture diminishes rather than enlarges language.

A similar distinction between *causa* and *usus* was made by the thirteenth- and fourteenth-century grammarians known as modistae, so called because of their treatises titled *De modis significandi,* the most elaborate achievement of Scholastic, speculative grammar. Modistic grammar, notorious among Renaissance humanists (including Vives, Thomas More, John Skelton, Erasmus, and Rabelais) is a synthesis of earlier developments in speculative grammar, whose fundamental principles were laid out by, among others, Roger Bacon.[40] Bacon advocated the study of grammar as a science; he proposed investigating the possible construction of a universal grammar describing language in general, irrespective of the grammars of individual natural languages. Modistic grammar fully realizes Bacon's ideas in its assertion of the complete interdependence of the structure of reality, the operations of the mind, and the structure of language in general, as opposed to the rules of specific natural languages. In the words of Boethius of Dacia, "There is but one logic for all tongues, and hence also just one grammar. The antecedent [*antecedens*, i.e., antecedent *causa*] is obvious, for were there not one logic in the many tongues, then we should have a logic specifically diverse from that which the philosophers handed down to us when they handed down the logic in Greek which we now have translated into Latin."[41]

The true underlying grammatical structure of language is logic, or the structure of thought based on things. It is thus an accident of history that Latin is the language modistic grammarians used to illustrate their linguistic principles. Indeed, modistic grammar is a perfect example of the dislocation of Latin as a culturally situated language, for the modistae were not interested in Latin as a natural, spoken

[40]For Scholastic views on general grammar that ultimately culminated in modistic grammar, see Norman Kretzmann, "History of Semantics," in *Encyclopedia of Philosophy,* ed. Paul Edwards (New York: Macmillan, 1967), VII, 374–75; G. L. Bursill-Hall, introduction to Thomas of Erfurt, *Grammatica Speculativa* (London: Longman, 1972), p. 22. Henry ("Two Medieval Critics," passim) examines the similarity between Anselm's linguistic views and those of the modista, Boethius of Dacia.

[41]Quoted in Henry, "Two Medieval Critics," p. 86. For a full description of modistic grammar, see Bursill-Hall's *Speculative Grammars,* his introduction to Thomas of Erfurt, *Grammatica Speculativa,* and his "Mediaeval Grammatical Theories," *Canadian Journal of Linguistics,* 9 (1963), 39–54.

language; rather, G. L. Bursill-Hall explains, they were interested in the grammatical structure of an idealized language of thought, a language that coincides with ontologically conceived categories of Latin grammar.[42] In this sense Latin was for them a metalanguage that embodied a general grammar independent of any utterance in the communicative situations in which language is determined by *usus loquendi*. That no one who actually used Latin as a natural language would ever utter the kinds of statements constructed by modistic principles, as the humanists were later to charge, would have made no difference at all to the modistae. Speech was the last thing they were concerned with.

The most complete extant modistic treatise is Thomas of Erfurt's *Grammatica Speculativa*,[43] a work known, and despised, in the sixteenth century by More, Skelton, and Rabelais but held in high esteem by Bishop Wilkins, perhaps the best-known seventeenth-century champion of philosophical language. Because Thomas elicited such strong reactions from linguistic thinkers of the sixteenth and seventeenth centuries—some vehemently rejected his work, others saw it as a model to be emulated—he has a critical role in the history of linguistic theory. Using some of the same vocabulary as terminist logicians, Thomas was primarily concerned with demonstrating how the mind's apprehension of reality generates language. Grammar is, accordingly, the study of how words signify things (*Grammatica est de signis rerum*) [p. 148]).

Thomas explains how words are constructed when a *vox* becomes a *dictio*, which in turn becomes a *pars orationis* through correspondence with an ontological category in reality. The basic starting point in grammar, as in logic, is the *vox*, the sound produced by human organs of speech. But, Thomas explains, the grammarian is concerned with *vox* only insofar as it is the material manifestation of the mind's ability to name things with signs. A *dictio* is a sign that signifies through a *vox*; it is the imposition of a meaning on an otherwise meaningless sound (*vox*) made by the human voice referring to some thing. (But each *dictio* exists in isolation from other *dictiones* in syntactical formations:

---

[42]Bursill-Hall, *Speculative Grammars*, pp. 35, 41, and introduction to Thomas of Erfurt, *Grammatica Speculativa*, p. 16. See also Alan R. Perreiah, "Humanistic Critiques of Scholastic Dialectic," *Sixteenth Century Journal*, 13 (Fall 1982), 13–14, 20.

[43]All references to Thomas of Erfurt's *Grammatica Speculativa* are from Bursill-Hall's edition, which includes both the Latin text and the English translation.

dicitur dictio formaliter per rationem signandi voci superadditam, quia dictio est vox significativa [p. 148]). As in terminist logic, a *dictio* is constructed through the process of *significatio* (p. 136).

The elements of language reach their full capacity to express meaning only when a *dictio* becomes a *pars orationis*, a part of speech. This transformation occurs when the mind assigns a *dictio* to its perception of a particular ontological category of a thing. A *dictio* becomes a noun when it signifies the perception of being, a verb when it signifies the perception of becoming; and a *dictio* so transformed into a *pars* can then be used in conjunction with other *dictiones*, which have similarly become *partes*.[44] Language thus attains full meaning when words have become correlates of reality in syntactical formations, in the logician's *proposition* (though Thomas does not use the word) which can be combined with other propositions to form syllogisms. (Thomas's distinction between a *dictio* and a *pars* bears a close resemblance to the terminist's distinctions between *significatio* and *suppositio* and between *vox* and *terminus*.) Modistic grammar, then, is based on the inherent correspondences among the categories of existence, the faculties of the intellect, and the human capacity for linguistic expression.[45]

These correlative categories in things, in the mind, and in language are Thomas's only reference points for linguistic meaning. His state-

[44]The modistae explained the mind's understanding of a particular category of reality expressed in grammatical categories as a relationship of *modi essendi* with *modi intellegendi* and *modi significandi*. For a concise description of this relationship, see Bursill-Hall, "Mediaeval Grammatical Theories." The *partes* emerging from this process originating in ontological categories are the declinables, roughly equivalent to the logician's categorematic terms. The explanation of nouns and verbs and their related *partes*, pronouns, adjectives, and participles, by far makes up most of Thomas's treatise. Indeclinable *partes* have no correlatives in reality and are thus roughly equivalent to the logician's syncategorematic terms. Thomas supplies no developed explanation of how the indeclinables are related to the connection between the modes of being, understanding, and signifying.

[45]In my claim that these correspondences generally prevail in scholastic logical and linguistic thought, I disagree with the view of Timothy J. Reiss, who argues that medieval discourse lacked the concept of a subjectivity that arranges its perception of reality in linguistic signs. This concept, Reiss claims, originated in the seventeenth century ("Medieval Discursive Practice," in *The Discourse of Modernism* [Ithaca: Cornell University Press, 1982], pp. 55–107). As Reiss's analysis depends on that of Michel Foucault, I also fundamentally disagree with Foucault's similar argument about preseventeenth-century discourse; see *The Order of Things: An Archaeology of the Human Sciences* (New York: Random House, 1970), pp. 17–45. Foucault all but ignores the Aristotelian tradition of language analysis.

ment that the modes of being, understanding, and signifying "speak" (*modus essendi dicit . . . , modus intellegendi . . . dicit . . . , modus signifi-candi . . . dicit* [p. 144]) is more than metaphoric. There is a kind of reciprocal process through which language maximizes its meaning when shaped by the ontological categories of reality and through which reality creates the possibility of meaning by realizing itself in acts of intellection and language. In both cases, things do in fact *speak*. But the language in which they speak is, as we have seen, a meta-language that materializes linguistic categories already inherent in things and in the mind. Though the modistae embodied this metalan-guage in the conventional *voces* of Latin, the Latin produced by modistic principles was used in the rhetorical circumstances of actual speech. Modistic Latin constructs the propositions that have only a tangential and accidental relationship to the norms of Latin consid-ered as a natural language.

The modistic approach to grammar is ultimately based on the realistic belief that the mind passively mirrors reality. This notion was opposed by the nominalist William of Ockham, who drew a greater distinction between things in reality and things in the mind than did the realists, and articulated in detail the problematic relationship between mental discourse and natural language. Ockham assigns to the mind an active role in the process of acquiring knowledge, par-ticularly regarding universals. For this reason Ockham's followers ridiculed modistic grammar.[46] Ockham himself tended to use con-cepts rather than things as the reference point of logic more than the modistae and most realists did. Nevertheless, like his modistic and terminist predecessors, Ockham regards logic as a *scientia sermocinalis* concerned with propositions whose truth value is based on their conformity to things, an idea he formulates in his theory of significa-tion and supposition. (As a nominalist, however, he is careful to stipulate that universals are abstractions that have no extramental existence.)[47]

---

[46]For Ockhamite reaction against the modistae, see Bursill-Hall, introduction to Thomas of Erfurt, *Grammatica Speculativa*, p. 18; and Mullally, p. lxxxii. Differences between nominalist and realist attitudes toward language and the perception of reality are admirably summed up by Michael McCanles, "Paradox in Donne," *Studies in the Renaissance*, 13 (1966), 266–87.

[47]Three essays by Philotheus Boehner, all in *Collected Articles on Ockham*, ed. Eligius M. Buytaert (St. Bonaventure, N.Y.: Franciscan Institute, 1958), examine different

Yet unlike most of his Scholastic predecessors, Ockham distinguishes sharply between the mental language of concepts and its spoken and written expression. For him the mental language prior to utterance in speech belongs to no spoken or written language and is separate from any *vox* made significant by convention. Ockham nonetheless describes a correspondence between the logical structure of concepts and the linguistic structure of natural language, as do his predecessors Peter of Spain, William of Sherwood, and Thomas of Erfurt. According to Ockham, concepts have a grammar that coincides with that of natural language. But for Ockham the logical criteria by which natural language is to be judged give it the same inferior status it has for all Scholastic logicians and grammarians.

Ockham begins his *Summa Logicae* by identifying the subject of logic as arguments (*argumenta*), which can be reduced, first, to propositions and, then, to terms. He divides terms into three kinds, which make up three kinds of propositions and three kinds of *oratio:* conceptual, spoken, and written (*concepta, prolata, scripta*), each of which separately and individually refers to things in the world. Ockham assigns primary importance to conceptual terms and conceptual propositions, by which spoken and written terms and propositions are to be judged.[48] Quoting Augustine's *De trinitate* XV, Ockham defines

---

aspects of Ockham's position. See "Ockham's Theory of Signification," esp. pp. 211–17; "Ockham's Theory of Supposition," esp. pp. 234–45, on Ockham's earlier development of the distinctions between scientific discourse about things themselves (physics) and a second order discourse about relationships between things (logic); and "Ockham's Realistic Conceptualism," on the argument against the incipient skepticism often attributed to Ockham. For a full treatment of Ockham's logic, see Ernest Addison Moody, *The Logic of William Ockham* (London: Sheed & Ward, 1935); and Gordon Leff, *William of Ockham: The Metamorphosis of Scholastic Discourse* (Manchester: University of Manchester Press, 1975).

[48]Ockham interprets Aristotle's connections among things, concepts, speech, and writing at the beginning of *De interpretatione* to mean that concepts, speech, and writing each directly signify things but that conceptual terms signify things primarily (*primo*) and that spoken and written terms signify things only secondarily and subordinately (*secundario, signa subordinata*). See Ockham, *Summa Logicae,* ed. Philotheus Boehner (New York: Franciscan Institute Publications, 1951), I, 8–9; all references to the Latin text are from this edition (hereafter cited as Boehner). The English translation appears in *Ockham's Theory of Terms: Part I of the Summa Logicae,* tr. Michael J. Loux (Notre Dame: University of Notre Dame Press, 1974), pp. 49–50. All references to the English text are from this translation (hereafter cited as Loux). Boehner explains this difficult concept of secondary signification of spoken terms in "Ockham's Theory of Signification," pp. 218–21. John Trentman argues for the pivotal importance of mental terms in Ockham's logic in "Ockham on Mental," *Mind,* 79 (1970), 586–90.

mental terms and the propositions they compose as "mental words which . . . belong to no language" (*verba mentalia, quae beatus Augustinus 15 De trinitate dicit nullius esse linquae*) and "reside in the intellect alone and are incapable of being uttered aloud" (*in mente manent et exterius proferri non possunt*) (Loux, pp. 49–50; Boehner, pp. 8–9). For Ockham, spoken terms, *voces* that "are externally pronounced" (*pronuntientur exterius*) (Loux, p. 50; Boehner, p. 9), are not an inextricable part of *oratio*, as they are for Peter of Spain and William of Sherwood, but form a separate kind of *oratio*, *oratio vocalis* as opposed to *oratio mentalis*.[49] The conceptual term in *oratio mentalis* is an "impression of the soul" which signifies "naturally," whereas "the spoken or written term signifies only conventionally" (*secundum voluntariam institutionem*) (Loux, p. 50; Boehner, p. 9). Most of the first thirteen chapters of Part I of Ockham's *Summa* are devoted to analyzing, explicitly or implicitly, the relationship between mental and conventional terms, distinguishing their foundation in logic and usage respectively, and proposing how to identify what in natural, conventional language has its correlate in concepts about things.

Ockham explains, for instance, to what extent the grammatical categories of spoken language correspond to the categories of mental language or to "the significative power of language" (*propter necessitatem expressionis inventa*) (Loux, p. 52; Boehner, p. 12). Some parts of speech in spoken language have correlates in mental language (e.g., nouns, verbs, pronouns, adverbs, conjunctions, and prepositions), while some (e.g., participles) do not, since they are peculiar to spoken and written language. The case and number, but not the gender of spoken nouns (*nomina vocalia*), have correlates in mental nouns (*nomina mentalia*).[50] Whatever element in spoken language does not correspond to mental language Ockham assigns to the dubious class of "the ornaments of language or some other cause" (*propter ornatum sermonis vel aliam causam*) (Loux, p. 52; Boehner, p. 12), switching to *sermo* as the word to designate spoken, conventional language. To a considerable degree, spoken words do have

---

[49]For Ockham's use of *oratio* outside logic as *vox significata ad placitum*, see Boehner, "Ockham's Theory of Signification," pp. 209–10.

[50]Ockham explains that the *figura* of nouns also has no correlate in mental terms. For example, *homo est alba*, instead of *albus*, while a grammatical mistake, does not alter the logical import of the spoken and written proposition, and so the error in agreement has no correlate in the mental proposition.

correlates in mental language, but many aspects of spoken language have characteristics peculiar to speech because they originate in convention rather than in the mind's apprehension of things. This conventional aspect of speech does not contribute to meaning.[51] Ockham explains the absence of correspondence between mental and spoken terms as the result of some irregularity of speech, whether it be an ornament or the poverty (*penuria*) of speech (Loux, p. 56; Boehner, p. 17). Characteristically devaluing external discourse, Ockham holds that Latin as a spoken, natural, conventional language does not in general measure up to the possibilities of mental language.

In his discussion of the discrepancies between mental language and the exterior language shaped by the convention of language users (*utentes*), Ockham provides a way to analyze usage into its logical components—the mental terms that alone give speech meaning. "In everyday speech" (*in vulgari locutione*) there is little awareness of the underlying mental terms that give spoken words meaning. Only in the speech of "philosophers and saints" is language used with this awareness (Loux, p. 65; Boehner, p. 29). Those "expert in logic" (*eruditi in logica*) thus habitually translate spoken terms into mental terms. The logician translates Latin as a natural language determined by usage into a correlate of the mental language that belongs to no specific language. If one were not able to do so, one could never know the intention of authors (*maxime necessarium est scire propter mentem auctorum habendam*) (Loux, pp. 67–68; Boehner, pp. 30–31). Meaning is communicated when one converts an author's conventional language (the written record of his *voces*) into written terms that correspond to mental terms. Usage, or the conventional *vox* of natu-

[51]Among the discrepancies between mental and spoken terms are the following: (1) the concrete nouns of mental, but not spoken, language all have corresponding abstract nouns (Boehner, pp. 17–18; Loux, pp. 56–57); (2) because synonyms are vocal terms signifying the same mental term, synonymy is characteristic of spoken, but not mental, language (Boehner, p. 19; Loux, p. 58); (3) some abstract vocal nouns are abstract only by virtue of the convention of language users (*utentes*), since their mental correlates are concrete nouns with disguised adverbial modifications (Boehner, p. 28; Loux, p. 65; see also Boehner, pp. 30–31; Loux, pp. 67–68); (4) equivocity, a word's ability to refer to more than one concept, is the result of convention and is not a property of mental terms (Boehner, pp. 41–42; Loux, pp. 75–76); and (5) the figurative use of language is a property of vocal terms, not mental terms (Boehner, p. 214; Loux, p. 220).

ral language (*signum ad placitum institutum*), is thus inevitably a distortion of meaning which one must adjust and correct by identifying underneath the exterior word the logical infrastructure responsible for meaning. The linguistic debris left when mental terms are subtracted from spoken or written terms is relegated to the "ornaments of speech," a category just slightly below the logician's disdain.

For Ockham, then, as for Abelard, Hugh of St. Victor, Peter of Spain, and William of Sherwood, the logician and his methods of analysis are ultimately responsible for explaining and preserving meaning in natural language by clearing away the distorting effects of speech which originate in usage and convention, although, to the logician's dismay, speech is not completely escapable, even in the discourse of logic. Finally, for the logician, accurate speech is possible only because it is the product of those processes that allow the phenomenal world to radiate through the mind's interior discourse, from which it falls into the conventions of *vox,* where it may still retain some gleams of its uncorrupted origins prior to utterance. Granted that speech can never be a transparent window through which we gaze at reality, and granted that for some Scholastic logicians the discourse of logic cannot exist without speech (as *vox*), complete linguistic transparency does exist as an ideal against which *vox* can be measured.

Nevertheless, for many Scholastic logicians, speech and thought are at odds. The act of speech is a moment of struggle between the mental articulation of a thought and its expression in the sounds of convention-bound speech. Suppositing terms, which for some logicians are inextricably bound up in speech, contain the seeds of their own undermining: since speech introduces elements that cloud the referential and logical function of terms, every spoken utterance can potentially render meaningless the meaning of which it is the necessary vehicle. If logic describes the principles for the accurate articulation of thoughts about things, then the materialization of such thoughts in speech always threatens to diminish the accuracy of those thoughts; especially for such logicians as Peter of Spain and William of Sherwood, the moment of speech is a threat to the very foundations of speech in logic. In its attempt to deculturate language to make it a transparent vehicle of thought about things, Scholastic logic presents a more anguished attitude toward spoken, natural language than does either Aristotle himself or Renaissance humanists. The most important theorists of language in the later Middle Ages regarded culture as in some basic way hostile to meaning. Indeed, at times they seem on the verge of declaring purely mental discourse as ineffable.

2 /

The Humanists:

The Primacy of Speech

SCHOLASTIC logicians and grammarians provided an ontological and epistemological framework that explains
the elements out of which language is constructed as an
instrument of knowledge, but their explanations leave the convention-bound *vox* of spoken language in an ambiguous position. Defining language as speech and locating its authority in social custom,
humanists by and large rejected the Scholastic evaluation of the spoken word, along with the reign of logic in the curriculum and what
they saw as the deleterious effect of Scholastic logic on grammar and
language study in general. Peter of Spain was often singled out for
derision, while Erasmus, Thomas More, John Skelton, Jean Des-
pautère, Jean Sintheim, and Alexander Hegius railed against the
modistae.[1] By the sixteenth century, medieval grammar textbooks

---

[1]See Charles Thurot, *Extraits de divers manuscrits latins pour servir à l'histoire des doctrines grammaticales au moyen âge* (1869; rpt. Frankfurt: Minerva, 1964), pp. 496–99; W. Keith Percival, "The Grammatical Tradition and the Rise of the Vernaculars," in *The Histo-riography of Linguistics*, vol. 13 of *Current Trends in Linguistics*, ed. T. A. Sebeok (The Hague: Mouton, 1975), pp. 240–41; E. J. Ashworth, review of Juan Luis Vives, *Against the Pseudodialecticians: A Humanist Attack on Medieval Logic*, tr. Rita Guerlac, and Juan Luis Vives, *In Pseudodialecticos: A Critical Edition*, tr. Charles Fantazzi, *Renaissance Quarterly*, 33 (1980), 744; Daniel Kinney, "More's *Letter to Dorp:* Remapping the Triv-ium," *Renaissance Quarterly*, 34 (1981), 182; Terence Heath, "Logical Grammar, Gram-matical Logic, and Humanism in Three German Universities," *Studies in the Renais-sance*, 18 (1971), 19. Ashworth and Kinney explain that Thomas of Erfurt was often mistakenly identified as Albertus, as in Skelton; see "Speak, Parrot," in *The Complete Poems of John Skelton, Laureate*, ed. Philip Henderson (New York: Dutton, 1959), p. 293. See also Rabelais, *Gargantua and Pantagruel*, tr. J. M. Cohen (Baltimore: Penguin, 1955), p. 70, though Rabelais does not mention Albertus.

had been banned from the schools, and the battle against Alexander
de Villa-dei's *Doctrinale*, the most popular scholastic school grammar
textbook, was won.[2]

The Role of Convention

Although the first extended humanist attack against the Scholastic treatment of Latin as a language came from Lorenzo Valla's *De
Lingua Latina Elegantiae*, among the attacks most directly relevant to
the linguistic program of the English humanists was Juan Luis Vives's
In Pseudodialecticos, a tract in the form of a letter to a friend.[3] Vives
tries to persuade his friend to take up humanistic studies and aban-
don the Scholastic vanities of Paris. Throughout the letter, Vives
examines the question of whether language norms are dictated by
logic or by usage, and he argues heatedly for usage, which makes
language a cultural artifact rather than an abstract philosophical
instrument. Vives agrees with the logicians that dialectic (the term he
uses in preference to logic, for reasons that become apparent later) is
a "science of speech" (*scientia de sermone*), but his definition of speech,
sermo, is diametrically opposed to the logician's *oratio*, although he
does not directly attack supposition theory itself.[4]

Sermo is not the materialization of mental concepts reflecting the
ontological nature of things in otherwise deficient conventional
sounds; it is the outer discourse of natural language and the spoken
vernacular. "Tell me," Vives asks, "what language [*sermo*] this logic of
yours belongs to? French, Spanish, Gothic, or Vandal perhaps? It is

[2]Thurot, *Extraits*, p. 492; and Heath, "Logical Grammar," p. 12.

[3]Charles Fantazzi argues that More was first attracted to Vives after reading *In
Pseudodialecticos* (introduction to Juan Luis Vives, *In Pseudodialecticos: A Critical Edition*
[Dordrecht: Reidel, 1979], pp. 7–8); hereafter cited as Fantazzi. Kinney, "More's
Letter," pp. 201–3, argues that in fact Vives wrote under the influence of More's letter
to Dorp. For helpful remarks on Valla, see Richard Waswo, "The 'Ordinary Language
Philosophy' of Lorenzo Valla," *Bibliothèque d'humanisme et renaissance*, 41 (1979), 255–
71.

[4]Alan R. Perreiah remarks that Valla was principally concerned with the reform of
"old logic," or that part of Scholastic logic derived from Aristotle which did not contain
the theory of the properties of terms ("Humanist Critiques of Scholastic Dialectic,"
Sixteenth Century Journal, 13 [Fall 1982], 7). Valla does nevertheless alter the orientation
of language analysis by giving classical usage such importance.

certainly not Latin."[5] A good deal of his subsequent answer is an explanation of what Vives the humanist means when he refers to Latin as a *sermo* in contradistinction to the Scholastic logician's Latin, the medium of logical propositions and syllogisms. Vives announces a shift in the linguistic elements that humanists believe constitute meaningful discourse, which, as we have seen, humanist grammarians generally identified as the medium of literature rather than logical or metaphysical predications.[6] Vives holds Aristotle's logic in as high esteem as any terminist but for a different reason: for him, Aristotle's logic explains and is expressed in the Greek language as spoken by Greek people (*ad uulgarem illam Graecum, quem totus populus loquebatur, accommodasse* [pp. 36, 37]). Far from rejecting logic, Vives returns to its classical source, which he believes the barbarous Scholastics have distorted.[7]

The language spoken by people (*sermo quam ceteri homines utantur* [pp. 36, 37]) is Vives's criterion for all language rules, even for the language of logic, and so he controverts the logicians' most fundamental linguistic claim: that they have made language accurate and precise and therefore suitable for statements of truth. Vives, like Erasmus, insists that, on the contrary, usage precedes and determines grammatical and logical rules, not vice versa. Thus he rejects the Scholastic grammarians' idea of the philosophical *primus inventor:*

> Language [*sermo*] was not twisted to suit the rules [*formulae*], but rather the rules followed the pattern of language. We do not speak [*loquimur*] Latin in a certain way because Latin grammar bids us so to speak; on the contrary, grammar recommends us to speak in a certain way because that is the way Latin is spoken. The same is true of rhetoric and logic, each of which is expressed in the same language as grammar. . . . Logic finds out truth, falsehood, or proba-

[5]Fantazzi, pp. 34, 35. All references to Vives are from this edition, which includes the Latin text (on even-numbered pages).

[6]As Perreiah puts it, humanists and Scholastics were generally interested in two different dialects of Latin, as it were: Latin as the natural language of classical antiquity, as opposed to Latin as a logical metalanguage ("Humanistic Critiques," p. 21). I am in essential agreement with Heath, "Logical Grammar," that literary texts become for humanists the purveyors of grammatical norms.

[7]For More's rejection of Scholastic additions to Aristotle rather than Aristotle himself, see Martin Fleisher, *Radical Reform and Political Persuasion in the Life and Writings of Thomas More* (Geneva: Droz, 1973), pp. 83–84.

bility in the common speech that everyone uses [*in hoc vulgari, & qui est omnium in ore sermo*].[8]

The argument is meant to refute the position of Hugh of St. Victor, for example, on the relationship between logical rules and spoken language.

Vives repeatedly accuses the Scholastic logicians of violating this commonality of language, the community based on *sermo*, by inventing their own language, an artificial language with no roots in the real source of language—the social matrix—or the conversation of actual speakers in social relationships. In the case of Latin, this matrix was of course the *populus Romanus*. Vives consistently maintained that the most important linguistic criterion is the *usus loquendi communis* (pp. 38, 39), the *consensus loquentium*, exactly the standard Scholastic logicians tried to eradicate through the theory of supposition. Instead of using "the stock vocabulary available to everyone from a common coinage" (*uulgaribus notisque uocabulis atque orationibus, quibus unusquisque uti debet tanquam nummis quibus publica forma est*), the logicians "have invented private meanings for words contrary to the customs and conventions of mankind" (*contra omnem hominum consuetudinem & usum* [pp. 38, 39; 40, 41]). The custom and convention of speakers preserve the public nature of language, *sermo*, the term Vives prefers over the medieval *oratio* or *vox*. Vives thus assigns to Latin the status of a vernacular.[9] Instead of providing resistance to meaning, culture is the only locus out of which verbal meaning can emerge. Vives does in fact refer once to the correspondence between word and reality in speech, but for the most part he is not especially interested in the axis that describes the referential coordinates of words and things. In-

[8]Pp. 36 and 37. T. W. Baldwin points out that Erasmus played a primary role in promulgating this idea in the northern Renaissance (*William Shakespeare's Small Latine and Lesse Greek*, 2 vols. [Urbana: University of Illinois Press, 1944], I, 75–117). For More's role in formulating this view in reaction against Scholastic logic, see Fleisher, *Radical Reform*, pp. 81–97.

[9]Vives uses the term *dialectic* over *logic* because of its association with spoken language, *dialect*, which he regards as the original meaning of the word (pp. 58 and 59). It should be noted, however, that Scholastics too stressed the oral process of learning through dialogue (i.e., dialectic) between student and master; see Perreiah, "Humanist Critiques," pp. 18–19; and Walter J. Ong, *Ramus, Method, and the Decay of Dialogue: From the Art of Discourse to the Art of Reason* (Cambridge: Harvard University Press, 1958), p. 155.

stead, he explains language by referring to prior acts of language which form a linguistic fabric that makes words comprehensible to groups of people sharing the conventions of a common language. For Vives that fabric is speech, *sermo,* and humanist grammar textbooks teach how to create it, though, as we shall see, humanists did consider the referential dimension of speech as well.

The new importance the humanists assigned to usage and common speech, *usus loquendi,* and their abandonment of Scholastic, terminist logic reoriented the disciplines of the trivium. For terminist logic humanists substituted a place-logic, also Aristotelian in origin but not concerned with the issues addressed by supposition theory and particularly suited to the needs of rhetoric and literary studies.[10] At the same time that rhetoric became thus allied with place-logic, grammar became separate from logic and was instead devoted to the rules of speech based on the usage of authors, the very principle that Scholastic speculative grammarians tried to nullify. The humanists conjoined grammar with the study of authors of literary, rhetorical, and historiographical texts, as it had commonly been conjoined before the rise of Scholastic philosophy in the eleventh century.

It would, however, be a mistake to see humanist grammar as the revival of principles entirely forgotten after the eleventh century. Though the humanists believed they were reacting against a specifically medieval form of grammar, their own grammar developed out of a grammatical tradition continuous since antiquity, a tradition alive even in the Scholastic Middle Ages and persisting alongside of and mostly independent from speculative grammar and the allied concerns of terminist logic.[11] But because the humanists deliberately

[10]Place-logic, whose introduction to humanist Europe is generally attributed to Agricola, teaches how to select preexisting commonplaces on a given topic ("invention") and to connect them into an argument ("judgment"), a logic particularly suited to the needs of rhetoric, to which it in fact became subordinated. On Agricolan logic, see Ong, *Ramus,* pp. 92–130; and, for its English adaptation, Wilbur Samuel Howell, *Logic and Rhetoric in England, 1500–1700* (Princeton: Princeton University Press, 1956), pp. 12–56. For the cultural significance of place-logic, see Lisa Jardine, *Francis Bacon: Discovery and the Art of Discourse* (Cambridge: Cambridge University Press, 1974), pp. 17–58. For the reorientation of the trivium, see Kinney, "More's *Letter*"; Heath, "Logical Grammar"; and Fleisher, *Radical Reform,* pp. 88–94.

[11]For late medieval grammar outside the Scholastic tradition of *grammatica speculativa,* see Percival, "Grammatical Tradition," pp. 231–33; James Jerome Murphy, *Rhetoric in the Middle Ages: A History of Rhetorical Theory from St. Augustine to the Renais-*

constructed their grammatical theory in opposition to Scholastic logic and modistic grammar, which, as we have seen, was meant to explain the very foundation of language, humanist grammar can profitably be examined as the cornerstone of the humanist linguistic program.[12] Indeed, humanists often use their discussion of grammar as a polemic for and exposition of their most fundamental assumptions about the grounds upon which language is constructed and which enable words to contain meaning.

Whereas the Scholastics expounded their linguistic views in logics and grammars to be used in the university curriculum, humanists frequently explain their program in educational treatises and Latin grammar textbooks, especially those designed to help the schoolmaster define a curriculum and instruct him on the day-to-day matters of teaching English spelling and Latin grammar in the petty school and grammar school, while preparing students for an education based primarily on literary subjects.[13] These textbooks, petty school manuals, and educational treatises of the sixteenth and early seventeenth centuries, written by English humanists or English writers affected by humanism, emphasize both the role of convention and the underlying logical relationship of things, thoughts, and speech, of inner and outer discourse.[14] English humanists reveal themselves to be much

sance (Berkeley: University of California Press, 1974), pp. 135–63; R. W. Hunt, "Oxford Grammar Masters in the Middle Ages," in *Oxford Studies Presented to Daniel Callus* (Oxford: Clarendon Press, 1964), pp. 163–93; Fr. Bonaventure, "The Teaching of Latin in Later Medieval England," *Mediaeval Studies*, 23 (1961), 1–20.

[12]My thesis is a corollary of Paul Oskar Kristeller's argument that humanism developed from issues first posed in medieval Italian grammar as well as rhetoric ("Humanism and Scholasticism in the Italian Renaissance," in *Renaissance Thought* [New York: Harper & Row, 1961], p. 100). For the centrality of grammar in Italian humanism, see Aldo Scaglione, "The Humanist as Scholar in Politian's Conception of the *Grammaticus*," *Studies in the Renaissance*, 8 (1961), 49–70.

[13]Helpful works on educational theory and practice in the English Renaissance include Kenneth Charlton, *Education in Renaissance England* (London: Routledge & Kegan Paul, 1965); Martin Lowther Clarke, *Classical Education in Britain, 1500–1900* (Cambridge: Cambridge University Press, 1959); Donald Leman Clark, *John Milton at St. Paul's School: A Study of Ancient Rhetoric in English Renaissance Education* (New York: Columbia University Press, 1948); Baldwin, *William Shakespeare's Small Latine;* Foster Watson, *The English Grammar Schools to 1660: Their Curriculum and Practice* (Cambridge: Cambridge University Press, 1908); William Harrison Woodward, *Desiderius Erasmus concerning the Aim and Method of Education* (Cambridge: Cambridge University Press, 1904).

[14]Timothy J. Reiss examines the construction of this humanist discourse in sixteenth-century tragedy (*Tragedy and Truth: Studies in the Development of a Renaissance and Neoclassical Discourse* [New Haven: Yale University Press, 1980], pp. 1–17, 40–77).

closer than is usually thought to Aristotle's formulation of the concordance between mental and spoken discourse, especially as it was further developed and extended by the Stoics. Stoic grammar codifies Aristotle's connection between logical and ontological categories in the spoken Greek recorded in the usage of good authors;[15] and one could argue that it was the Stoics rather than the skeptics who were the true intellectual forebears of the English humanists, even though the skeptics are often considered the ancient inspiration for Renaissance rhetoric. But humanists modified their inherited belief in the logical—Aristotelion or Stoic—basis of language by identifying literary language, rather than logical proposition and syllogism, as the discourse that can contain and express truth. For humanists, literary language conveys the ontological stability of the world. The language of authors is a witness to the knowability of the phenomenal world, and *sermo* affirms that the phenomenal world is predictable. The language humanist Latin grammars teach students to construct is identical to the language of the literary subjects of the humanist curriculum—poetry, history, oratory—a language everywhere esteemed in accord with the humanist reverence for the very idea of the author. This shift in the privileged disciplines of the curriculum will ultimately be accompanied by a shift in the categories and objects of knowledge themselves.

One treatise that outlines the linguistic goals and methods of the English grammar school is William Kempe's *Education of Children in Learning* (1588), which T. W. Baldwin characterizes as the "clearest presentation of the underlying philosophy of the [Elizabethan] grammar school curriculum" in a "coordinated and philosophized form."[16] Using a method that precisely accommodates his understanding of how language is constructed in general, Kempe describes, year by year, a grammar school curriculum almost entirely devoted to teaching Latin language and literature. In the petty school, the Elizabethan schoolboy learns to master English words or *voces:* he begins to learn the pronunciation of the sounds of letters and syllables while also practicing written letters representing those sounds.[17] Thus pre-

---

[15]See Michael Frede, "Principles of Stoic Grammar," in *The Stoics,* ed. John M. Rist (Berkeley: University of California Press, 1978), pp. 27–76.

[16]Baldwin, *William Shakespeare's Small Latine,* I, 436–37.

[17]William Kempe, *The Education of Children in Learning: Declared by the Dignitie, Utilitie, and Method Thereof* (London, 1588), sigs. F2r–F3v. All references are from this edition.

pared, the schoolboy enters grammar school, where he starts the first form by declining the Latin parts of speech and, gradually acquiring the rules of syntax, then learns to read Latin (sigs. F3v–F4r). In the second form, he studies grammar by examining Latin authors, while translating English sentences into Latin and Latin sentences into English. The third form is devoted to paraphrasing Cicero's letters in Latin and then using them as the basis of double translation, which Kempe calls imitation, a practice that likewise occupies the next two forms, though the material is longer and more difficult. (The entire process is described on sigs. F3v–G1v.)

In describing the second form of this representative humanist curriculum, Kempe makes a remark that connects the course of study to the process by which language itself is constituted: "Wherefore in reading, [the student] learned letter by letter, syllable by syllable, so heere [in spoken dialogue with his schoolmaster, an important component of the method] let him learn word by word, phrase by phrase, untill he have all the partes, which are equall to the whole, as may be expressed in this manner of talke between the Maister and the Schollar" (sig. F4v). The material covered in the several years of Kempe's graduated curriculum corresponds to the materials out of which discourse is assembled step by step from the speech sounds signified by letters and syllables that constitute words, to the syntactical construction of whole sentences assimilated by studying authors, and finally to extended discourses learned through double translations of Cicero. In the process, the student's command of Latin approaches the level of "talke," or spoken, exterior discourse, equivalent to the written language of literary authors. Kempe's description of the progress from letter and syllable to speech is the counterpart of the construction of linguistic elements from *sonus* and *vox* to *terminus*, proposition, and syllogism which appears in the opening of Peter of Spain's *Summulae*, although the humanist and the scholastic obviously emphasize different elements. Kempe's curriculum guiding the student through the several stages that lead to the mastery of speech manifests a concern completely different from the Scholastics' preoccupation with semantic and referential criteria. Kempe, moreover, places *vox* at the center rather than the periphery of language. His curriculum is a tribute to what John Colet called "makynge latynes." (Colet used the phrase in the preface to his short treatise, published a half century earlier, on the parts of speech, the *Aeditio* [1527], which became part of the official Tudor Latin textbook, Lily's *Grammar*, which also defines its concern for language as "speche.") The method of Kempe, Colet, and Lily marks the victory of the humanist interest in natural language over Scholastic attempts to devalue Latin as a natural language.

This insistence on language as speech is reflected in a new and intense interest in orthography, a subject taught in the petty school. The humanists of course had other reasons for being concerned with spelling, but certainly spelling was part of a linguistic program that constantly reminded students that language is sounded speech transcribed into writing. This principle was one of the first things a schoolboy learned in the petty school, and it became a commonplace in humanist discussions of language, making its way even into popular manuals such as Sir Thomas Hoby's translation of Castiglione's *Courtier*, which devotes several pages to the subject.[18] Debates over the nature and reform of spelling were thus the occasion for discussions of the nature of language itself, and although the language at issue was English, the conclusions reached in the spelling debates were just as applicable to Latin (indeed, to language in general) and in fact prepared the way for definitions of Latin as a natural language. The humanist discussion of spelling—incorporated into the first stage of Kempe's curriculum, where students learn to construct words from letters and syllables—thus contrasts sharply with the Scholastic logicians' and grammarians' refusal to consider *vox* apart from *significatio*.[19]

Advocates of spelling reform sought a theory of orthography, a *ratio* for spelling, that would regularize the chaotic condition of English spelling by making it correspond more accurately to actual pro-

[18]Baldassare Castiglione, *The Book of the Courtier*, tr. Sir Thomas Hoby (London: Dent, 1928), pp. 50–53. See p. 50: ". . . wryting is nothing els, but a maner of speach, that remaineth still after a man hath spoken."
[19]See Thomas of Erfurt, *Grammatica Speculativa*, ed. G. L. Bursill-Hall (London: Longman, 1972), pp. 148, 149. See also Aquinas's comments in *Aristotle: On Interpretation. Commentary by St. Thomas and Cajetan*, tr. Jean Oesterele (Milwaukee: Marquette University Press, 1962), pp. 21–22, and for the Latin version, Thomas Aquinas, *Opera Omnia*, vol. 18, *In Aristotelis Stagiritae Nonnullos Libros Commentaria* (Parma: Fiaccadoro, 1865; rpt. New York: Musurgia, 1949), p. 2. Aquinas bases his view on the authority of Aristotle's *De anima*.

nunciation and by adding new letters to the alphabet to further facilitate that correspondence. But even those who argued against such
reform agreed with their opponents that writing imitates speech, and
that letters, the basic components of words, stand for sounds. As D. G.
Scragg points out, sixteenth-century spelling reform aimed at bringing "the spoken and written language into close alignment."[20] The
implications of this attempt bear further examination, and a close
comparison of reformist and anti-reformist views on orthography
reveals the seriousness with which the humanists regarded spelling:
the spelling controversy was a vehicle for formulating the public,
social nature of language as speech conveyed in common usage. The
participants in the spelling debate placed phonological values at the
center of their linguistic interests.

The most important works on English orthography—Thomas
Smith's *De recta et emendata linguae Anglicae scriptione, dialogus* (1568),
John Hart's *Orthographie* (1569), Alexander Gil's *Logonomia Anglica*
(1619), and Charles Butler's *English Grammar* (1633)—all called for
the reform of English spelling. Smith initiated the movement for
spelling reform after working with Erasmus on the proper pronunciation of ancient Greek. Smith's ideas were disseminated in English
by Hart, one of his students.

The main import of Hart's argument is that English spelling is
seriously deficient because it has been dominated by "custome" rather
than by "reason." Custom has preserved obsolete spellings even when
letters no longer match the sounds of the words, laments Hart, following Smith's formulation of the "reason" of spelling.[21] It is no
accident that Hart sees orthography as part of a grammatical program designed to teach the student the art of speaking well (sig. B2r).
Letters, Hart argues, were created by man as marks of "voices" or
sounds; words and sentences are a series of such voices (sig. C1v).
"Letters," he explains, "are the figures and colours wherewith the
image of mans voice is painted" (sig. C2r), a fact that the Romans
realized in their creation of letters to imitate the sounds of their
speech (sig. F1r). Hart thus gives the *vox* of the Scholastic logician a

[20]D. G. Scragg, *A History of English Spelling* (Manchester: University of Manchester Press, 1974), p. 61.

[21]John Hart, *An Orthographie* (London, 1569; facs. rpt. Menston: Scolar Press, 1969), sigs. A3r–A3v, C1v–D3r. All references to Hart are from this edition.

new life at the pre-semantic level. He can even conceive of words as the vibration of breath produced by the relative position of the speech organs (sig. H2v). Although the Scholastics relegated this aspect of language to the physicist, Hart sees it as vital to language as a cultural phenomenon, for when letters are correctly matched to the sound produced by the mouth, tongue, and throat, they can preserve the words of any language over time, even if the meaning of the words has long been forgotten (sig. B1v)—so much importance does Hart assign to pre-semantic sounded speech, which may be recorded in written letters, totally subordinate to spoken language.[22]

Hart's most formidable opponent in the orthography debate was Richard Mulcaster, who expounded his opinions in *The First Part of the Elementarie* (1582). Mulcaster devotes a large portion of this work to refuting Hart's arguments, though he does not mention Hart by name. Yet Mulcaster agrees with many of Hart's premises, particularly that letters were invented by man to express "euerie distinct sound in voice" and so preserve speech in writing, which must therefore imitate speech.[23] Nevertheless, Mulcaster's emphasis on "consent" and convention in spelling clearly distinguishes him from Hart. At the root of the debate between the two orthographers is their disagreement about which facet of the humanist conception of language deserves greater emphasis: language as sounded speech or language as conventionally agreed upon norms. The particular letters invented to represent sounds, Mulcaster insists, were themselves chosen by consent, not because of any intrinsic qualities of their own; and although they may have originally matched the sound of words accurately and "reasonably," pronunciation often changes while spelling remains the same through custom. For Mulcaster, then, custom is by no means a pernicious influence; rather it prevents spelling from constantly changing and is thus a stabilizing linguistic force. That is, custom acts to preserve as much as possible of the initial match between letter and sound against the constant threat of linguis-

---

[22]The near complete identification of words with their sounds is probably related to the popular compilation of alphabetized word lists. In his Epistle Dedicatorie to the *Palace of profitable Pleasure* (London, 1621; facs. rpt. Menston: Scolar Press, 1967), John Evans sees his alphabetized list as a guide to teaching spelling (sig. A5v), since it "enforceth the learner to rely wholly vpon the sound of the Letters" (sig. A3v).

[23]Richard Mulcaster, *The First Part of the Elementarie* (London, 1582; facs. rpt. Menston: Scolar Press, 1970), p. 65. All references to Mulcaster are from this edition.

tic change (pp. 66–72). Mulcaster's concept of speech thus retains both custom and reason. (Ironically, humanist orthographers such as Hart and Mulcaster stress language as speech for a reading public that was increasingly encountering language in print.)[24] By grounding the first stage of language construction in consent and custom, Mulcaster gives language a public, social nature that affects it at every level, for consent can be conferred only where people live and communicate in social circumstances. The Scholastic logician would have had great difficulty understanding the kind of significance humanists attributed to *vox*, as the cultural importance of phonological values shifted drastically in the Renaissance.

To base orthography on custom is to give spelling a history and to justify present spellings on the basis of prior spellings. The notion that language depends on prior acts of language is central to the humanist concept of speech and is the rationale not only for erecting words out of letters and syllables, that is, the first stage in the Tudor curriculum, but for learning Latin in the grammar school, the curriculum's second stage. The principles underlying natural, spoken language remain the same in Latin as in English, though they are discussed on a much larger scale.

The humanists' notion that Latin is to be meaningfully considered only as spoken utterance is illustrated by their use of Roman comedy in teaching Latin grammar. The first English textbook based on this notion was the *Uulgaria quedem abs Terencio in Anglicam linguam traducta,* a collection of phrases from Terence put together about 1483, probably by John Anwykyll, a schoolmaster at Magdalen College, one of the early humanist centers that developed new techniques for teaching Latin.[25] In creating this textbook based on the Latin *sermo* of authors, Anwykyll was among the very first Englishmen to exemplify

[24]For a description of the identity of the reading public in this period, see David Cressy, *Literacy and the Social Order: Reading and Writing in Tudor and Stuart England* (Cambridge: Cambridge University Press, 1980). That humanists so emphatically defined language as sounded speech must qualify Ong's view that humanists were concerned mostly with written language (*Ramus,* pp. 92, 154–55), though Ong is of course aware of the humanist interest in speech.

[25]See William Nelson, "The Teaching of English in Tudor Grammar Schools," *Studies in Philology,* 49 (1952), 121; and Beatrice White, introduction to *The Vulgaria of John Stanbridge and the Vulgaria of Robert Whittinton,* EETS, no. 187 (London: Kegan Paul, Trench, Trubner, 1932), p. xvi. Subsequent references both to White's introduction and to the *Vulgariae* will be given as White.

the method that Vives would later enunciate as a principle. Nicholas Udall, headmaster of Eton, wrote a similar textbook for his students, *Floures for Latine speaking* (1533). Udall provided a line-by-line translation of three plays by Terence, appending commentaries on Terence's grammatical constructions to the translation of individual lines. This method of instruction remained in use into the seventeenth century.[26] Both Anwykyll and Udall thus anticipated Kempe's prescription for introducing students to Latin grammar through the study of actual literary texts. Sixteenth-century annotations of Latin comedy assume that Latin is a natural language whose norms must be sought in the conventions of "*author*ity," since rules of grammar do not exist in the abstract but rather in the usage, the actual utterance, of speakers—that is, literary authors—who define the canon of correctly constructed *sermo*.

John Colet took much the same position in his *Aeditio*. In the preface he explained: "For in the begynnynge men spake not latyn because such rules were made but contrariwyse, bycause men spake such latyn. Vpon that folowed ye rules were made. That is to saye latyn speche was before the rules not the rules before the latyn speche."[27] In a point almost identical to that Vives makes in *In Pseudo-dialecticos*, Colet here implicitly argues against the speculative grammarian's claim to have outlined a universal system of precepts for grammatical constructions independent of and more accurate than the *usus loquendi* of Latin speech.

Because for Colet Latin means Latin speech, *usus* is its only guide. Accordingly, the rules for declining the parts of speech provided but the barest introduction to grammar, which the student can best learn by observing the usage of great authors: "Let hym [the student] aboue all besyly lerne & rede good latyn authours of chosen poetes

---

[26] Just as Latin comedy was used to teach Latin speech, the method was also reversed by translating Latin comedy into English, as John Palsgrave describes his translation of *Acolastus* on the title page (*The Comedy of Acolastus*, tr. John Palsgrave, ed. P. L. Carver, EETS, no. 202 [London: Oxford University Press, 1937]); quoted in White, p. xliv.

[27] John Colet, *Aeditio* (n.p. 1527; facs. rpt. Menston: Scolar Press, 1971), sig. D7r. For the authorship and textual history of Lily's *Grammar*, universally recognized as not having been written by Lily alone, see C. G. Allen, "The Sources of 'Lily's Latin Grammar': A Review of the Facts and Some Further Suggestions," *The Library*, 5th ser., 9 (1954), 85–100; Baldwin, *William Shakespeare's Small Latine*, I, 95–98; Vincent Joseph Flynn, *The Grammatical Writings of William Lilly, ?1468–?1523* (New York: Bibliographical Society of America, 1943).

and oratours, and not[e] wysely how th[e]y wrote and spake and studi alway to folowe them: desyring none other rules but their examples [since] imitacyon with tongue and penne more avayleth shortly to gete the true eloquent speeche than al the tradicions rules and preceptes of maysters."[28] The need for a preexisting linguistic model arises when one considers language as speech, as a "tongue" recorded by "penne." Colet introduces the term "imitation" to describe this process of acquiring language without recourse to referential or semantic concepts. Colet's grammatical imitation constructs a series of linguistic signs based on other linguistic signs, illustrating what contemporary linguists call a semiotic—as opposed to a mimetic—concept of language.

The *Vulgaria*, a list of Latin phrases and sentences translated into English, was the kind of textbook typically chosen by early humanists to teach Latin as exterior discourse, as *speech*. One such book, compiled in 1519 by Anwykyll's student, John Stanbridge, was in fact adopted by Lily for use in St. Paul's. In the same year, William Horman, in introducing his more extensive *Vulgaria*, rejoiced over the recovery of Latin "speche" rediscovered by "redynge of substanciall authors."[29]

Even a grammarian such as Robert Whittinton, who took issue with an exclusive reliance on example, advocated teaching Latin as speech. A student of Stanbridge and translator of Cicero, Seneca, and Erasmus, Whittinton hoped he rather than Colet and Lily would become the author of England's standard grammar textbook. In his *Vulgaria* (1520) he, like other humanists, appealed to Cicero as his authority on the importance of grammatical precept (just as his opponents appealed to Cicero to make the opposite case for example).[30] But for

[28]Colet, *Aeditio*, sigs. D6r–D7r.

[29]Quoted in White, p. xxvi. For Stanbridge's *Vulgaria* at St. Paul's, see White, p. xix. Reiss too sees the sixteenth century as the beginning of a new approach to language, but he does not deal with the implications of the imitation of other texts. Reiss follows Foucault's epistemic models, although he places the beginning of "classical" discourse in humanist tragedy, whereas Foucault locates it in the seventeenth century. In his provocative explanation of sixteenth-century attitudes to language (one I disagree with, however), Reiss sees the determining consideration of this discourse in the disappearance of God as final arbiter of signs in the created world itself. After preclassical discourse, man becomes the controller of signs, analyzing and appropriating reality in his own signs, including language signs (*Tragedy and Truth*, chap. 1).

[30]For Whittinton's quarrel with Lily, see White, p. xxviii.

all his emphasis on precept, Whittinton sought to teach Latin as a *vulgaris & quotidiana sermo* whose conventions were established by the *usus loquendi* of classical authors.[31] More concerned with syntax than the parts of speech, Whittinton presents each rule in two, often three, ways. The rule is first stated as a general precept, then illustrated by exemplary sentences.[32] Many though not all rules are also illustrated by a passage from a classical author cited in a section titled "Authoryte." The presentation of a grammatical construction, then, moves from an abstract rule to a hypothetical utterance invented by Whittinton and finally to an actual utterance of a classical author. The *author*ity of grammar precepts are thus the particular acts of language of sanctioned authors incorporated into general precepts. Each time a student creates his own syntactical construction in accordance with the rules, he is in effect imitating the example of a classical author. Moreover, because Whittinton's examples, including those from classical "Authoryte," range in subject and tone from moral aphorism to the most conversational level of discourse (for instance, how to state the price of malt), the student is constantly reminded that literary language and ordinary speech have the same source, and that he is learning Latin *speech*.

The humanists' interest in the "reason" of grammar centered on the proper relationship between precept and example in a rationalized method of teaching grammar rules based on usage, what Colet in the preface to his *Aeditio* called learning "not by rote, but by reason,"[33] though this "reason" had nothing to do with the Scholastic *causa* of grammar. Perhaps the most extreme expression of the humanists' subordination of precept to usage and convention appeared in the works of Joseph Webbe in the early seventeenth century.[34] Webbe

[31]White, p. 33. It is interesting that Ascham, who shared these views about language, should refer to the *Vulgariae* of both Horman and Whittinton as "beggarlie gatheringes" (*The Schoolmaster*, in *English Works*, ed. William Aldis Wright [Cambridge: Cambridge University Press, 1904], p. 259). All quotations are from this edition.

[32]By this point the student knows enough Latin not to need translation. In this sense, the written book teaches how to read itself as speech.

[33]Colet, *Aeditio*, sig. A3r.

[34]Webbe was well enough known to be identified as an exemplary language teacher in John Webster, *Academarium Examen* (London, 1653; facs. rpt. in Allen G. Debus, *Science and Education in the Seventeenth Century: The Webster-Ward Debate* [New York: American Elsevier, 1970]). The context in which Webbe worked is discussed in two articles by Vivian Salmon: "Problems of Language-Teaching: A Discussion among

argues against any standard grammar text—he is implicitly referring to Lily's *Grammar*—on the very grounds the humanists had established as the only valid criteria for language norms, usage and convention. Webbe sees language as the artifact of a particular society whose idiom is determined only by the speakers of that society. And because this idiom is constantly changing, it is incapable of being contained in any set of rules.[35] Webbe urges language teachers to dispense with all grammar rules and to replace them with the study of usage in literary authors alone. Thus Webbe takes the consequences of defining language as speech to a greater extreme than did most humanist grammarians before him. Webbe insists that in speaking, we do not utter isolated words but groups of words, which he calls "clauses" (what we might call phrases). This view severely diminishes the importance of the parts of speech, so essential to most rationalized methods of classifying grammatical categories, whether of the speculative or the humanist grammarian.

Webbe puts his theoretical formulations into practice in his several Latin textbooks, all of which are "claused" translations of Latin classics. Claiming Cicero as the ancient source of his method—which he regards as a continuation of the tradition of Erasmus, Julius Caesar Scaliger, and Daniel Heinsius—Webbe uses a visual, typographic technique: he breaks up the Latin sentences into clauses and supplies corresponding clauses in English translation.[36] The textbooks, how-

---

Hartlib's Friends," *Modern Language Review*, 59 (1964), 13–24, and "Joseph Webbe: Some Seventeenth-Century Views on Language Teaching and the Nature of Meaning," *Bibliothèque d'humanisme et renaissance*, 23 (1961), 324–40. Both are reprinted in Vivian Salmon, *The Study of Language in Seventeenth-Century England* (Amsterdam: John Benjamins, 1979).

[35]Joseph Webbe, *An Appeale to Truth* (London, 1622; facs. rpt. Menston: Scolar Press, 1967), p. 21. All quotations are from this edition. Webbe was a friend of Samuel Hartlib, whose help he sought in establishing his own grammar school founded on his own methods of language teaching. See Salmon, "Problems of Language-Teaching," for the details of Webbe's attempts to establish a school. His application to parliament for a license is presented in his *Petition to the High Covrt of Parliament* (London, 1623). All quotations from the *Petition* are from this edition.

[36]Webbe's textbooks include claused translations of Cicero's *Ad Atticum* (*Lessons and Exercises out of Cicero Ad Atticum*) (1627), *Pueriles Confabulatiunculae* (1627), Terence's *Andria* (1629) and *Eunuchus* (1629). For his identification of Cicero as his source, see *Petition*, pp. 4–5; for his awareness of his place in the humanist tradition, see the preface to his translation of *The First Comedy of Pub. Terentivs, called Andria* (London, 1629; facs. rpt. Menston: Scolar Press, 1972) sig. ¶3r. Each of the translations divides the page down the middle, with Latin clauses on the left, one to a line, and their corresponding English clauses on the right, one to a line. Each also contains instruc-

ever, do not primarily teach students how to read Cicero or Terence but how to construct proper Latin sentences by recombining the clauses. Webbe promises that this method will produce effective and quick results for those who wish to learn any language, including the vernaculars.[37] His method is in fact an ambitious application of the theory espoused by most humanists; ultimately one learns Latin by studying the *sermo* of authors. All the verbal units necessary to construct any act of speech are already present in the clauses of authors, Webbe maintains in his *Petition to . . . Parliament.*[38] In the preface to the *Andria,* he energetically argues that his claused translation of Terence can generate all possible utterances (except modern place names) in the style of Terence.[39] So powerful is his method, he believes, that he warns teachers not to use claused versions of inferior authors, lest students be impressed with inferior clauses and so become inferior stylists.

In the *Petition to . . . Parliament,* Webbe considers the objection that he is actually teaching a form of "theevery" or plagiarism. He confidently replies, "if you marke it wel, all speech runnes in this maner, and every man speakes each others clauses" (pp. 19–20). For Webbe, all acts of language are imitations of prior utterances, though he would like to control which prior utterances are to be imitated. Strange as his scheme is, it rests on an insight to which Scholastic logicians and grammarians paid little heed: cultures encode the proper norms of language in their sanctioned texts and place limits on the possibilities of meaning within the parameters of those texts. For language to mean, it must reverberate through preceding acts of language—conventional usage—institutionalized by a society. This reverberation between present and past utterances is what humanists regard as "speech," a distinct contrast to the logician's *oratio* constructed out of *significationes, suppositiones,* and *termini,* which may be secondarily transmitted through the conventions of *impositiones vocum.*

---

tions and exercises for writing compositions by using clauses found in the work translated. For a discussion of the visual component of Webbe's textbooks, see Chapter 4 below.

[37]See *Pueriles Confabulatiunculae, or Childrens Talke* (London, 1627; facs. rpt. Menston: Scolar Press, 1968), sig. *2v.

[38]Webbe, *Petition,* p. 10.

[39]Webbe, *Andria,* sig. ¶¶2v.

Webbe's insistence on language as speech ultimately has significant implications for the language of literature. Since we cannot hear Latin as a spoken language, he explains in *An Appeale to Truth* (p. 31), we must depend exclusively on classical authors for our knowledge of the usage of those who perpetuate the conventions of Latin speech, "the Roman nobility, the men of authority, the Gentry, and the learnedest citizens" (p. 22). The written record of authors is to be regarded as the transcription of speech, he points out, untroubled by his perception that written texts regulate his attempt to reinstitute Latin speech; accordingly, in *An Appeale to Truth* Webbe advises his reader to "*speake* [emphasis added] after the example of *Cicero, Liuius, Salustius, Virgilius, Ouidius, Plautus, & Terentius*" (p. 17). Later in the work, he argues more strenuously: "for, wee must . . . speak . . . as most excellent Authours have written. Makest thou any doubt of following that which *Cicero, Varro, Liuius, Florus, Valerius,* and both the *Plinij,* and others of the purest Authours have spoken? Do'st thou as yet imagine, that he that vseth *Ciceros* and *Virgils* words, doth speak improperly?" (p. 47). Like many another humanist, Webbe considers the poetry of Virgil and the prose of Livy and Sallust to represent the same kind of language as the dramatic speech of Plautus and Terence, that is, spoken, sounded discourse, even though "we cannot hear or imitate the Custome of their native Tone, their accent and delivery" (p. 31).[40]

Perhaps the most significant implication of Webbe's work is that speech is tantamount to the language of literature, literature in the humanist sense that encompasses not only poetry but the literary arts as a whole, including history and oratory. The humanists in general conceive of literary language as a network whose threads weave together a linguistic consensus—common usage, convention—that emerges from a social intercourse; literary language is the common medium that binds a *gens* together and expresses its cultural values,

[40]Ascham too judges classical writing as speech: the speech of Caesar, Cicero, and Demosthenes is superior to that of Sallust and Thucydides because the former expressed themselves while living in the center of spoken Latin and Greek (*The Schoolmaster*, pp. 155–61). The fact that Webbe and Ascham include aureate stylists among the speakers recorded in writing should alter accepted notions about plain style imitating speech and the high style imitating an abstract pattern of eloquence. Virgil and Spenser, Livy and Hooker, are speakers as much as John Donne and Robert Burton are.

which, as many in the Renaissance were aware, rested on the support of political institutions. In his recommendations for teaching Latin, Webbe makes explicit what is implicit in most of the grammarians I have been discussing, namely, the connection between grammatical form, literary language, and speech. Webbe emphatically brings to the fore the humanist principle that to speak well is to utter the language of literature. Nothing could be further removed from the *oratio* of the Scholastic logician and grammarian.

As eccentric as Webbe may at times appear, the literary implications of his theory had already been institutionalized by the standard grammar nationally adopted in the sixteenth century, Lily's *Grammar*. This work presents rules inductively abstracted from the literary usage of classical authors; its basic premise is that to follow grammar rules correctly is by definition to imitate classical authors and thus to become part of the literary and linguistic network of antiquity, as well as its extension among other contemporary authors similarly imitating ancient usage. The preface of Lily's *Grammar* in fact indicates the dual function of the work by describing it as the "beste and certaynest guyde, bothe of reading and speakinge." Books, which for the authors of Lily mean classical literature and its modern imitations, are characteristically part of the same linguistic spectrum as spoken, sounded speech. To learn to read is to learn to speak, even *by* learning to read. The theoretical connection between the two skills justifies their pedagogical conjunction: the rules presented in the grammar text are to be taught along with readings from Latin authors and exercises in speaking Latin.[41] Reading Latin books and translating English books into Latin—both orally and in writing—were inseparable processes in Lily's program of instruction, in Kempe's, and in that of Roger Ascham, the most widely known exponent of the humanist educational program. Ascham's *Schoolmaster* is probably best understood within the context of this grammatical tradition that ex-

---

[41]William Lily [et al.], *A Shorte Introduction of Grammar* (London, 1567; facs. rpt. New York: Scholars' Facsimiles and Reprints, 1945), sigs. Aiir, Aiiir, Aiiiv. A similar conjunction of speaking and reading authors, with an emphasis on convention, appears in John Brinsley, *Ludus Literarius: or, The Grammar Schoole* (London, 1612; facs. rpt. Menston: Scolar Press, 1968), passim; and James Cleland, *The Institution of a Young Noble Man* (Oxford, 1607; facs. rpt. New York: Scolars' Facsimiles and Reprints, 1948), pp. 78–81, though Cleland strongly emphasizes reading authors of historical works.

tends from Anwykyll, Udall, Whittinton, and Lily all the way to Webbe.

The Schoolmaster pursues the larger cultural implications of regarding *sermo* as literary language. Ascham is keenly aware that speech reflects the social consensus from which language conventions derive and that speech is part of an extensive linguistic network of which each individual author is a particular representative. In his outline of an educational plan devoted mainly to literary study, Ascham repeats most of the characteristically humanist positions on language: grammar rules are abstractions from usage (pp. 184, 259); "vtterance" can be produced "either by pen or taulke" (pp. 263, 277); the written classics are "wise talke" that can be "hear[d] or read" (p. 283); classical, literary Latin is the public, common usage of Roman speakers available to moderns in ancient literary documents (pp. 297–99). Accordingly, the written eloquence of Caesar and Cicero derives from their contact with Rome, the center of spoken Latin, whereas Sallust's inelegance can be attributed to the fact that he lived and wrote in the provinces (pp. 300–301). One learns to write well, that is, as one learns to speak well, by hearing the speech of "the best and wisest" (p. 264). Double translation from Latin to English and from English back to Latin, far from being the mechanical, pedantic exercise it is sometimes made out to be, is a way of hearing Latin properly spoken in the absence of actual speakers. Like Webbe's clausing, Whittinton's divisions of precept, example, and authority, and Udall's grammatical annotations of Terence, double translation is the practical and pedagogical embodiment of the humanist theory of literary grammar which explains how language is constructed.

As is well known, the imitation of the best and the wisest (for Ascham, that means Cicero) is the heart of Ascham's pedagogic program. But the cultural and linguistic significance of such imitation has not always been recognized. Ascham argues that great Latin (i.e., classical literary Latin) was written for only about one hundred years, reaching its purest expression with Cicero (pp. 286–87). The Latin written during this particular historical period then became the model for writers in all subsequent periods. Eloquent expression is not an abstract concept based on abstract principles; it is a practice based on the particular usage of certain authors who wrote at certain times. The possibility of eloquence exists, then, because certain writers have spoken eloquently at a particular moment in history, a truth implicitly assumed by the humanist grammatical tradition. Ascham firmly places language in a concrete historical lineage that would have been irrelevant to the terminist logician, but Ascham is not interested in locating the aboriginal moment of eloquence by creating a myth of origins. For Ascham the humanist, the great historical literary writer replaces the Scholastic's primeval *primus impositor,* a philosophor.

Ascham was also aware that the great literary writer's opportunity for eloquence exists within the equally strong propensity of language to decay. According to Ascham, a nation may preserve its language at its best and even improve it by incorporating the standards of some earlier exemplary era. The Romans, for example, achieved literary eloquence in Latin by imitating the usage of the Greeks; to understand how Latin achieves eloquence, one must know the sources of its conventions in Greek authors, as Cicero did (p. 273). On the same principle, the English too may achieve Latin eloquence, by assimilating the linguistic conventions of Rome. And eloquence in English itself may be achieved in the same way—through the adaptation of Latin conventions to English. (Ascham does not bother to identify the source of Greek eloquence, nor is he bothered by the possible infinite regress his theory implies.) The student of eloquence, in other words, must recognize that speech, unlike the logician's *oratio,* has a history. The necessity for imitation does not simply arise from the desire of native English speakers to recover a language no longer spoken but is inherent in the very nature of language itself.

Ascham's double translation thus brings together three, even four, linguistic cultures through literary imitation. Every utterance in eloquent English or Latin speech (that is, in the English and Latin literary network) produced by a sixteenth-century Englishman contains inscribed within it a history of the conventions of eloquence; every eloquent utterance is a cipher of the origins of its own eloquence, preserved in a literary tradition. Ascham thus pushes to its ultimate conclusion the humanist formulation of language as speech arising from preestablished conventions and giving rise to a common usage established through social consent. The humanist grammatical program, from its elementary stages in orthography to its advanced stages in double translation, is part of a social (and ultimately a political) order whose speech (in the ideal grammar school curriculum) is built up from sounded letter and syllable to extended discourse, a discourse preserved in literary texts.

Speech, Things, and Reason

Francis Bacon's criticism of humanist attitudes toward language has too often been taken at face value, and scholars have too often assumed that humanists were concerned with words instead of things or that they were interested in abstract patterns of eloquence regardless of the matter they were writing about.[42] Similarly, in their attempt to rehabilitate the language philosophy of the Middle Ages (in reaction to the humanist legacy of denigrating Scholastic logic), historians of linguistics and logic often overemphasize the humanists' concern for convention to the complete exclusion of semantic criteria, which, they argue, were lost to the humanists because of their lack of interest in the deep structure of language.[43]

But just as Scholastic logicians generally saw some connection between the *impositiones vocum* and *oratio*, so humanist linguistic thinkers generally acknowledged the role of the mental language representing things in spoken, natural language. Vives, who regarded language as preeminently conventions of speech, was an exception among sixteenth-century English humanists. Even Stanbridge translated *partes orationis* as the "partis of reason," presumably synonymous with the parts of *speech*.[44] The position of Thomas More was

[42]In most of his essays contrasting Ciceronian and Attic prose styles, Morris Croll considers seventeenth-century styles to have things and reason as their referents, whereas sixteenth-century styles are governed by sensuous and aural factors that make things and reason extraneous; see essays two through five in *Style, Rhetoric, and Rhythm: Essays by Morris W. Croll*, ed. J. Max Patrick, et al. (Princeton: Princeton University Press, 1966), pp. 51–233. See also Marion Trousdale, "Recurrence and Renaissance: Rhetorical Imitation in Ascham and Sturm," *English Literary Renaissance*, 6 (1976), 156–79. Heath, "Logical Grammar," also argues that humanists *displaced* things with literary usage as the arbiter of language. For opposing views, see Thomas M. Greene, "Roger Ascham: The Perfect End of Shooting," *ELH*, 31 (1969), 609–25; and Alvin Vos, "'Good Matter and Good Utterance': The Character of English Ciceronianism," *Studies in English Literature, 1500–1900*, 19 (1979), 3–18. Vos also argues against the centrality of skepticism in Ascham's linguistic humanism.

[43]See, e.g., I. M. Bochenski, *A History of Formal Logic*, tr. and ed. Ivo Thomas (Notre Dame: University of Notre Dame Press, 1961), p. 12; and Pieter A. Verburg, "Vicissitudes of Paradigms," in *Studies in the History of Linguistics*, ed. Dell Hymes (Bloomington: Indiana University Press, 1974), pp. 198–205.

[44]John Stanbridge, *Accidence* (London, c. 1496; facs. rpt. Menston: Scolar Press, 1969), sig. Air.

typical of that held by most humanists: More included *ratio* as a criterion for common usage, but he also argued that meaning cannot subsist in some fixed relationship between word and thing alone.[45] For humanists, a theory of language based on things and reason complements rather than contradicts a theory based on convention.[46] Although humanists categorically rejected the philosophical apparatus of Scholastic linguistic thought, they retained, albeit in a position of secondary importance, much of its underlying foundation in Aristotle's *De interpretatione* and its Stoic elaboration, particularly the idea that the categories of speech are in some way connected to the categories of mind and reality.

Even as English humanists emphasized the imitative nature of language transmitted through prior acts of speech culturally fixed in literary conventions, they warned against empty eloquence, words devoid of matter. This topos recurs throughout Cicero and was forcefully proclaimed by Erasmus, Thomas Elyot, and Gabriel Harvey.[47] "Matter," or the Latin *res,* in such contexts usually refers to subject matter, as A. C. Howell has noted, but it sometimes takes on broader connotations suggesting "things" as the constituents of an extramental reality, the sense it had for the Scholastic logical and grammatical elaborators of Aristotle's *De interpretatione.*[48] For instance, Richard Sherry, whose *Treatise of the Figures of Grammer and Rhetorike* discusses the importance of wisdom in eloquence, calls for a correspondence

[45]See Kinney, "More's *Letter*," pp. 188–92; and Fleisher, *Radical Reform,* pp. 86, 88. In works other than *In Pseudodialecticos,* Vives does hold that *res* is the foundation of *verba.* In his survey of Vives's linguistic ideas, Eugenio Coseriu even finds continuities with modistic grammar ("Zur Sprachtheorie von J. L. Vives," in *Festschrift zum 65. Geburtstag Walter Monch,* ed. Werner Dierlamm and Wolgang Drost [Heidelberg: F. H. Kerle, 1971], p. 247). See also Vives's analysis of the interconnections among reason, things, speech, and authors, in *Vives: On Education. A Translation of the De Tradendis Disciplinis,* tr. Foster Watson (1913; rpt. Totowa, N.J.: Rowman & Littlefield, 1971), pp. 90–115.

[46]For an approach to Renaissance language studies which for the most part regards conventions as arbitrary, see Lawrence Manley, *Convention, 1500–1750* (Cambridge: Harvard University Press, 1980).

[47]The classical origins of this topos are discussed by Jerrold Siegel, *Rhetoric and Philosophy in Renaissance Humanism: The Union of Eloquence and Wisdom, Petrarch to Valla* (Princeton: Princeton University Press), pp. 3–30.

[48]See A. C. Howell, "*Res et Verba:* Words and Things," *ELH,* 13 (1946), 131–42; and Perreiah, "Humanist Critiques," p. 7, who points out that Valla, in reformulating Aristotle's ten categories, uses *res* to "include substances, qualities, and actions simply in virtue of their common feature of existence." For *res* as an extramental existent in Peter of Spain, see Ong, *Ramus,* p. 66.

between the conventions of speech and "things," using "things" to mean sometimes subject matter, sometimes *res* in the Scholastic sense, as in the following passage: "Every speach standeth by usual wordes, that be in use of daily talke, and proper words that belong to the thing, of which we shall speake. Neither be properties to be referred only to the name of the thyng, but more to the strength & power of the signification: and must be considered not by hearing but by vnderstanding."[49] Sherry refers to the commonplaces of the humanist notion of language as speech preserved in the conventions of usage, but in this difficult and at points obscure passage, he also assumes that speech is based on another level of language, an inner discourse. This mental discourse, the deep structure of conventional speech, assigns names to things, not arbitrarily, but according to their properties. Consequently, this order of language is perceived by the understanding rather than the ear—or perhaps it is perceived through the ear—which deciphers in speech the properties of things embedded in the significations and names of conventional usage.

This combination of language determined on the one hand by convention and usage and on the other hand by the nature of things also appears, surprisingly, in Mulcaster. After devoting the better part of the *Elementarie* to an explanation and defense of custom in language, Mulcaster suddenly shifts to an analysis of language based on things. In his own version of the two levels of language, he distinguishes between "the words and the forces which theie haue" and "the vttering thereof by pen & voyce" (p. 167). It is difficult to ascertain exactly what Mulcaster means by the "force" of words, but it seems related to the idea that words are "appointed upon *cause* [emphasis added]" (p. 167), the scholastic word for the basis of language in the metaphysical nature of things. (This concept was developed by the humanist Scaliger and referred to in the title of his theoretical work on Latin grammar, *De causis linguae Latinae*.)[50] Mulcaster boasts,

---

[49] Richard Sherry, *A Treatise of the Figures of Grammer and Rhetoric* (London, 1555), fols. iiiv–iiiir.

[50] For a defence of the Aristotelian, philosophical approach to grammar, see the preface in Julius Caesar Scaliger, *De causis linguae Latinae* (Lyons, 1540), sigs. (:)iiijr–(:)viir. Manuel Breva-Claramonte discusses Scaliger's literary and speculative approaches to grammar in "Sanctius' Theory of Language: A Contribution to the History of Renaissance Linguistics" (diss., University of Colorado, 1975), pp. 144–81. The speculative approach to grammar in the Renaissance is discussed by W. Keith Percival,

"We nede not to prove by *Platoes Cratylus*, or *Aristoteles* proposition as by best authorities, . . . that words be . . . appointed by cause." We have instead a "better warrant" that testifies to this fact about language, Adam's naming the animals. In one of the relatively rare references to Adamic language in humanist writings, Mulcaster observes:

> For even God himself, who brought the creatures, which he had made, vnto that first man, whom he had also made, that he might name them, according to their properties, doth planelie declare by his so doing, what a cunning thing it is to giue right names, and how necessarie it is, to know their forces, which be allredie giuen, bycause the word being knowen, which emplyeth the propertie of the thing is half known, whose propertie it emplyeth. [pp. 167–69 (mispaginated)]

Mulcaster does in fact espouse a referential theory of language based on correspondence, a theory similar in its fundamental assumption to that of Aristotle and his Scholastic grammatical and logical elaborators. Though Mulcaster believes in the truth of Adamic naming, he does not think it inconsistent with his view that language is humanly instituted rather than divinely created, as many proponents of the Adamic language did. Moreover, Mulcaster stops short of claiming the divine creation of words themselves.[51] He does, however, con-

---

"Deep and Surface Structure in Renaissance and Medieval Syntactic Theory," in *History of Linguistic Thought*, ed. Herman Parret (Berlin: De Gruyter, 1976); and Vivian Salmon, review of *Cartesian Linguistics* by Noam Chomsky, *Journal of Linguistics*, 5 (1969), 165–87. For the importance of Franciscus Sanctius in the Renaissance continuation of Aristotelian linguistic analysis, see Breva-Claramonte, "Sanctius' Theory of Language"; and Percival, "The Grammatical Tradition," pp. 239–40. For the survival of Scholastic logical analysis of language in the Renaissance, see Lisa Jardine, "The Place of Dialectic Teaching in Sixteenth-Century Cambridge," *Studies in the Renaissance*, 21 (1974), 31–62; E. J. Ashworth, *Language and Logic in the Post-Medieval Period* (Dordrecht: Reidel, 1974), and "The Doctrine of Supposition in the Sixteenth and Seventeenth Centuries," *Archiv für der Geschichte der Philosophie*, 51 (1969), 260–85.

[51]Waswo, " 'Ordinary Language Philosophy,' " p. 266, points out that Valla proposed an Adamic theory of language according to which words are humanly instituted, an idea that may derive from the Stoics. See Frede, "Principles of Stoic Grammar," pp. 68–69, on the Stoic understanding of the origin of language. That grammatical regulation of the vernaculars became necessary after the confusion of tongues at Babel is a Renaissance commonplace; see Webbe, *Appeale*, p. 38, and Whittinton, as quoted in Elizabeth Jane Sweeting, *Early Tudor Criticism, Linguistic and Literary* (Oxford: Blackwell, 1940), p. 83.

sider uttered speech to be closely connected to the *causae* of words in things: "Therefore," he concludes, "the argument of words, speche, & pen [is] so necessary," for the underlying meaning of spoken words preserved in custom is ultimately determined by its correspondence to the nature of things.

The idea that every language comprises both a natural language determined by the usage of speakers and authors, and, at the same time, an underlying discourse determined by the properties of things is also embedded in the grammatical tradition itself. Authors of Renaissance Latin grammars characteristically begin with a definition of grammar as the art of speaking well but, untroubled by any apparent contradiction between a referential and conventionalist approach to language, they often go on to define a noun as the name of a thing. Even Peter Ramus, usually noted for his structural, morphological approach to grammar, defines a word as "a note whereby a thing is called" and proceeds to explain that words are made up of syllables, which are in turn made up of letters, which represent sounds that can be transcribed in writing.[52] In his *Petie Schole with an English Orthographie*, Francis Clement defines words in a manner that encompasses language as uttered sounds in speech whose meaning is based on things: "A Word is an absolute & perfect voice, whereby some thing is ment and signified."[53] In this introduction to the most elementary stage of language instruction, Clement thus echoes, in an almost Scholastic way, the Aristotelian premise that language originates in things as understood by the mind ("ment") expressed in the spoken utterance of natural language, which for Aristotle is conventionally instituted by man. Clement's main concern, orthography as the transcription of sound, is thus theoretically grounded in the nature of things.

In his analysis of humanist grammatical theory, G. A. Padley incisively remarks on the humanists' retention of Scholastic semantic criteria:

> From their models they inherited a mixed approach in which both formal and semasiological criteria were employed. . . . Here, the

[52]Peter Ramus, *The Latine Grammar of P. Ramus: Translated into English* (London, 1585; facs. rpt. Menston: Scolar Press, 1971), pp. 1–2.
[53]Francis Clement, *The Petie Schole with an English Orthographie* (London, 1587; facs. rpt. Menston: Scolar Press, 1967), p. 11.

early Humanist grammarians go beyond Roman practice, . . . towards ever more semasiological definition. Particularly in the work of Nebrija and the later grammarian Melanchthon, is this flight from formal to semantic criteria evident. The semantic approach to grammar is not an invention of the seventeenth century, but the harvest from seeds set at the very beginning of the New Learning.[54]

Padley sees this same tendency in Scaliger and in the sixteenth-century Spanish grammarian Franciscus Sanctius, as well as in Colet's definition of the noun in *Aeditio:* "the name of a thynge that is. and may be seen felte herde or understande [*sic*]."[55] For Padley such a definition is "a witness to the belief that to each separate entity in the world there corresponds a name. Here again a typically seventeenth-century preoccupation, the urge to undertake a conceptual classification of the universe with a one-to-correspondence between names and things, has its counterpart in sixteenth-century grammar." As Padley argues, "by the end of the sixteenth century, . . . Aristotelian criteria are increasingly in use even by grammarians who otherwise stay within the conservative Humanist tradition."[56]

The humanist practice of combining usage and semantic criteria to explain grammatical categories is exemplified by Thomas Granger's *Syntagma Grammaticvm,* whose title page announces that it, like so many grammars of the period, is an "explanation of Lillies Grammar."[57] In his long introduction, addressing schoolboy and schoolmaster alike, Granger places himself in the humanist tradition of teaching Latin grammar as an introduction to the study of literature, to writing in a literary style, and to speaking Latin. Granger similarly defines words within the orthographic tradition, linking them to sounded, spoken utterance, while at the same time appealing to a se-

[54]G. A. Padley, *Grammatical Theory in Western Europe, 1500–1700: The Latin Tradition* (Cambridge: Cambridge University Press, 1976), p. 30. Nevertheless, Padley does not quite see semantic criteria as essential to humanist linguistic thought, but only as a vestige of scholastic views and a halfway house for seventeenth-century views, which truly do, according to Padley, analyze language semantically. See Breva-Claramonte, "Sanctius' Theory of Language," pp. 37–38, for ancient linguistic views that maintain the importance both of usage and of an underlying logical level of language.

[55]Colet, *Aeditio,* sig. Avir.

[56]Padley, *Grammatical Theory,* pp. 38–39, 36. A full discussion of the issue appears on pp. 30–39.

[57]Thomas Granger, *Syntagma Grammaticvm* (London, 1616; facs. rpt. Menston: Scolar Press, 1971). All quotations are from this edition.

mantic concept of language in which words refer to things. Granger distinguishes between "significatiue" words (nouns and verbs, which have referents in reality) and "explanatiue" words (the parts of speech that have no referents in reality) (sigs. D1r, I8r), a distinction close to the Scholastic definition of categorematic and syncategorematic terms. (His use of such words as "consignifie" [sig. G5r] also suggests a familiarity with medieval speculative grammar.)

Using again the terminology of Scholastic logicians, Granger remarks, "In a word are to be considered the matter, and signification, which is the forme. The matter of a word is divided into letters and syllables" (sig. C2r), and he proceeds to define letters and syllables as sound. Like Clement in his *Petie Schole*, Granger attempts to connect the naming, signifying power of words and their expression in sounds; out of the nature of things, as signified by words, emerge the spoken sounds of speech, the Scholastic's *vox significans*. In this way, Granger supplies a philosophical explanation for Lily's conventionalist literary grammar of speech based on the reading of authors.

Despite humanist denunciations of Scholastic logic and grammar, Scholastic concepts of language were preserved in grammars identified with the literary tradition of language study institutionalized in Lily's *Grammar*. Granger of course does not rank in influence with grammarians such as Whittinton, Colet, and Lily, but he does develop the implications of the humanist concern with both convention and things as the basis of speech, and he demonstrates the distance a humanist grammarian may go in the direction of speculative grammar. Granger develops more fully a view also expressed by John Brinsley in his *Ludus Literarius* (1612), a comprehensive educational treatise that helped to transmit the humanist language program and educational ideals to the early seventeenth century. Brinsley prescribes the characteristic humanist method of teaching Latin in stages that proceed from letter to syllable to word, sentence, and finally composition, a method reminiscent of Kempe's. Brinsley's primary pedagogical device, double translation of classical authors, indicates his humanist understanding of language as usage and all that that implies. Yet, like so many others in the humanist tradition, he regards the parts of speech as semantic entities, and separates nouns and verbs from the other parts, since they alone have the power to "signify."[58] The ultimate object of the *sermo* that Brinsley teaches his pupils to achieve through the study of classical literary usage is the power of language to name things: "in Speech which men vtter, there is nothing but words to cal or know things by, and setting or ioyning of words together. Like as it is in our English tongue, so in the latine & so in other tongues."[59] To be sure, Brinsley would have his students devote most of their efforts to the "ioyning of words together" by imitating the syntactical style of classical authors; nevertheless, he suggests that at the lexical level of words themselves, things govern the nature of language.

The prevalence of this joining of two concepts of language so apparently divergent as spoken utterance and philosophical naming is perhaps attested by its expression in popular form, in the English translation of La Primaudaye's *French Academie*. La Primaudaye in fact proposes as close a one-to-one correspondence between spoken word and thing as may be possible: "We cannot speake without certaine words and names to name and signifie things by, whereof wee minde to speake. For if wee haue no wordes and names to make them knowen by, we must alwayes have the things themselves present that wee may point at them with the finger, which is impossible."[60] Echoing Aristotle and anticipating Swift's Lagado academicians, La Primaudaye describes words as a direct substitute for things.

The referential view of language most completely intermeshes with the conventionalist view in the linguistic theory of Joseph Webbe— surprisingly so, since, as we have seen, Webbe was one of the strongest supporters of the primacy of usage, even among humanists. For Webbe, "clausing" is not only the most pedagogically effective means to teach Latin, or any other language; it is also the most semantically accurate. In his *Petition to Parliament*, Webbe argues that the founda-

---

[58]Brinsley, *Ludus*, pp. 132–33. In his grammar textbook, *The Posing of the Parts* (London, 1612; rpt. Menston: Scolar Press, 1967), Brinsley makes explicit distinctions, as well as connections, between words and things, especially in his definition of a noun, sig. B1v.

[59]Brinsley, *Ludus*, p. 55.

[60]Pierre de La Primaudaye, *The Second Part of the French Academie*, tr. T[homas] B[owes] (London, 1594), p. 98. The passage echoes Aristotle's *Sophistical Refutations*, 165a, 6–7. See Miriam Therese Larkin, *Language in the Philosophy of Aristotle* (The Hague: Mouton, 1971), p. 10.

tion of his method lies "in that wherein all languages of the world agree," namely, in their reference to things, as he proceeds to explain: "the grounds of speech are laid in things, in the meanings of which things all tongues meet. Therefore as they are all meanings of things, so they are all the meanings of one another" (p. 6). This intertranslatability of all languages is the basis of Webbe's argument for the referential nature of language.

Webbe describes the several stages by which language is built up from letters to locate the point at which articulations become meaningful. He begins with the physical components of written letters, "points" and "right & crooked lines," which delineate "literall characters [i.e., letters] produced of these points and lines." These characters are the elements with which words and syllables are constructed. Here Webbe reaches the stage, individual words, that most Scholastic logics and humanist grammars identify as the starting point of meaningful language (pp. 6–7). Webbe, however, insists that meaning begins only with the unit of language that can be translated into another language. He identifies this unit as the clause, since word-for-word translation usually produces unintelligible nonsense. It is the clause, then, that has the power to signify by referring to things, and, as the basic semantic unit, it is a near equivalent of the logician's "term." Further, Webbe argues in almost all his works, it is the clause that determines the conventional nature of language: students learn proper speech by imitating the usage of classical authors through the practice of recombining their clauses. The clause thus becomes the minimal unit of meaning that defines language as, on the one hand, referential and based on things and, on the other, as conventional and based on authors' usage. Reference to things, the conventions of speech, and the possibility of translation are all interrelated and reinforce each other. Syntactic forms—clauses—thus are ultimately, though indirectly, connected to things.

Among the *causae* of language, the Scholastics included not only the categories of reality but also the categories of the mind. Humanists too define *sermo* as a product of reason and sometimes explore the relationship between speech and mind without considering things as a coordinate of discourse. Such is the case in Thomas Linacre's *De emendata structura Latini sermonis* (1524), which Padley credits as the first theoretical treatment of Latin grammar by an English humanist.

Padley argues that Linacre recognizes "an underlying mental structure which can be variously actualized by items of discourse." The idea is suggested most clearly in Linacre's treatment of the ellipsis as an uttered linguistic structure that expresses an underlying mental concept. Usage is thus a manifestation of logical concepts in the mind. Linacre's analysis contains, as Padley observes, an "implied recognition of a 'deep' and a 'surface' structure to language, a *verbum mentis* underlying the *verbum oris* of actual discourse."[61]

In arguing for a combination of wisdom and eloquence, of "good matter and good vtterance" (p. 265), Ascham too presents a kind of two-level concept of language. He attributes good language not just to the use of proper conventions but also to the quality of mind that issues words. Ascham explains that one aim of education should be to teach boys to "speake so, as it may well appeare, that the braine doth gouerne the tonge, and that reason leadeth forth the taulke" (pp. 185–86). In his best-known pronouncement he warns against a "diuorce betwixt the tongue and the hart" (p. 265). For Ascham the relationship between tongue and heart, or tongue and brain, is typically governed by moral categories; he draws a further connection between heart, language, and manners (one's outward behavior manifested in action), a connection between "ill thoughtes," "lewde taulke," and "ill deedes" (p. 266).

This moralization of the relation between inner and outer discourse is characteristic of humanist observations about language. "Language most shewes a man," Ben Jonson says, quoting Vives, because it is "the image of the parent of it, the mind." Similar sentiments guide James I in his advice to his son in *Basilikon Doron*. In the Proheme to *Of the knowledg which maketh a wise man*, Thomas Elyot explains his purpose in *The Governor*: "I intended to augment our Englyshe tongue, whereby men shoulde as well expresse more abundantly the thynge that they conceyved in theyre hertis (wherefore language was ordeyned) havynge wordes apte for the purpose." In

<hr/>

[61]Padley, *Grammatical Theory*, pp. 21, 54–56. Padley's helpful discussion of Linacre appears on pp. 21–24 and 39–45. Linacre's linguistic views bear, at the very least, a resemblance to those of Ockham. For Linacre's rivalry with Lily for authorship of a national grammar, see D. F. S. Thomson, "Linacre's Latin Grammars," in *Essays on the Life and Work of Thomas Linacre, c. 1460–1524*, ed. Francis Maddison et al. (Oxford: Clarendon Press, 1977), pp. 24–35.

his *Ciceronianus,* Gabriel Harvey records his abandonment of slavish imitation of Cicero for the view that language conventions are valid only as they express the mind. The idea was popular enough to find its way into behavior manuals such as Hoby's translation of *The Courtier,* Henry Peacham's *Compleat Gentleman,* where the idea is explicitly attributed to Cicero's *De oratore,* and Richard Brathwait's *English Gentleman.*[62] Given the widespread currency of the idea, it is not surprising that it appears in a work that tries to square English with Lily's *Grammar,* John Hewes's *Perfect Survey of the English Tongue.* Grafting English *sermo* onto the conventionally established categories of the exterior Latin discourse, Hewes reminds his reader of the moral nature of inner discourse governing speech: *"Hominis character eius est oratio.* Speech (saith one) is the Character of a man, or the expresse image of his heart or minde."[63]

At times, however, sixteenth-century writers on language propound something close to a full-fledged Aristotelian position on the relationship between reality, mind, and speech. In a popular version of this view of language, La Primaudaye explains the relationship between interior, mental discourse prior to utterance, an "internal [speech] of the minde," and exterior utterance in speech, "external [speech], which is pronounced": the external, he says, "is the messenger of the internall, that speaketh in the heart."[64] He goes on to

[62]See Ben Jonson, *Discoveries,* in *Works,* ed. C. H. Herford, Percy and Evelyn Simpson (Oxford: Clarendon Press, 1947), VIII, 625; James I, *Basilikon Doron,* ed. James Craigie (Edinburgh and London: Blackwood, 1944), I, 86–87; Thomas Elyot, *Of the knowledg which maketh a wise man, A disputacion Platonike* (London, 1533), p. 4, rpt. in Kurt Schroeder, *Platonismus in der Englischen Renaissance vor und bei Thomas Eliot* (Berlin: Mayer & Müller, 1920); Gabriel Harvey, *Ciceronianus,* tr. Clarence A. Forbes, ed. Harold S. Wilson (Lincoln: University of Nebraska Press, 1945); Hoby (tr.), *Book of the Courtier,* p. 56; Henry Peacham, *The Compleat Gentleman, The Truth of Our Times, and The Art of Living in London,* ed. Virgil B. Heltzel (Ithaca: Cornell University Press, 1962), p. 43; Richard Brathwait, *The English Gentleman* (London, 1630), pp. 82–83, 89. All references to Brathwait, unless otherwise noted, are from this edition.

[63]John Hewes, *A Perfect Survey of the English Tongue* (London, 1624; facs. rpt. Menston: Scolar Press, 1972), sig. x4r. See also Sherry, *Treatise,* fol. iiir. For a variation of this argument see Nicholas Gibbens, *Questions and Disputations Concerning the Holy Scriptures* (London, 1602), p. 427. Gibbens explains that after Babel, the language of the "soule and reason," which is "the *image & character* of the mind," remained the same for all, while "speech and voice" now differ from one nation to another. Gibbens thus presents a biblicized account of Aristotle's inner and outer discourse.

[64]Pierre de La Primaudaye, *The French Academie,* tr. T[homas] B[owes] (London, 1586), pp. 126–27. See also La Primaudaye, *The Second Part,* pp. 91–92.

complete the Aristotelian triad of mind, reality, and speech by including "things" in the connection between internal and external discourse: "For before the thought can vtter any outward speech by meanes of the voyce, first the minde must receiue the images of things presented vnto it by the corporall senses. And then . . . reason must discourse to knowe and to consider them well." When the mind controls speech, reason (itself a discourse judging thoughts about "things") shapes "the aire framed in voyce."[65] La Primaudaye restores Aristotle's *logos* as the intersection of thought and vocal expression, in contrast to the Scholastic *oratio*, expressed in but distorted by *vox*.

Granger takes much the same position as La Primaudaye. In his *Syntagma Grammaticvm*, Granger observes that "a word is a signe or note whereby we declare the meaning of the minde in naming, or calling something" (sig. C2r). Moreover, the grammatical categories founded on the mind's power to signify things is "naturall to the Soule, infused into it in the creation" (sig. A6r). Thus Granger can end his preface on methods of teaching Latin grammar through readings of literary texts with the motto: *A Deo, & natura, non ex phantasia, aut more* (sig C1r). Granger appears to claim that usage defined by conventions of literary Latin has its origins in the natural capacity of the mind to perceive the categories of things. Epistemological categories of the mind, ontological categories of reality, and linguistic conventions of literature all rest neatly within each other in Granger's "significatiue" words.

Finally, Webbe, in explaining the theoretical underpinnings of his clausing of Cicero's *Ad Atticum,* describes the relationship between words and things in a manner that any Scholastic grammarian would have applauded: "For as words are but characters and shadowes of mens conceptions, and these conceptions are but right or crooked shadowes of truthes and realities, so this purity of these words . . . brings us neerer the truthes of thinges and their realities."[66] The more Webbe explains his conventionalist, humanist approach to speech, the more he appeals to the Aristotelian, perhaps Stoic, formulation of the philosophical foundation of language in thoughts about things, thoughts uttered in the "pronounced" speech of the

[65]La Primaudaye, *The Second Part,* pp. 88–89.
[66]Webbe, *Lessons and Exercises,* Appendix, sig. b2r.

"voice" framing the air, as La Primaudaye put it. Webbe thus envisions natural language as the convention-bound speech containing *oratio* (*oris ratio*) within it as its rational *causa* and forming the discourse of literature.

In opposing the Scholastic view that speech distorts the articulation of thought, Renaissance humanists posited the concept of the literary *logos* as the vehicle of a culture's assimilation of the world in countless face-to-face encounters between self and world. These encounters are regularized, validated, and institutionalized in the verbal conventions of a morally superior culture, classical Latinity. The sounds of speech preserved in the literary *logos* guarantee that the space between mind and reality is bridgeable, and these sounds form a chain of linguistic conventions linking the centuries between antiquity and the Renaissance.

The moral burden of connecting mind and reality in the sounds of speech is intimated by Richard Brathwait in some brief remarks about the virtues of silence in *The English Gentleman*. Brathwait is particularly sensitive to the fact that sounded speech is anchored in the moral intelligence of the human heart. As "*Speech* . . . [is] *the image of life*," an "*Index of the Minde*," he says, it is also "called the *object* of the *eare*" (p. 89). (In his *Essaies vpon the Five Senses* Brathwait constructs a communicative model of language based on this idea: the heart's language is pronounced by the mouth to be received by the auditor's ear, which in turn relays it to the auditor's heart.)[67] In *The English Gentleman* he suggests true speech always confronts the temptation to "shroud and conceale . . . thoughts" in deceitful words (p. 89), but because deceit is so prevalent, he periodically offers the prospect of silence as a superior alternative to speech itself. Suspicious of rhetoric and indiscriminate imitation, he refers to "*fooles* which carry their *Hearts* in their *Mouthes*," as opposed to "*wise men*, which carry their *Mouthes* in their *Hearts*" (p. 82). For Brathwait, in fact, wise speech often turns out to be a kind of silence (see pp. 83, 89, 90). Nevertheless, one case in which speech is the clear victor in this agon between speech and silence is the speech of the Christian preacher and Ciceronian orator, who are ultimately obliged to break out of Pythagorean silence to maintain the moral and spiritual integrity of society and

[67]Richard Brathwait, *Essaies vpon the five senses* (London, 1610), pp. 6–8.

humanity (p. 90). The ultimate value of *vox*, then, is moral. It is the constituent element of a *sermo* of a culture, a *populus*, communicating its moral ideals to itself. In contrast to the Scholastics, whose ideal was an abstract, transparent articulation of thought in the *oratio* of an isolated mind, humanists generally held that *sermo* (which includes *oratio*) gathers its meaning through its accumulated reverberations in a community of literary texts and moral beings.

The debate between the Scholastics and the humanists provides a framework for the discussions of speech, writing, and print in the chapters that follow. Humanists recognized the difficulty of making the right convention properly signify in speech, as the prose of Thomas Elyot and Roger Ascham and the poetry of Ben Jonson illustrate. Further, the humanist theory of speech was constantly encroached upon by writing: it was made possible by the recovery of classical texts; it was practiced mostly in written rather than spoken performance; and it was circulated so widely because of print. The humanists could use written performance to complement the theory of speech, as in their adept use of the printing press to manipulate an effective textual space, the written manifestation of speech. But writing could also provide a model of signification rivaling speech, which could falter precisely because human speech is defective. This interplay of speech and writing occurs in George Herbert's hieroglyphic poetics. Similarly, writing could provide a linguistic model openly hostile to humanist speech. This sort of model, which was proposed by Francis Bacon, would accommodate a renewed Scholastic desire for pure representation outside the human voice and outside the social community. Both models relied on writing in an attempt to fulfill the Scholastic wish to signify without language. In Bacon's language scheme especially, writing removes the barrier of convention that, for the Scholastics, stood between reality and its representation. But even as we move from the humanists to Herbert and Bacon and observe the authority of language shift from speech to writing, we can see how the very success of print in disseminating language challenged the authority of both speech and writing. One response to this challenge is represented by Robert Burton, for whom the proliferation of books is the source of a philosophical skepticism.

3/

Elyot, Ascham, Jonson, and the Frailty of Speech

T HE interlacing of imitative and referential views of
speech in humanist grammar holds intact the interaction between culture and the phenomenal world. But
it does so in two distinctive ways. On the one hand, it directs the
purpose of language toward social communication; on the other, it
defines the concept of social speech as ethical. La Primaudaye, in
explaining that interior language consists of the mind's names for
things and that exterior speech is the vocal expression of interior
language, concludes that the ultimate purpose of both these levels of
language is for one person to instruct another: "In a worde, God hath
given this benefite to man, by meanes of the tongue and the eares,
that they can represent one to another, and cause each other to know
and understand as well diuine things as humane." Similarly, La Primaudaye insists that "all talke ought to have reason for a foundation,
and the loue of our neighbor for a marke to aim at." The individual
speaker who can participate in social communication has moral and
semantic integrity; he has "the same thing in the mouth which [he
has] in the thought," as opposed to *"men of double hearts, and double
tongues,* that are not upright in heart, not true and certaine in word."[1]
Much the same argument is made by Richard Brathwait and by
Nicholas Gibbens, whose biblical moralization of speech is echoed in

---

[1] Pierre de La Primaudaye, *The Second Part of the French Academie,* tr. T[homas]
B[owes] (London, 1594), pp. 98, 128, 90–92.

70

the opening pages of Thomas Wilson's *Rule of Reason*.[2] Indeed, the moral imperative of speaking is commonplace in the period, and the works of Elyot, Ascham, and Jonson in particular will reveal the degree to which speech depends on social and political contingencies that render the moral integrity of speech vulnerable and frail in its dependence on the virtue of rulers or society in general. The moral concerns of these writers are tellingly similar to those implicit in Augustine's treatment of language in *De Trinitate*, which provides an illuminating philosophical context for their ideas.

Augustine, Elyot, and Ascham

An extensive articulation of the moral relations between interior and exterior discourse appears in Augustine's *De Trinitate* XV, mentioned by Ockham and almost certainly known by English humanists. Here Augustine presents a linguistic scheme that in some respects resembles Aristotle's, though he goes beyond Aristotle in his belief that the union of word and thing depends on the spiritual condition of the mind.[3] He distinguishes between mental and spoken words (whether actually sounded or just silently articulated in the mind): "if we utter . . . [the contents of our knowledge] in words, [*dicere velimus*] we can only do so by thinking them. For although there were no words [*verba*] spoken [*sonent*], at any rate, he who thinks speaks [*dicit*] in his heart." And he adds, "we call thoughts speeches of the heart [*locutiones cordis*]."[4] The spoken word, on the other hand, constitutes the natural languages, "the tongues of nations [*linguae gentium*], of which our Latin tongue is one." But to materialize the word of the heart by speaking it is to debase it. The written word is yet a further

[2]Thomas Wilson, *The Arte of Rhetorique* (London, 1553), sigs. A3r–A4v, facs. rpt., ed. Robert Hood Bowers (Gainesville, Fla.: Scholars' Facsimile and Reprints, 1962).

[3]For additional material on Augustine's linguistic views, see Eugene Vance, "Saint Augustine: Language as Temporality," in *Mimesis: From Mirror to Method*, ed. John D. Lyons and Stephen G. Nichols, Jr. (Hanover, N.H.: University Press of New England, 1982), pp. 20–35 (hereafter cited as *Mimesis*).

[4]The discussion appears in Augustine, *On the Trinity*, tr. Arthur West Haddan, rev. W. G. T. Shedd, in *A Select Library of the Nicene and Post-Nicene Fathers of the Christian Church*, ed. Philip Schaff (1887; rpt. Grand Rapids, Mich.: Eerdmans, 1974), pp. 208–210. All references are to this edition. References in the original Latin are from Migne, *PL* 42. 1070–72.

debasement of the spoken word. This successively lowered status of the word of the heart in material signs of sounds and writing is nevertheless necessary for communication (see also *De doctrina Christiana*, bk. II, chaps. 1–4), which for Augustine is a moral necessity, if God's word is to be spread.

Like Aristotle, and unlike the humanists, Augustine gives place of honor to the interior word, but not for the same reason Aristotle and his scholastic followers did. For Augustine, the word of the heart "is begotten from the knowledge that continues in the mind, when that same knowledge is spoken [*dicitur*] inwardly according as it really is." [The inward word, that is, comes closest to a perfect representation of the mind.] Augustine, in fact, frequently stresses that the interior word actually partakes of the mind's knowledge. It is born from, and shares the same nature as, the mind's knowledge: "For the thought that is formed by the things [*res*] which we know is the word [*verbum*] which we speak [*dicimus*] in the heart: which word is neither Greek nor Latin, nor of any other tongue." The source of the mind's knowledge can be either interior (the mind reflexively thinking about its own contents) or exterior (sense perceptions or written or oral reports from other people) (p. 212). In general, however, Augustine is more interested in the relationship between the mental word and the mind than in the extramental source of language. Indeed, he typically speaks of interior divine illumination as the source of all knowledge, whether it be the mind's knowledge of itself or of the external world (p. 130).

Augustine's particular interest in the relationship between the mind's knowledge and the interior word accords with the moral and spiritual status he attributes to language, which is ultimately expressed in spoken language and even in human action. Augustine does assert that "a word [*verbum*] is not true unless it is born of a thing [*de re*] that is known" (p. 213; *PL* 42. 1077), but in Book IX he asks whether we can conceive a word from knowledge we dislike.[5] There is, he insists, some connection between the spiritual status of the mind and the interior word that partakes of the mind's contents. That connection is apparent in the assent one gives to the mind's contents and its interior verbal expression. The heart, or mind, can speak

[5]The discussion appears in *On the Trinity*, pp. 131–32; *PL* 42. 968–69.

spiritual truths only when it is one with those spiritual truths, but it may also truly speak spiritually repellent words "when we rightly dislike and rightly censure them." It is possible, however, for a word to be conceived "either by desire [*cupiditas*] or by love [*caritas*]," that is, in accordance with one's spiritual attitude toward the object of knowledge and the contents of language. The inner word thus always indicates the absence or presence of *caritas* in the speaker. The primal act of interior discourse, Augustine seems to imply, always accompanies an acknowledgment that the object of knowledge exists either through itself or through God. In the former case, one conceives words through *cupiditas*, in the latter through *caritas*.

True words, however, can be conceived only through *caritas*, which connects both the conceiver and the objects of his words with the divine order of things. "Therefore love [*amor*] . . . conjoins our word [*verbum*] and the mind from which it is conceived, and without any confusion binds itself as a third with them, in an incorporeal embrace."

And again: "A word [*verbum*], then, . . . is knowledge together with love [*amor*]. Whenever, then, the mind knows and loves itself, its word [*verbum*] is joined to it by love. And since it loves knowledge and knows love, both the word is in love and love is in the word, and both are in him who loves and speaks [*dicit*]" (p. 132).

Augustine here links the truth and efficacy of the human word with the spiritual state of the mind that conceives interior discourse. And we may presume that spiritually upright speech, exterior discourse, is also the result of this "incorporeal embrace." Augustine extends the moral connection between mind and speech to the conditions of human action, whose source he regards as the inner word: "there are no works [*opera*] of man that are not first spoken [*dicantur*] in his heart" (p. 210; *PL* 42. 1073). The moral connection between word, thought, and action is clear in such statements as: "Now a word [*verbum*] is born, when, being thought out, it pleases us either to the effects of sinning, or to that of doing right" (p. 131; *PL* 42. 968).

Augustine thus ultimately provides a way of looking at interior discourse in a manner strikingly different from Aristotle. For Aristotle, the interior word is a spontaneous, almost physiological, response to an external stimulus—the world. For Augustine, the word depends on the quality of mind that conceives it. Only through *caritas* can the mind fill itself with perceptions of objects in the world, objects created by the same *caritas* that illuminates the mind (see p. 209). Aristotle's linguistic model produces philosophical speakers; Augustine's produces Christian moralists. Moreover, though Augustine does not actually mention the Fall, his model leaves open the possibility that one might misspeak because of the mind's fallen condition. It is difficult to say whether Augustine specifically is a source for the humanist concept of the two discourses, but he does offer a theoretical model that ties together many of the elements that were to express the moral foundation of language for the humanists. The humanists differ from Augustine, however, in emphasizing the ethical as opposed to the spiritual context of language.

The humanists' moralization of the relationship between interior and exterior discourse profoundly changes the foundation of the relationship between words and things. The connection between words and things becomes a matter of human will ultimately determined by the speaker's moral disposition. Marion Trousdale has skillfully argued that, for humanist rhetoricians, language represents things only contingently, not inherently. For humanists, "language use was by definition a conscious endeavour and . . . there was always a recognized gap between the thought or the *res* and the words on the page."[6] Trousdale largely follows Lisa Jardine in considering the Renaissance use of place-logic the result of a proclivity toward skepticism.[7] That gap between reality and the mind's ability to name it in words is bridged, in the individual, by his moral status, which stands in some relation to the moral status of his society at large. Good societies produce good speakers, and good speakers shape good societies. The humanist view is an ethical and social version of Augustine's "incorporeal embrace" between the soul and the word, a version that recognizes the need to anchor *caritas* in some larger public institution.

Richard Mulcaster, for example, in explaining the importance of custom in language norms, sometimes speaks as if language is the public possession of the national commonweal. He identifies the

---

[6]Marion Trousdale, *Shakespeare and the Rhetoricians* (Chapel Hill: University of North Carolina Press, 1982), pp. 24–31.

[7]Lisa Jardine, *Francis Bacon and the Art of Discourse* (Cambridge: Cambridge University Press, 1974), pp. 1–65.

conventions of speech with "the custom of your cuntrie"; whoever challenges a nation's linguistic conventions thus doubts the national wisdom.[8] Mulcaster's extension of the citizen's obligations as public servant to linguistic behavior reflects his view that the well-being of language depends on the political conditions of the society in which it is spoken:

> doth not speche alter sometime to the finer, if the state where it is vsed, continew it self, and grow to better countenaunce, for either great learning, or other dealing, which vse to proin a tung? And doth it not sometime change to the more corrupt, if the state where it is vsed, do chance to be overthrown, and a master tung comming as conqueror, command both the peple and the peples speche to?[9]

To define language as consent, as Mulcaster does, makes it dependent not only on social groups that provide consent but also on the political organization of that society ("the state"). For Mulcaster the very idea of usage is intimately connected with concepts of political legitimacy and the common weal. In following the conventions of his nation, the speaker signals his place in a political as well as a social unit.[10] Ultimately, the force responsible for creating a society in which it is possible for a speaker to unite word and thing is the monarch, who is responsible for the political fortunes of his kingdom. The connection between morally disposed political power and the verbal health of a nation may have its origins among the Stoics, who held that the initial imposition of a name or thing occurs under a good king and deteriorates over the course of history as the moral virtue of the kings' declines.[11]

The linguistic responsibility asked of English Renaissance monarchs is well documented. Henry VIII received high praise for his

---

[8]Richard Mulcaster, *The First Part of the Elementarie* (London, 1582; facs. rpt. Menston: Scolar Press, 1970), p. 101; John Brinsley, *Ludus Literarius: or, The Grammar Schoole* (London, 1612; facs. rpt. Menston: Scolar Press, 1968), p. 22.

[9]Mulcaster, *First Part*, p. 101.

[10]The idea is a common theme in Shakespeare studies. See, e.g., Lawrence Danson, *Tragic Alphabet: Shakespeare's Drama of Language* (New Haven: Yale University Press, 1974), 1–21; and Timothy J. Reiss, *Tragedy and Truth: Studies in the Development of Renaissance and Neoclassical Discourse* (New Haven: Yale University Press, 1980), pp. 40–77.

[11]Michael Frede, "Principles of Stoic Grammar," in *The Stoics*, ed. John M. Rist (Berkeley: University of California Press, 1978), pp. 68–70.

involvement in establishing a uniform Latin grammar for all of England and was thus regarded as the guardian of Latin teaching, as the translator John Palsgrave announced in his preface to the Latin comedy *Acolastus*. Joseph Webbe considered it James I's duty to support his language-teaching schemes as a way of strengthening the nation. These are just two of many examples of the connection between language pedagogy and monarchy.[12] Thomas Elyot and Roger Ascham offer more poignant treatments of the prince's influence on language, fully aware of the ruler's power to corrupt as well as improve language.

One of the earliest English humanist investigations of the relationship between language and political legitimacy appears in Thomas Elyot's *Of the knowledg which maketh a wise man*, a five-part "Platonike dialog" whose main subject is the definition of wisdom as the proper ordering of the soul through self-knowledge.[13] The linguistic context of wisdom is evident in Elyot's contention that the well-ordered soul issues well-ordered thoughts expressed in well-ordered words accompanied by well-ordered actions in society. Elyot's interest in the linguistic dimension of individual wisdom and social action is apparent at every turn in the dialogue. Just about every moral, social, and political issue he raises is placed in the context of how to formulate that issue in words. It is no accident that the form Elyot chose to discuss the nature of wisdom is a dialogue between Plato and Aristippus about a past dialogue between Plato and Dionysus, the tyrant of Sicily. Elyot was keenly aware that ideas have a moral impact only when expressed in speech, and the work is shot through with the problem of communicating moral intelligence. Ideas about wisdom appear in the work only as they are spoken by one person and understood by another. Through the present conversation with Aristippus, Plato continually refers back to their past conversations and repeatedly commends Aristippus for his ability to both speak and

---

[12]*The Comedy of Acolastus*, tr. John Palsgrave, ed. P. L. Carver, EETS, no. 202 (London: Oxford University Press, 1937), p. 2; Joseph Webbe, *Petition to the High Covrt of Parliament* (London, 1623), p. 2. For the relation between politics and verbal representation, see Timothy J. Reiss, "Power, Poetry, and the Resemblance of Nature," in *Mimesis*, pp. 215–47.

[13]Thomas Elyot, *Of the knowledg which maketh a wise man: A disputacion Platonike* (London, 1553); rpt. in Kurt Schroeder, *Platonismus in der Englischen Renaissance vor und bei Thomas Eliot* (Berlin: Mayer & Müller, 1920).

listen reasonably. Plato's compliments reverberate against Dionysus' inability to speak and listen with moral intelligence. They also reverberate against Elyot's self-defense in the Proheme in answer to his critics' misunderstanding of, and false accusations about, his own words in *The Governour*. The themes of the work are thus embedded in a series of conversations extending from that between Plato and Dionysus to that between Plato and Aristippus and, even further, to a kind of dialogue between Elyot and the critics of his other work.

Elyot frequently expresses both the political and linguistic themes of the work in terms that reflect the humanist and Augustinian understanding of how the mental word, the word of the heart, is externalized. At one point he refers to "the harte of man" as "the soules booke, wherein all thoughtes be wrytten" (p. 57). The work in general can be regarded as a probing of the relationship between inner and outer discourse in political circumstances. In fact, in the Proheme Elyot bases his license to speak on the authority of Henry VIII.[14] Elyot's confidence in his own verbal authority stands in marked contrast to Plato's punishment at the hands of Dionysus, who ruthlessly inhibits the expression of truth in language. In the dialogue itself Plato recounts that while traveling in Sicily, he was invited to Dionysus' court because of his reputation as a wise man capable of explaining the meaning of wisdom. Plato articulates his moral dilemma in Dionysus' court as one concerning speech: to speak the truth would bring him real personal harm because he would have to tell Dionysus that his political tyranny is contrary to real wisdom, but not to speak the truth would allow his words to be "incensed and stered" by the affections rather than reason (p. 104), and they would thus deny his quest for, and his claim to possess, wisdom.

Plato's evaluation proves correct. He speaks the truth, and Dionysus jails him and then sells him into slavery. Plato's recollections of his past conversation with Dionysus are filled with regret about his total failure. Musing over the past, he repeatedly resorts to images of the inefficacy of his speech. He imagines how difficult it would have been for "one of the philosophers of Inde, or of other countrayes speakynge no greke" to instruct Dionysus through an interpreter. He conjures up the image of "Zeno Eleates offer that he had byt of his

[14]Ibid., p. 4.

owne tongue, and spyt it in the face of the tyrant that tourmented hym" so that Zeno could communicate with him only through dumb "signes and tokens." He is exasperated by the thought that all the conditions of moral coordination between his heart and tongue were useless in the face of political tyranny, and appealing to Aristippus, he asks, "But supposest thou Aristipp, that any man can better inter-prete an other mans sentence, eyther spoken in a strange language, or signified by tokens, than I could expounde myne owne intent or meanynge?" (p. 98).

Plato—like Elyot—is haunted by the possibility that the secure relationship between word and thought in the morally upright heart may be ineffectual without the support of a morally ordered political structure overseen by a morally upright monarch. Augustine's vision of *caritas* binding word and heart, when translated into the secular terms of civil society, is not enough. For all the effect his words had, Plato might just as well have bitten off and spit out his tongue. The terrifying specter of silence looms behind Plato's apprehension about how to deal with Dionysus. Elyot is acutely aware of the interdepen-dence of the linguistic and political orders; he recognizes the political dimension of the moral relationship between exterior words and the interior word inscribed in the book of the heart. Even his own exterior words might perish, he suggests in the Proheme, if not for his own relationship with his monarch.

Ascham was preoccupied with similar concerns, as we can see in his *Report and Discourse . . . of the Affaires and State of Germany and the Emperour Charles his Court . . .*, his historical analysis of the Emperor Charles's fall from the favor of his erstwhile German allies.[15] Ascham attributes the emperor's political misfortune to a moral failing, his "vnkyndnes" to his allies (p. 128). But this moral theme is enmeshed in the verbal communication among the protagonists participating in the events and implied in the language of the spectators observing those events. Ascham, so aware of his sources of information, sees political history as largely a record of verbal statements made about political events, not a description of battles, military maneuvers, or overt actions in general. For Ascham, historical action usually means

---

[15] All references are from Roger Ascham, *A Report and Discourse . . . of the Affaires and State of Germany and the Emperour Charles his Court . . .*, in *English Works*, ed. William Aldis Wright (Cambridge: Cambridge University Press, 1904).

diplomatic communications, that is, political advice and general political maneuvering transmitted through language, what we might now
call speech acts. International affairs take place in an elaborate verbal
network. A ruler's moral stature, in fact, is very often judged against
his use of, and attitude toward, language. Consistent with Ascham's
Tudor anti-Catholicism, those characters in the dialogue who use
deceitful language tend to be Catholic (among them, the emperor
and the pope), whereas the just users of language, in particular the
German princes, tend to be Protestant.[16]

For instance, the emperor's virtuous former allies who turn against
him are the linguistically pure Protestants, the Marches Albert and
Duke John Frederick, both of whom are described in terms that recall
the Augustinian concept of inner and outer discourse. Ascham portrays Albert as a heroic figure, whose heroism is defined by the
relationship between his heart and tongue. Indeed, he is like Achilles,
for "when he talketh he so frameth hys toung to agree with his hart, as
speakyng and meanyng seemeth to be always at one in hym" (p.
147). From Homer's portrayal of Achilles, Ascham deduces that Homer regarded heroic virtue as the moral coordination of thought,
speech, and action. Again like Achilles, "a Prince of noble courage
should have his hart, his looke, hys toung, and his handes so alwayes
agreeyng together in thinkyng, pretendyng, and speakyng, and
doyng, as no one of these foure should at any tyme be a iarre with an
other" (p. 147). Ascham remarks that Albert's relative, Johannes,
Marches of Bradenburg, is also such a prince: "in Religion a Christian
Prince, with hart toung & honesty of lyfe" (p. 145).

Duke John Frederick receives similar praise in the same vocabulary
derived from the Augustinian and Renaissance moralization of Aristotelian semantic theory: he "would, y^t wordes should be so framed
with the toung, as they be alwayes ment in the hart" (p. 155). John
Frederick's version of the Augustinian moral embrace of inner and
outer discourse is also the basis of moral action: he

thincketh nothyng which he dare not speake, nor speaketh nothyng
whiche hee will not do. Yet hauyng thoughtes grounded vppon

---

[16]Duke Maurice is something of an exception. A German Protestant who at first
betrays those close to him, he later reforms when the emperor verbally tricks his
guardian (whom he had also turned against) and justly shifts back his allegiance.

wisedome, his talke is alwayes so accompanied with discression and his deedes so attende vppon true dealyng, as he neither biteth with wordes, nor wringeth with deedes, except impudency follow the fault, which *Xenophon* wittely calleth the farthest point in al doyng. [p. 155]

In this description, as so often in Ascham, the moral and linguistic relation between heart, tongue, and action is presented with some classical text in the background, some cultural and literary model that guarantees a just relationship between heart, tongue, and action.

In contrast to the linguistically heroic Protestants, the Catholic emperor consistently breaks his pledges and convenants, and often exercises his political power through language. In fact, the entire narrative is set in motion when the emperor breaks his treaty with the Turkish sultan. Moreover, he forces the Germans "in their owne countrey to vse straunge toungs for their private sutes, wherein they could say nothyng at all, or nothyng to the purpose" (p. 144). But, in general, the emperor's estrangement from his German allies is the result of his continual severing of heart, tongue, and hand in his "vnkyndnes."

That Ascham himself should be capable of such moral discernment is no accident, for his discourse—the relationship of his inner and outer word—is guaranteed by the sponsorship of his Protestant sovereign, King Edward (p. 127), just as Elyot's words were validated by the authority of Henry VIII. In the end, all the words in and about Ascham's German history derive their authority from the religious and political virtue of the English monarch. Edward provides the political context that makes possible both Ascham's moral embrace of inner and outer discourse and the referential embrace of these discourses with events.

The political context of language also figures prominently in Ascham's *Schoolmaster,* whose historical perspective is considerably longer than that of his *Report,* which describes events that take place over a period of only two years. In the *Schoolmaster,* Ascham presents a clearly marked out historiography that explains the relationship between political and linguistic history.[17] Like most Renaissance histo-

---

[17]Roger Ascham, *The Schoolmaster,* in *English Works,* pp. 223–24. That languages reach their highest perfection during periods of high political fortune is implied by much of the discussion in Book II.

rians, Ascham, following his classical models, regards history as the history of political affairs. Nations rise and fall over time because of changing political fortunes, which are reflected in the development and deterioration of language. By imitating the language of exemplary eras, a nation preserves an eloquence that can transcend the vissicitudes of its political history and, Ascham implies, can even act as a stabilizing political force itself. Further, because the proper use of language depends so heavily on imitation of historically prior models, eloquence usally contains within itself a history of eloquence. The sixteenth-century Englishman's eloquent Latin and English are inscribed with a history of language conventions. But that history is also a political history, a history of epochs in which morally disposed political authorities nurtured the proper use of language, thus allowing citizens to speak with their mouths what was in their hearts. The problem is, to locate the ideal historical moment worthy of imitation, one must already have sufficient moral acumen. That acumen depends on the political climate of the epoch and nation in which the imitator lives. In Ascham's historiography, classical Rome and sixteenth-century England occupy roughly the same position on the wheel of historical fortune (an upswing of good fortune), and so the Roman linguistic model is applicable to the contemporary political setting in England. Indeed, in both the *Schoolmaster* and the *Report,* Ascham makes it clear that Protestant England, armed with its newly recovered classical literary models, had achieved just the political condition that could be expressed and preserved in its linguistic institutions modeled on classical usage.[18]

Jonson as Humanist

Similar interconnections among language, society, and classical culture are at the heart of the thought and poetry of a major literary humanist of the seventeenth century, Ben Jonson. Jonson too was aware of the frailty of language in the face of adverse social and political forces, but his view of language is more complex and perhaps more pessimistic than that of Elyot and Ascham.[19] However aware

[18]For the relation between Protestantism and language in Ascham, see Alvin Vos, "'Good Matter and Good Utterance': The Character of English Ciceronianism," *Studies in English Literature, 1500–1900,* 19 (1979), 3–18.

[19]Questions about the political feasibility of the humanist language program, at least

Elyot and Ascham were of the dangers that language may face, for them humanism was the catalyst of both a new social and a new linguistic order. For Jonson humanism is often the possession of a select few in a generally hostile environment. Further, while Ascham considered contemporary England to be comparable to the classical era at its peak, Jonson treated the highest moral and cultural values of antiquity as if they were antithetical to those of his England. As a result, there is a basic tension in Jonson's treatment of classical civilization and traditional humanist ideas as, on the one hand, morally central yet, on the other, socially peripheral—at least in the actual social reality he portrays in his poems.[20]

To be sure, Jonson repeats the general stock of humanist ideas about language and society, especially in *Discoveries*, whose pronouncements on language combine Aristotelian, Augustinian, and Stoic ideas. Jonson appeals to the Aristotelian idea that language and reality are connected via the mind. It is clear that Jonson was familiar with Renaissance grammarians such as Scaliger and Vives who modified medieval philosophical grammar for their own purposes, since he refers to them in *Discoveries* and in his *English Grammar* (which itself, however, shows no interest in philosophical grammar). A modified Aristotelian formula appears in *Dirrecons for Speech and Style* (c. 1599) written by John Hoskyns, a lawyer and rhetorician whom John Aubrey described as Jonson's intellectual father.[21] Jonson quotes Hoskyns verbatim in *Discoveries:*

---

in its application to the public forum of the court, do of course appear with the rise of humanism itself: see, e.g., Thomas Wyatt's "Mine own John Poins" and Thomas More's *Utopia*. For an illuminating treatment of the politically problematic nature of language at court, see Cesare Vasoli, "Francesco Patrizi and 'The Double Rhetoric,' " *New Literary History*, 14 (1983), 539–51; and Heinrich F. Plett, "Aesthetic Constituents in the Courtly Culture of Renaissance England," *New Literary History*, 14 (1983), 597–621. For the threat of dislocation in the referential use of language, see Murray Krieger, "Presentation and Representation in the Renaissance Lyric: The Net of Words and the Escape of the Gods," in *Mimesis*, pp. 110–31; and Thomas M. Greene, *The Light in Troy: Imitation and Discovery in Renaissance Poetry* (New Haven: Yale University Press, 1982), pp. 111–15.

[20]I have discussed this issue at greater length in "Words, Things, and Names: Jonson's Poetry and Philosophical Grammar," in *Classic and Cavalier: Essays on Jonson and the Sons of Ben*, ed. Claude J. Summers and Ted-Larry Pebworth (Pittsburgh: University of Pittsburgh Press, 1982), pp. 91–104.

[21]The passage Jonson quotes from Hoskyns appears in *The Life, Letters, and Writings of John Hoskins, 1566–1638*, ed. L. B. Osborn (New Haven: Yale University Press, 1937), p. 116.

The conceits of the mind are Pictures of Things, and the tongue is the interpreter of those pictures. The order of Gods creatures in themselves, is not only admirable, and glorious, but eloquent; then he who could apprehend the consequences of things in their truth, and utter his apprehensions as truly, were the best Writer, or Speaker. Therefore Cicero said much, when he said, *Dicere recte nemo potest, nisi qui prudenter intelligit.*[22]

Through Hoskyns, Jonson refers to the world of things, "the order of Gods creatures," as an "eloquent" language in itself, to be reflected in human language in turn made eloquent by the mind's apprehension of the order of things. Thus Jonson and Hoskyns justify eloquence by referring to the Aristotelian basis of philosophical grammar (though, interestingly, they appeal to a rhetorician—Cicero—rather than the philosopher). Although neither Hoskyns nor Jonson was interested in the elaborate technical details of speculative grammar, both made the Aristotelian relationship between mind, language, and reality the theoretical underpinning of their humanist concern for eloquence.

Like other humanists, Jonson understands the relationship of mind, reality, and language in a moral context. Jonson's statements about language suggest his belief that language names a moral reality and that the ability to name that reality depends on the ethical condition of the mind that assigns words to things. "Language most shewes a man," he declares, quoting Vives, because it is "the Image of the Parent of it, the mind" (p. 625). A moral dysfunction of the mind manifests itself in what Hoskyns called, as Jonson quotes him, "Negligent speech," or misappareled thought, which "doth not onely discredit the person of the Speaker, but it discrediteth the opinion of his reason and judgement" (p. 629). Jonson's emphasis on the quality of the perceiving subject that appropriates words to the world is particularly pronounced.[23]

[22]All references to Ben Jonson's poetry and prose are from vol. 8 of the *Works*, ed. C. H. Herford and Percy and Evelyn Simpson (Oxford: Clarendon Press, 1947). This passage appears on p. 268.

[23]The emergence of the autonomous perceiving subject and its relationship to this language paradigm is discussed in Michel Foucault, *The Order of Things: An Archaeology of the Human Sciences* (New York: Random House, 1970), pp. 46–165; and Timothy J. Reiss, *The Discourse of Modernism* (Ithaca: Cornell University Press, 1982), pp. 55–107. This idea is applied to Jonson by Don E. Wayne, "Poetry and Power in Ben Jonson's *Epigrammes:* The Naming of 'Facts' or the Figuring of Social Relations?" *Renaissance and Modern Studies*, 23 (1979), 79–103.

Jonson also follows other humanists in coupling this moralized Aristotelianism with an insistence on the social nature of language. The stylistic and semantic issue of *res et verba* has social and political implications for Jonson too. In typical humanist manner, he regards language as "the Interpreter of Society" (as he says [p. 621], again quoting Vives), the vehicle of moral perception. The larger social conditions of language are as important to Jonson as the moral condition of the individual speaker's mind. For him, as for Ascham and Mulcaster, the state of language depends on the state of the commonweal. The moral function of language in fact attains its fullest being primarily in the social domain, and the connection between word and thing in that domain is best preserved by custom. Jonson defines his sense of custom in *Discoveries:* "*Custome* is the most certaine Mistresse of Language, as the publicke stampe makes the current money" (p. 622). He goes on to explain: "But that I call Custome of speech, which is the consent of the Learned; as Custome of life, which is the consent of the good" (p. 622). The link between the moral and social context of language is fast: as words do not exist apart from speakers, speakers do not exist apart from society. Jonson subscribed to the humanist idea that, at least ideally, good societies produce good speakers, as good speakers produce good societies.

This view of language is reflected in Jonson's poetry, which frequently probes the interrelationship of moral, social, and linguistic orders. In so doing, it translates a referential theory of language into a theory of poetic diction and poetic authorship. One of Jonson's typical strategies is to portray a particular individual who acts in society with "Custome of life" as defined by "the good" and "Custome of speech" as defined by "the Learned." Jonson often appeals to classical culture as his most reliable guide for this strategy: classical ideals and classical diction, as the products of a superior civilization, furnish models for custom of speech and life in many of Jonson's poems.

In the epigram "To William Camden" (*Epigrammes,* XIV), for example, Jonson uses naming nouns and adjectives whose etymologies stem from Augustan, Virgilian Latin ("graue," "name," "faith," "authoritie"), as well as words of English origin with strong classical associations ("things," "weight"). Similarly, that quality of the poet's moral being which enables him to identify Camden's ethical nature is also associated with classical Roman origins, namely, his "pietie," a virtue Jonson most likely learned from Camden himself, his humanist teacher. The poet's subject, the poet's word, and the poet himself are all interrelated through classical ethical ideals.

Etymologies, in other words, here anchor the moral nature of both the poet and his subject in the common medium of classical ethical institutions. In this sense, the moral reference of the poet's *verba* to the *res* of Camden's moral being is a dimension of humanist theory, just as Camden's naming of Britain is an act of the historical understanding. As the repository of ethical ideas that can be emulated in Renaissance England, classical antiquity also provides the linguistic guarantee of the connection between an English *verbum* and its referent, its *res*. The ethical authority of antiquity stretches across centuries in English diction based on Augustan words. The poem's classical ideals, then, shape its words, their referent (Camden), and the mind that assigns one to the other (the poet's "pietie").

Looming over both Jonson and Camden is the Britannia named by Camden, a Britannia that is part of the Roman tradition providing the moral climate for right language.[24] Jonson's praise of Camden typifies his use of representative English figures of the day as models of the proper union of word (or name) and moral referent in their very lives, a union illustrated by the fact that they live up to their aristocratic names. In all probability Jonson acquired this interest in names from Camden himself, who on several occasions in both *Britannia* and *Remaines Concerning Britaine* explains the origins and etymologies of British names, almost always including in his remarks some reference to Plato's *Cratylus*.[25] Although Jonson shows little interest in the Cratylist etymologies of either common or proper names, he does share Plato's and Camden's thesis that the name (or, perhaps more important, a noble title) of a person in some way reveals his essence (for Jonson, a moral or social essence). By reminding people of their names and titles, Jonson reminds them of their obligation to live up to, and provide an example of, the social and

---

[24]F. J. Levy, *Tudor Historical Thought* (San Marino, Calif.: Huntington Library, 1967), pp. 152–54.

[25]See William Camden, *Britain*, tr. Philémon Holland (London, 1637), p. 23, and *Remaines Concerning Britaine* (London, 1614), pp. 46–53. (On p. 36 of the *Remaines* Camden refers to a view of language based on Aristotle's semantic theory.) See also "A posthumous Discourse . . . By Mr. Camden," in *Camden's Britannia . . . with large additions and improvements*. Published by Edmund Gibson (London, 1695), col. 189.

moral ideals represented by those names, so that, as Camden commands, "wee faile not to be answerable to [our names], but be Nostris nominis homines."[26]

The names of important English nobles and intellectuals appear throughout Jonson's poetry, a characteristic Jonson draws attention to in *Epigrammes*, IX and in the dedication of the *Epigrammes* to the Earl of Pembroke. For Jonson, a name may variously represent ideals associated with a renowned family, a title defined by a place, or simply one's reputation; and it is these associations of names and ideals in particular which indicate the moral and social implications of Jonson's Aristotelian view of the relationship between words and things. For instance, Jonson's funereal praise of Margaret Ratcliffe's virtues (*Epigrammes*, XL), in which each line emanates acrostically from the letters of her name, is more than just a flashy trick.[27] The proper political and moral arrangements allow language to discover and express moral essence, almost as a property of language itself. Here, as in Mulcaster's descriptions, the social and Adamic approach to language merge. The acrostic expresses an almost ritual identification of name and moral nature as perceived and celebrated by the poet. This theme, which Jonson uses in many poems, is elegantly exemplified in the Cary-Morison ode, where celebrated aristocratic names become the generic names of virtues:

> You liv'd to be the great surnames,
> And titles, by which all made claimes
> Unto the Vertue. Nothing perfect done
> But as a CARY, or a MORISON.
>
> [ll. 13–16]

To project the name of a noble personage as a generic name of virtue, Jonson once again relies on classical values. Jonson frequently uses members of the Sidney family as shining examples of the connections between nominating words, classical culture, and the nobility. In the epigram "To Mary Lady Wroth" (CV), addressed to the niece of

---

[26]Camden, *Remaines*, p. 53. For Camden's remarks on the representation of moral ideals in Christian names, which "stir men up to the imitation of them whose names they bare," see p. 48.

[27]For James's interest in acrostics and pattern poems, see Graham Parry, *The Golden Age restor'd: The Culture of the Stuart Court, 1603–42* (New York: St. Martin's Press, 1981), pp. 24–25.

Sir Philip Sidney, Jonson praises Mary Wroth as the epitome of classical feminine grace. If all classical literature were lost, her very person would be a reconstruction of the classical goddesses. She would, in fact, restore not only their charms but also their very names out of her own being. Those who would see her wearing "the wheaten hat" would call her Ceres; those who would see her "keeping [her] due state" would call her Juno, and so on. Jonson adds, "But euen their names were to be made a-new, / Who could not but create them all, from you." Mary Wroth contains within her character all of classical "fable" regarding women. The classical virtues persist in the person of a noble lady related to the poetic Sidney; she links the classical past to the English present, making classical matter and names perennial, as if they inhered in nature. At the same time, her embodiment of classical names and natures justifies her life on a country estate (signaled by a host of classical nature deities) and her position in the political hierarchy (signaled by Juno) as part of the natural order of things. Classical allusions thus help to legitimate the social and political status of the nobility codified by words (here names). The classics inhere in nature, and classical values, because perpetuated in the noble personages living off the land, can withstand all attacks.[28]

Jonson's use of classical motives in the epigram to Mary Wroth appears to be an extension of his role as court poet. He endows the nobility with symbols of their power and celebrates the legitimacy of their position, as he did for James in the coronation entertainments and in his masques.[29] In fact, Jonson reminds his readers at the beginning of the *Epigrammes* that his authority to comment on social matters stems from the king. The volume contains several poems to James, but *Epigrammes*, IV, "To King James," makes the clearest connection between poetic language and the royal presence, especially as James is both king and poet:

> How, best of Kings, do'st thou a scepter beare!
> How, best of *Poets*, do'st thou laurell weare!
>
> [ll. 1–2]

---

[28]The relationship between land tenure and Roman law is mentioned by Brian Paul Levack, *The Civil Lawyers in England, 1603–1641: A Political Study* (Oxford: Clarendon Press, 1973), p. 149.

[29]Jonson's role in the Royal Entry is discussed at length in Parry, *Golden Age restor'd*, pp. 3–24.

It is not suprising, then, that Jonson should regard James as the authorizing force behind his poetry:

> Whom should my *Muse* then flie to, but the best
> Of Kings for grace; of *Poets* for my test?
>
> [ll. 9–10]

Like Ascham and Elyot, Jonson points to the monarch as the guarantor of his word, though he does not go to the extreme of seeing his entire poetic being as constituted by the authority of the king.[30]

Jonson and the Problem of Consensus

Despite Jonson's conventional humanist use of classical themes to celebrate the king and his virtuous nobles, a closer look at his treatment of language, the nobility, and the classics reveals darker, more ambivalent feelings about society in general and the court in particular. Jonson criticism has been divided on the question of Jonson's attitude toward his aristocratic subjects. He has been regarded both as the spokesman for the values of traditional English society and as an embattled figure whose apparent ease in aristocratic society is often belied not merely by ambivalence but by hostility toward those around him. Some critics have even claimed that, far from being the conservative figure he is often made out to be, Jonson in fact transcended the society of his aristocratic patrons and was the harbinger of a new social and literary order.[31] And while those schol-

---

[30]For contrasting views of Spenser and Jonson in this regard, see Jonathan Goldberg, *James I and the Politics of Literature: Jonson, Shakespeare, Donne, and Their Contemporaries* (Baltimore: Johns Hopkins University Press, 1983), pp. 1–17, 219–30.

[31]Those who emphasize Jonson's role as a representative spokesman of his society include Edward Partridge, "Jonson's *Epigrammes:* The Named and the Nameless," *Studies in the Literary Imagination,* 6 (1973), 153–98; Hugh Maclean, "Ben Jonson's Poems: Notes on the Ordered Society," in *Essays in English Literature from the Renaissance to the Victorian Age, Presented to A. S. P. Woodhouse,* ed. Millar MacLure and F. W. Watt (Toronto: University of Toronto Press, 1964), pp. 43–68; Geoffrey Walton, *Metaphysical to Augustan: Studies in Tone and Sensibility in the Seventeenth Century* (London: Bowes & Bowes, 1955), pp. 23–44; L. C. Knights, *Drama and Society in the Age of Jonson* (London: Chatto & Windus, 1937). Those who stress Jonson's ambivalence about the social context in which he wrote include E. Pearlman, "Ben Jonson: An Anatomy," *English Literary Renaissance,* 9 (1979), 64–93; Jonas A. Barish, "Jonson and the Loathed

ars who believe Jonson was at ease with the aristocratic values he celebrates tend to see in his poetry a smooth, unambiguous appropriation of classical values into contemporary English culture,[32] those who emphasize Jonson's ambivalence see—more accurately, I believe—his use of the classics as expressing a disparity between the classical past and the English present.

This disparity is the result of Jonson's basic discomfort in his society, a discomfort that separates him from many of his humanist predecessors who saw in speech based on classical authority the embodiment of a social consensus and political cohesion derived from the educational and intellectual prestige of legitimate rulers. Jonson, however, frequently resorts to classical values to express his ambiguous position in his society; his preference for marginality, whether geographical, social, or intellectual, is telling. Moreover, Jonson conveys a sense of pervasive moral and social decay that ultimately isolates not only him but his lauded nobles from the social and moral environment, undermining the possibility that the praise of their virtuous names will resound very far.

Stage," in *A Celebration of Ben Jonson*, ed. William Blisset et al. (Toronto: University of Toronto Press, 1973), pp. 27–53; Isabel Rivers, *The Poetry of Conservatism, 1600–1745: A Study of Poets and Public Affairs from Jonson to Pope* (Cambridge: Rivers Press, 1973), pp. 21–71; Arthur Marotti, "All about Jonson's Poetry," *ELH*, 39 (1972), 208–37; and, most notably, Don E. Wayne, *Penshurst: The Semiotics of Place and the Poetics of History* (Madison: University of Wisconsin Press, 1984). Among the most suggestive outlines of the complexities of Jonson's attitude toward self and society is Annabel Patterson's *Censorship and Interpretation: The Conditions of Writing and Reading in Early Modern England* (Madison: University of Wisconsin Press, 1984), pp. 126–44. For Jonson as a harbinger of a new bourgeois social order, see Jonathan Haynes, "Festivity and the Dramatic Economy of Jonson's *Bartholomew Fair*," *ELH*, 51 (1984), 645–88; and Wayne, "Poetry and Power," and *Penshurst*.

[32]See, e.g., D. J. Gordon, "*Hymenaei:* Jonson's Masque of Union," in *The Renaissance Imagination*, ed. Stephen Orgel (Berkeley: University of California Press, 1975), pp. 157–84, esp. pp. 174–79; Wesley Trimpi, *Ben Jonson's Poems: A Study in the Plain Style* (Stanford, Calif.: Stanford University Press, 1962); G. A. Hibbard, "The Country House Poem of the Seventeenth Century," *Journal of the Warburg and Courtauld Institutes*, 19 (1956), 159–74. (Gordon does, however, point out that Jonson is not always successful in appropriating the Roman past for the English present.) Thomas M. Greene, Richard S. Peterson, and George Parfitt, who are sensitive to the tension of Jonson's process of assimilating the classics, tend to see his poetry as a resolved union of the antique and the English. See Greene, *Light in Troy*, pp. 264–93; Peterson, *Imitation and Praise in the Poems of Ben Jonson* (New Haven: Yale University Press, 1981); Parfitt, "Compromise Classicism: Language and Rhythm in Ben Jonson's Poetry," *Studies in English Literature, 1500–1900*, 11 (1971), 109–23.

The epigram to Pembroke (CII) is an apt example of the social isolation of the morally good. As in the Cary-Morison ode, Jonson treats his subject's name as the generic name of virtue:

> I doe but name thee PEMBROKE, and I find
> It is an *Epigramme*, on all man-kind;
> Against the bad, but of, and to the good:
> Both which are ask'd, to haue thee vnderstood.
>
> [ll. 1–4]

And Jonson regards not only Pembroke's name but Pembroke himself as an act of language that projects moral virtue. Word (or name) and referent are bonded together because of Pembroke's moral character; his "noblesse keeps one stature still" (l. 13). But Pembroke inhabits a society that pays little heed to his virtue. He is surrounded by people who "follow vertue, for reward, to day; / To morrow vice, if shee give better pay" (ll. 9–10). As a result, Pembroke himself is "besieg'd with ill / Of what ambition, faction, pride can raise" (ll. 14–15). Most people cannot possess Pembroke's name, because they evade any fixed and therefore real commitment to virtue (a characteristic of many of the unnamed figures in Jonson's satirical epigrams). And though the ultimate reason for publicly proclaiming Pembroke's virtuous name is that "they, that hope to see / The common-wealth still safe, [may] studie thee" (ll. 19–20), Jonson portrays himself and Pembroke as two of the few people capable of real virtue, the few bound to each other but separate from the "common-wealth" at large. Indeed, many of Jonson's poems are marked by this dynamic tension in which he holds up an exemplary noble to public praise, only to present him or her as exceptional and inimitable by the unworthy crowd.[33]

Although Jonson does celebrate the public good brought to the commonwealth by the king's appointees, such as Robert Cecil (*Epigrammes*, LXIII, LXIV) and Thomas Elsmere (*Vnder-wood*, XXXI), not surprisingly he rarely celebrates rituals of broad social communion. His humanist topoi often serve as attempts to preserve what he

---

[33]For Jonson's treatment of virtue as restrictive rather than invitational, see Stanley Fish, "Authors-Readers: Jonson's Community of the Same," *Representations*, 7 (Summer 1984), 26–58.

perceives as the remnants of a social order threatened from within by corruption and from without by mercantile values, among other dangers.[34] The very theme of naming someone in order to praise him is characterized by a rhetoric of divisiveness that delineates a moral hierarchy from which most of his compatriots are excluded; "few, / Be of the best" (ll. 13–14), he remarks in an epigram to the Countess of Bedford (XCIIII).

One of Jonson's typical strategies of praise is to separate those who deserve celebration from those who do not. Frequently, as in the epigrams to Nevil (CIX) and Shelton (CXIX), Jonson praises his subjects by elevating them above their more typically corrupt contemporaries in a corrupt society. The very act of singing an individual's fame sets him off from a society that at times offers no support to the virtue that merits the fame. The poet must sing Salisbury's fame (*Epigrammes*, XLIII), for example, so that the rest of the nation will not fail to do so; he must sing Mounteagle's fame (*Epigrammes*, LX) because the rest of the nation has in fact already failed to do so. In the epigram to Cary (LXVI), Jonson goes so far as to say that the nation is incapable of recognizing virtue to begin with: "this our time, / Durst valour make, almost, but not a crime" (ll. 5–6). The fame Jonson bestows on his selected nobles is quite different from the renown of classical epic heroes, for example, whose praiseworthy deeds reinforce and solidify their place within society rather than elevate them above society.

Thus the concept of right language based on convention is more problematic for Jonson than for Mulcaster, Elyot, and Ascham. The pervasive moral and social decay that Jonson portrays in his poetry repeatedly puts his poetic practice at odds with his theoretical statement in *Discoveries* that "*Custome* is the most certaine Mistresses of Language." Jonson's poetry often insists on the loss of the "consensus" that humanist grammarians regarded as the basis of all lan-

[34]Alvin B. Kernan's observation is relevant here: "Jonson's rigid classicism, moral authoritarianism, and stout insistence upon form and realism seem as much desperate defenses raised against disaster as rational aesthetic positions freely chosen" ("Alchemy and Acting: The Major Plays of Ben Jonson," *Studies in the Literary Imagination*, 6 [1973], 8); quoted by Pearlman, "Ben Jonson," p. 394, n. 27. Pearlman's view, p. 375, is also to the point: "Caught between the classes," Jonson turned to aristocratic values of selfhood, almost as a defensive reaction to emerging middle-class Protestant patterns of selfhood.

guage, the social "agrement" (to use Mulcaster's term) that institutionalized moral norms and thereby linguistic norms—though
Jonson never questions the moral authority of the king. Jonson fundamentally accepts the notion of language as speech, to be understood in a moral and social context, but he presents himself as skeptical of the social "agrement" that makes just speech reflect just social
norms. Many of his poems dislocate the basic humanist notion of
speech as the language norms provided by the moral and social
leadership of the noble classes. The question his poetry poses is, How
is the language of moral intelligence (i.e., speech) maintained in the
face of what he perceives as the loss of community that makes speech
possible? A half century earlier, Ascham had posed a different version of the same question in his analysis of historical cycles that pull
language down along with declining political fortunes. He had an-
swered that such declines could be forestalled by the perpetuation of
classical imitation in English educational institutions. For Jonson the
solution to the problem of linguistic decline was less simple. Virtuous
nobles who embodied classical values could be found, but by situating
them in geographically and socially marginal places, Jonson implicitly
limits their influence on their surrounding society.

The attenuated connection between select nobles and classical culture on the one hand and the larger society of court and city on the
other is highlighted in Jonson's poems praising great country houses,
especially those connected with the Sidney family, such as "To Robert
Wroth" and "To Penshurst."[35]

In Jonson's ode to Sir Robert Wroth (*The Forrest,* III), as in the
epigram to Sir Robert's wife, Mary Lady Wroth, classical allusions
justify the social universe of Wroth's landed estate. Jonson caps his
description of the Wroths' country seat (ll. 13–46) with an account of
the "rites" (l. 47) of classical nature gods that restore the golden age
("Saturnes raigne" [l. 50]) to the land, an occasion celebrated with
"Apollo's harpe, and Hermes lyre" (l. 51) in the presence of the Muses
themselves (perhaps a reference to Lady Wroth's patronage of poets).
This classical celebration of the land and the arts follows a survey of

[35]It is noteworthy that as a writer of court masques for James, Jonson employed
classical motives to celebrate the very center of his society, James's court, the site of a
translatio imperii; see Parry, *Golden Age restor'd,* p. 49.

the estate's seasonal production of food, gathered by harvest and hunt, with which the Wroth family feed themselves and their guests. (Wroth was known as a great huntsman and sportsman.) The society sustained by the fruitful Wroth estate, a pastoral world untouched by the corruption of city and court, is legitimated by the classical allusions, which suggest it is just, natural, and part of an ancient, even mythological, historical order.

But the legitimacy of the estate also depends in part on its separation from (or, perhaps more accurately, its marginal relation to) the official society of the court, where ostentatious feasts and entertainments feed ambition, pride, and vice in general (ll. 5–12). In fact, in most of the second half of the poem, Jonson derides the active life altogether (ll. 61–90). Jonson thus again invokes a classical ideal— pastoral country retirement—to separate the virtuous few from the corrupt multitude.

This place on the moral and geographical periphery of the national center ("so neere the citie, and the court" [l. 3]) becomes the center of its own social communion. The description of the classical nature "rites" that mark Wroth's aristocratic connection to the land is directly followed by a scene in which distinctions of social rank are blurred:

> The rout of rurall folke come thronging in,
>   (Their rudenesse then is thought no sinne)
> Thy noblest spouse affords them welcome grace;
>   And the great *Heroes,* of her race,
> Sit mixt with losse of state, or reuerance.
>   Freedome doth with degree dispense.
>   [ll. 53–58]

The closer the atmosphere comes to that of classical pastoral and the farther away it moves from that of city and court, the less important social distinctions become. Jonson crowns his list of moral corruptions in aristocratic society with a description of city and court as places where people strive for "place and honour" (l. 87). The denigration of "honour" is an ironic reversal of Jonson's own praise of a noble's honor—his name. The hierarchical organization of official society—unsupported by firm moral values—is an indication of that society's decay and contrasts with the "losse of state" in the country house, especially at the table where "the jolly wassal walkes the often round" (l. 69). The site of this ritual of social communion, characteristically for Jonson, is associated with the consumption of food. [36]

Whatever social leveling may be effected in the feasting on the estate, there is no suggestion here of democratic sentiment. In the ritual that Jonson portrays, social stratification depends on its temporary dissolution, a process well known to anthropologists.[37] Ritually celebrating the essential unity of all elements in a society diffuses potential conflict within the social hierarchy and even reinforces distinctions of rank when participants return to their various social strata after the ritual is completed. Though such rituals may result in a change in the established order, they can also move through a transitional state to end in a renewal of the *status quo ante*. Such is the case in the ode to Wroth, a poem which is after all the celebration of a noble family whose members are part of a local ruling elite.

But Jonson's portrait of the Wroth estate precludes an exit to a larger social world. The estate becomes a protective enclosure as Jonson criticizes nearly everything outside its grounds. The communion enacted on the estate cannot embrace a larger social community because, for Jonson, all bonds both of communion and of the legitimate social structure have been lost in the corruption of the social world outside Wroth's domain.[38] The Wroth estate as Jonson pictures it is inner-directed, its setting emblematic more of a wish to protect its way of life from impending and threatening social change than of the hope of extending that way of life to the world at large.[39] Significantly, in Jonson's poem the social renewal represented by the coun-

[36]On the theme of consumption in "To Penshurst," see Raymond Williams, *The Country and the City* (New York: Oxford University Press, 1973), pp. 27–34.

[37]Though I have not used Victor Turner's terms in the following analysis, I am indebted to his formulations. For Turner's concept of structure, anti-structure, *communitas*, and liminality in social rituals marking a transition from one phase of life to another—including rituals of personal, social, or political transformation—see *Dramas, Fields, and Metaphor: Symbolic Action in Human Society* (Ithaca: Cornell University Press, 1974).

[38]Fish, "Authors-Readers," observes that Jonson's poetry "withholds itself and closes its face to anything outside its circle" (p. 40); his moral declamation "functions less as a means of expanding the community than as a device for closing the door in the face of those who are not already 'sealed,'" (p. 38).

[39]For a discussion of this theme of protectiveness in Jonson's poetry, see George Parfitt, *Ben Jonson, Public Poet and Private Man* (New York: Harper & Row, 1977), esp. chap. 8.

try life is not eventually transferred to the court (a characteristic exchange of, say, a Shakespeare comedy); the court in fact comes to the estate. A central event in the poem is a visit from King James, who "makes [the] house his court" (l. 24). Even James is brought into the estate's social communion and made part of its almost self-contained world. Ultimately, then, the poem's stance is divisive, its underlying vision exclusionary: it separates the blameless from the blameworthy, admitting only the blameless into the privileged, sanctioned, peripheral world of the country estate. The poem's classical setting does not represent a "custome of life" for a total society or even the governing class as a whole but for only a saved remnant.[40] As Stanley Fish has said, opposing the commonly held view of Jonson's poetry, "rather than embracing society, [Jonson's poems] repel it."[41]

Jonson's choice of classical pastoral to sanction the morally privileged world of the country estate offers a clue to his concept of social and linguistic convention, for the force that Jonson's classical allusions gather when applied to this peripheral space makes them culturally peripheral too.

The connection between classical allusion and marginality is more complicated than might at first be supposed, however, since Jonson's portraits of his subjects often cannot be taken at face value. It would be a mistake, for example, to conclude that the ode to Wroth expresses a genuine rejection of the court. Here, as so often in Jonson's poetry, the nobles he portrays as retired to the country were in fact active at court. Although Robert Wroth himself was apparently devoted to a leisurely country life and performed no active service other than that of sheriff of Essex, his wife was a member of an influential court circle.[42] Further, Jonson's depiction of the feudal society on the Wroth estate is generally a fiction, for it represents a manner of life that no longer existed in England at that time.[43] Indeed, so far was

---

[40]For a treatment of Renaissance Latin which emphasizes social exclusivity, though in a different context, see Walter J. Ong, "Latin Language Study as a Renaissance Puberty Rite," in *Rhetoric, Romance, and Technology: Studies in the Interpretation of Expression and Culture* (Ithaca: Cornell University Press, 1971), pp. 113–41.

[41]Fish, "Authors-Readers," p. 39.

[42]For details of the lives of Robert and Mary Wroth, see *Dictionary of National Biography (DNB)*, s.v. "Lady Mary Wroth."

[43]See William Alexander McClung, *The Country House in English Renaissance Poetry* (Berkeley: University of California Press, 1977), p. 5.

the estate from the feudal, non-moneyed, self-sufficient world portrayed by Jonson in the poem that, when Robert Wroth died, Mary
Wroth was left with a large debt.[44] Thus to decry the court and to
praise the Wroths was still in a real sense to praise the court. Jonson's
critical stance in this poem and elsewhere is not a repudiation of the
courtly world that in fact sustained him but, often, a form of socially
sanctioned dissent, what Jonathan Goldberg calls a "contained re-
bellion."[45]

I would qualify Goldberg's remark and suggest that Jonson represents the Wroth estate as a marginal place that expresses his *own*
ambivalence. As we have seen, Jonson derides the court, but celebrates the king's arrival with the court. Although it is ambiguous
whether James legitimates or is legitimated by Wroth's estate, from
one perspective his presence can be understood as the monarchical
legitimation of country values inimical to courtly life. Jonson disdains
the active life but praises Wroth for his service to his country (disin-
genuously so, since Wroth's main activities seem to have been hunt-
ing and sporting). At the time Jonson wrote *The Forrest,* court and
country were beginning to quarrel in parliament about the source
and nature of the king's authority and power, and the tension created
by that quarrel is perhaps reflected in the poem. But Jonson's insin-
uation of the king in a country estate whose lady is an active member
of the court suggests that he may not particularly favor the country
faction that opposed James's claim to absolute power, a claim James at
times based on Roman civil law, in contrast to the English common
law invoked by his opponents among the gentry.[46] Jonson's continual
association, here and in "To Penshurst" of the country with things
classical may have a political context if the classical is implicated in
James's classicizing Roman absolutism. At any rate, the marginality
Jonson imputes to the country estate, in reality an extension of the
court, is his own creation, a way of claiming allegiance to the court
while professing aloofness.

[44]*DNB,* "Lady Mary Wroth."

[45]Goldberg, *James I and the Politics of Literature,* p. 220.

[46]See Perez Zagorin, *The Court and the Country: The Beginning of the English Revolution
in the Mid-Seventeenth Century* (New York: Atheneum, 1970), and qualifications by
Derek Hirst, "Court, Country, and Politics before 1629," in *Faction and Parliament:
Essays on Early Stuart History,* ed. Kevin Sharpe (Oxford: Clarendon Press, 1978),
pp. 105–37.

Jonson uses the motif of marginality in the same way in "To Pens-hurst." In this poem, however, Jonson contrasts the virtuous life of the estate, Robert Sidney's Penshurst, with the socially degenerate life of the ostentatious rich in the surrounding countryside rather than with the corrupt society of city and court.[47] The peripherally situated estate, partly feudal, partly pastoral, represents the rare lord who is virtuous. The poem begins by distinguishing Penshurst from the many houses "built to enuious show" (l. 1) and then moves on to describe the lush pastoral grounds and the social communion among the various classes which takes place at the "liberall boord" (l. 59). As in the ode to Wroth, the classical pastoral celebrating abundance marks the lord's just maintenance of, and attachment to, the land, as well as his role in providing an ideal society.

The way Jonson merges Penshurst's specifically English landscape with a classical literary setting is a critical commonplace. Appropri-ately, the point at which the estate becomes a prototypical emblem of quintessentially English values—when James visits—is also the mo-ment when it realizes itself as a Roman household. On his approach to Penshurst, James sees the hearths aflame as if they were Penates, the Roman household gods that Aeneas carried with him from Troy and that informed him of his mission to found Rome (*Aeneid* III, 147–71)—an apt emblem of both the domestic and the royal nature of James's visit. What is remarkable about the Roman setting of the poem, however, is the way it substitutes for, rather than enhances, the English society at whose head Penshurst might otherwise seem to stand. For while, in the poem, Penshurst is culturally validated by Jonson's allusions to Roman institutions, in fact it is (as Jonson em-phasizes from the beginning) detached from the surrounding English society littered by "proud, ambitious heaps" (l. 101).[48] For Jonson, Penshurst is a place where the present meets the classical past, but only because much of the present is rejected; the cultural guardians of the house partake of the values of Roman antiquity because they recognize the distance between antiquity and "the times," the present.

---

[47]See McClung, *Country House,* chap. 3, for a discussion of this issue in relation to English country architecture.

[48]For a parallel view of Jonson's concept of the just man, see Thomas M. Greene's influential essay, "Ben Jonson and the Centered Self," *Studies in English Literature, 1500–1900,* 10 (1970), 329–48; and Peterson, *Imitation and Praise,* p. 126.

However much Jonson may use classical values to mark Penshurst off from its surrounding society, the poem reveals the same ambivalence underlying the ode to Wroth. Jonson praises Sidney and his wife as the epitome of "manners, armes, and arts" (l. 98), a gesture toward their participation in the active life inconsistent with the general picture of the estate as separate from society. Furthermore, the "ancient" feudal world portrayed by Jonson in Penshurst is really a fiction first promulgated by Sidney's father, himself the son of a new man created by the Tudor monarchy.[49] The entire poem celebrating the self-contained estate is at odds with Sidney's public and diplomatic career, as if, in an almost willful distortion of Sidney's real position as an active courtier, Jonson portrays him as a retiring country squire.[50] As in the companion poem to Wroth, Jonson finds it difficult to take a straightforward stance toward his subject.

Clearly, the model of classical imitation established by Ascham and the humanist grammarians does not quite work for Jonson. Jonson may invoke Roman antiquity, but often he does so out of a sense of loss and nostalgia, not because he has confidence in its living presence. Jonson's classical allusions present the Wroth and Sidney estates as utopias in order to highlight them, not as models of social perfection to be followed throughout the commonweal, but as loci of regret.[51]

Of course, on numerous occasions Jonson does emphatically proclaim the contemporary significance of the classics. One important influence on Jonson, for example, was Camden's view of the English present arising out of Roman-British remains.[52] And in his Epistle to Selden (*Vnder-wood*, XIV), Jonson praises Selden's *Titles of Honour* for its "Newnesse of Sense, Antiquitie of voyce" (l. 60). Other examples are too well known to repeat.

Nevertheless, Jonson's poems repeatedly intimate that those who

---

[49]See Wayne, *Penshurst*, pp. 81–115.

[50]Sidney's courtly career is carefully documented in Millicent Hay, *The Life of Robert Sidney, Earl of Leicester (1563–1626)* (Washington, D.C.: Folger Shakespeare Library, 1984).

[51]Here I paraphrase Gérard Genette's remarks on Valéry's notion of a linguistic paradise; see "Valéry and the Poetics of Language," in *Textual Strategies: Perspectives in Post-Structuralist Criticism*, ed. Josué V. Harari (Ithaca: Cornell University Press, 1979), p. 313.

[52]See Peterson, *Imitation and Praise*, pp. 57–58.

share moral and cultural values with antiquity isolate themselves from society at large instead of contributing an ethical intelligence that could shape social morality. Jonson's doubt that the classical past can penetrate into the present even through the noble and learned classes is apparent in his epigrams to two translators of classical history, Sir Henry Savile (*Epigrammes*, XCV) and Clement Edmonds (*Epigrammes*, CX, CXI). Jonson presents Savile as a reincarnation of Tacitus. Savile not only translates the Roman historian; he also fills in lost parts of Tacitus' narrative. Savile's scholarly connection to Tacitus and Sallust gives him the wordly understanding and political acumen necessary to write an English history:

> We need a man, can speake of the intents,
> The councells, actions, orders, and euents
> Of state, and censure them: we need his pen
> Can write the things, the causes, and the men.
>
> [ll. 31–34]

Savile's mastery of classical history also gives him the moral courage to speak truth in adverse circumstances; Jonson's implication is that there are few such men around and many adverse circumstances:

> But most we need his faith (and all haue you)
> That dares nor write things false, nor hide things true.
>
> [ll. 35–36]

In other words, the moral and expressive qualities—the two are really one—that Savile has acquired through classical learning distinguish him precisely because he is not the norm and precisely because the times do not support the classics as a model of truth expressed in language.

Jonson portrays Clement Edmonds, the translator of and commentator on Caesar's *Gallic Wars,* in much the same way. Though Edmonds's scholarship may help us see that "What the'antique souldiers were, the moderne bee" (*Epigrammes*, CXI), Jonson characteristically laments that the lessons of antiquity are lost to most. Referring to Caesar's books, he exclaims: "whose good / How few haue read! how fewer vnderstood!" (*Epigrammes*, CX). Jonson's association of the classics with exclusiveness rather than with "consensus" is expressed more bitterly in "An Ode. To himselfe" (*Vnder-wood*, XXIII). He answers in the affirmative to the questions,

> Are all th'*Aonian* springs
> Dri'd up? lyes *Thespia* wast?
> Doth *Clarius* Harp want strings,
> That not a Nymph now sings?
> Or droop they as disgrac't,
> To see their Seats and Bowers by chattring Pies defac't?
> [ll. 7–12]

For Jonson the absence of a true classical voice among his contemporaries is proof enough of the surrounding literary wasteland, where only he has the talent to "take in hand thy Lyre" (l. 25) in poetry (rather than drama), safe from a hostile world of the "wolves black jaw, and the dull Asses hoofe" (l. 36). The loss of a classical literary culture—apart from Jonson's own perpetuation of it—is an index of what Jonson presents as his own separation from the larger literary and cultural milieu. Jonson's use of the classics is an inversion of that form of imitation, described by Thomas Greene and G. W. Pigman, in which the imitator recognizes his distance from his model, in some cases, as in Jonson's, his historical distance.[53] Such imitation usually involves either implicit criticism or a modification of the classical model to adapt it to the present. Jonson, however, reverses this situation: assimilating an idealized past to the present requires an adjustment of the present, not the past. This necessity produces Jonson's ambivalence toward the present cultural (as well as social) milieu as a whole and compels him to restrict his praise to the few contemporary exemplars whose manners and morals coincide with an idealized past. Accordingly, as a consensus of the noble and learned classes (custom in its synchronic dimension) and as the historical example of ancient models (custom in its diachronic dimension), custom does not generate quite the authorizing force for Jonson that it did for Renaissance grammarians, primarily because of the deficiencies of the present. The result of Jonson's modification of the typical Renaissance idea of custom is that his poems become the stage of his own self-projection.

---

[53]See Greene, *Light in Troy*, p. 40; and G. W. Pigman III, "Versions of Imitation in the Renaissance," *Renaissance Quarterly*, 33 (1980), 1–32.

Marginality and Jonson's Authorial Voice

In Jonson's poetry this felt absence of a custom codified by humanist grammarians in classical authority leads to various dislocations in the process of naming and in the morally appropriate use of language in general, dislocations that often tend to place Jonson at the center of his poems. Jonson sees himself writing poetry under the conditions outlined by Seneca, whom he quotes in *Discoveries:* "Wheresoever, manners, and fashions are corrupted, Language is. It imitates the publicke riot. The excess of Feasts, and apparell, are the notes of a sick State; and the wantonnesse of language, of a sick mind" (p. 593). The "publicke riot" endangers the referential function of language; Augustine's *caritas* is not institutionalized deeply enough in Jonson's society to bind together word, mind, and thing. In shaping his own poetic personality, Jonson determines that individual courage—his own—is necessary to replace a faltering consensus. The result is the strident voice of the poet proclaiming his own office in poem after poem.[54] Jonson's tone alternates between what Richard Helgerson aptly calls "an air of achieved being"[55] and a dislocated voice trying to center itself. Jonson at some times perceives his poetic office as supported by moral and political authority (as in the epigrams to James I, Camden, and Elsmere) and at other times as alienated from a larger society that should, but does not, support his moral vision and the power of his words. He sometimes portrays this alienation as his own, sometimes as shared with a true nobleman or noblewoman who, like himself, is unaffected by the insidious encroachment of vice.

Jonson's off-centered voice is audible as well when he plays the celebrant in a social ritual, a guise he often assumes in celebrating the virtue signified, again, by a noble name. But Jonson's ritual language differs from truly ritual language, which usually mutes any personal voice in the repeated proclamations of widely accepted values, as in Middle English religious lyrics, whose images and metaphors are based on associations sanctioned by the community as a whole.[56] Jon-

---

[54]On Jonson's self-presentation, see Richard Helgerson, *Self-Crowned Laureates: Spenser, Jonson, Milton, and the Literary System* (Berkeley: University of California Press, 1983), chap. 3.

[55]Ibid., p. 169.

[56]See Greene, *Light in Troy*, p. 22, and his reference to Paul Ricoeur on p. 298, n. 34.

son's ritual voice is intensely personal, foregrounding itself against the absence of proper communally shared values. In the *"Epistle* to Elizabeth Countess of Rutland" *(Forrest,* XII), for example, Jonson frequently refers to his own position in the poem as that of a classical poet-priest: the poem is an "offring" (l. 30) and (in the suppressed lines) a "sacrifice"; he writes with a "sacred pen" (l. 56) while "rapt with rage diuine" (l. 63). Nevertheless, he does not perform his priestly duty by ritualizing communally accepted values. Instead, he and Elizabeth are guided by values of another society, another age:

> whil'st gold beares all this sway,
> I, that haue none (to send you) send you verse.
> A present, which (if elder writs reherse
> The truth of times) was once of more esteeme,
> Then this, our guilt, nor golden age can deeme,
> When gold was made no weapon to cut throtes,
> Or put to flight ASTREA, when her ingots
> Were yet vnfound, and better plac'd in earth,
> Then, here, to giue pride fame, and peasants birth.
>
> [ll. 18–26]

Here, as in the ode to Sir Robert Wroth, Jonson plays on the association of nobility with a classical golden age, which he opposes to the greed for monetary gold which characterizes contemporary society. Jonson allies himself to the heiress both of a noble name (Elizabeth is Sidney's daughter) and of right language. It is therefore appropriate that he recalls to her the importance of classical poets as purveyors of fame. Once again, the classical world becomes an emblem of an unappreciated nobility, though here the problem explicitly involves the failure of a society to create an atmosphere that fosters the proper use of language. Jonson's ritual voice strives to unite Elizabeth and himself against a court where appearance and flattery rule, where inferior "versers" gain "account" (ll. 68–69), and where "noble ignorants . . . / Turne, vpon scorned verse [Jonson's, that is], their quarter-face" (ll. 28–29). Against this background the classical, priestly voice of Jonson establishes itself, in association with Sidney's daughter, who, isolated among sycophantic courtiers, alone recognizes the real worth of his poetry.

In contrast to the *"Epistle* to Elizabeth" the *"Ode.* To Sir William

Sidney" (*The Forrest,* XIIII) addresses a noble individual whose name has become detached from its proper referent. This situation is a sign not only of a society whose corruption vitiates the force of words but of William Sidney's own irresponsible behavior. The poem's unspoken scandal is that Sidney himself shows no indication of living up to what "will be exacted of [his] name" (l. 41). Though the poem itself is not explicit, the facts of Sidney's sometimes violent life suggest he did not "liue in honor, as in name" (l. 51).[57] But while Jonson reprimands Sidney for not living up to his aristocratic duty, he presents himself as the only one in Sidney's company who recognizes what that duty is. "Sidney," the most potent noble name in Jonson's poetry, representing a humanist civic, moral, and poetic ideal, may in this case be empty. The incongruity between the Sidney name and William's way of life is tantamount to a threat to a cultural institution, the erasure of one of the few remaining signs of the ideals represented by the Sidneys in Penshurst and the Wroth estate.

The occasion of the ode is a birthday party celebrating Sidney's majority. In light of the facts of Sidney's life, however, the celebration is morally empty. Jonson attempts to restore the Sidney virtue through his office as classical poet-priest: his Horatian lyric stanza is inspired by waters from the "*Thespian* Well" (l. 11), and he divines "what / This day / Doth say" (ll. 12–13). His task will be not to praise the Sidney name but to urge William to act in accord with the name's traditional associations: the honorable life and action of the Sidney family. Jonson's ritual function in the poem is to transform the evening into a morally significant social event—the naming of Sidney—so that Sidney may in actual fact "live in honor as in name," unlike those "that swell / With dust of ancestors, [and thus] in graues but dwell" (ll. 39–40).

Jonson's ministrations to cure Sidney of his moral, even metaphysical, privation (and thus to uphold a desperately needed cultural and linguistic symbol) turn on changing the referent of his name. The ritual poet attempts this combined linguistic and social task in his moral advice to Sidney, which culminates, appropriately, in a trick of

---

[57]For the facts of William Sidney's life, see Lisle Cecil John, "Ben Jonson's 'To Sir William Sidney on his Birthday,'" *Modern Language Review,* 52 (1957), 168–76; and Claude J. Summers and Ted-Larry Pebworth, *Ben Jonson* (Boston: Twayne, 1979), pp. 170–71.

language that fixes the meaning of the birthday celebration. In the last line of the poem Jonson transforms the opening line's metaphoric personification of "the harths . . . crown'd with smiling fire" into its literal realization:

> And with the flame
> Of loue be bright,
> As with the light
> Of bone-fires. Then
> The Birth-day shines,
>   when logs not burne, but men.
>   [ll. 56–60]

By appealing to the etymological meaning of bonfire, the symbol of public celebration, Jonson names the meaning of the event as he asks Sidney to be a man of his name. If Sidney were to heed Jonson's advice, he would, like the other Sidneys in Jonson's poetry, become an embodiment of moral, social, and linguistic decorum: his moral behavior would match his name; *res* would fit *verbum*. Further, Jonson sees the mirth of the birthday banquet as an indication that it is celebrated by those unperturbed by its emptiness, those content with the physical light of burning logs rather than the moral luster of virtuous men. In his vain ministrations Jonson the classical poet-priest stands aside, alone, to define what should be the real meaning of the event in a poetic fiat unaided by either Sidney's surroundings or by Sidney himself.

Jonson again plays the role of poet-priest in the "*Epistle.* To Katherine, Lady Avbigny" (*Forrest,* XIII), where he celebrates Lady Aubigny's family name and heritage on the occasion of the impending birth of her child. Characteristically, he praises "[her] name, and goodnesse of [her] life" (l. 109). Katherine's name—her noble birth and title—is matched by her virtue, as is not the case with many whose titles are empty "sounds" (ll. 45–50). In contrast to those who have names without virtue, she will pass on the virtuous essence of her father's name, although, ironically, as a daughter, she cannot pass on the name itself. And just as Lady Katherine's name that truly speaks her virtue renders her "Not fashion'd for the court" (l. 115), so does Jonson's moral integrity isolate him from self-seeking flatterers and false accusers as a lone figure capable of speaking truth. He "professe[s] [him] selfe in loue / With every vertue, wheresoere it moue, / And howsoeuer" (ll. 7–9). Indeed, the poet's own moral excellence is prerequisite to his ability to perceive and name the moral excellence of his subject.

In a world that misrepresents the connection between word and thing, where it is "almost a danger to speake true / Of any good minde, now: There are so few" (ll. 1–2), it is an act of moral—and linguistic—courage for Jonson to bid Lady Aubigny to "see / In my character, what your features bee." Jonson here plays on "character" in the Theophrastian sense: Lady Aubigny is an exemplar of virtue. But he is also referring to a character as both a letter of the alphabet and a hieroglyphic emblem. Like the perfectly congruous connection between a hieroglyphic sign and its referent, the letters of Jonson's verse create a morally just connection between *res* and *verba* in praising Lady Aubigny's name, for the name truly does contain the moral reality Jonson ascribes to it. Jonson's words thus become Lady Katherine's "glasse" (ll. 26, 122). The poem (and by implication the poet's moral perception) and Lady Katherine are mirror images of each other in their virtue (ll. 122–24).[58]

The reflection of the one in the other is particularly poignant since Jonson thinks of the moral action of naming Lady Aubigny as a way of naming himself. To be identified as one "at fewd / With sinne and vice" is to be "in this name" (i.e., of poet, social critic), and as poet and critic, Jonson is, he says, "giuen out dangerous" by those who "for their owne cap'tall crimes . . . *indite* my wit" (emphasis added). The more Jonson identifies with what he presents as his subject's moral marginality in her social world, the greater the authority he acquires for his own voice.

Jonson's claim to moral authority as the basis of his authorial voice has been approached with increasing skepticism. There is a growing recognition among contemporary critics that Jonson's poems are in many ways disingenuous not only about his own self-proclaimed virtue but also about the virtue of those he praises. His praise, in other words, cannot be taken at face value.[59] And while Jonson's portrayals

[58]Fish, "Authors-Readers," sees this mirroring as the fundamental strategy of Jonson's poetry in general.

[59]See Wayne, "Poetry and Power," pp. 86–87; and Paulette Goll, "Jonson's Epigrammes: Fact and Fiction," *Seventeenth-Century News*, 42, nos. 1–2 (1984), 6–8.

of the isolated country estate are at odds with historical fact, his projection of his sense of marginality similarly seems an inaccurate reflection of his favored status in the court of James. Writing apparently well-received poems to some of the most influential figures of the day, employed as the king's poetic spokesman, Jonson was not a man barred from the center of power and prestige, at least during the Jacobean reign. How then can we account for what amounts to Jonson's adopted sense of marginality?

There are several possible explanations. Jonson may have adopted this stance out of a basic frustration with his literary profession, with, as Helgerson argues, his inability to find a suitable genre to fulfill and project his literary self-image as laureate poet.[60] But that frustration may itself have been the result of Jonson's displaced social position. E. Pearlman has characterized Jonson's feeling as an unease in his society expressed as ambivalence toward authority, or what Isabel Rivers describes as the "curious amphibiousness" of his "antipathy to and conscious support of his society."[61] Perhaps Jonson's ultimate gesture of social ambivalence was his choice of the very format in which to present his work—and himself, namely, print.[62] For, while the printed folio of 1616 was an effective way of claiming his status as a serious professional author independent of the vagaries of courtly patronage, his conspicuous listing on the title page of the nobles to whom each of the works was dedicated still signaled his connection— no matter how uncomfortable—to the court.[63] Whatever the psycho-

<hr/>

[60]Helgerson, *Self-Crowned Laureates*, chap. 3.

[61]See Pearlman, "Ben Jonson," pp. 367–82; and Rivers, *Poetry of Conservatism*, p. 71.

[62]For the relationship between Jonson's use of print and his authorial self-projection, see Timothy Murray, "From Foul Sheets to Legitimate Model: Antitheater, Text, Ben Jonson," *New Literary History*, 14 (1983), 641–64; and Richard C. Newton, "Jonson and the (Re-)Invention of the Book," in *Classic and Cavalier: Essays on Jonson and the Sons of Ben*, ed. Claude J. Summers and Ted-Larry Pebworth (Pittsburgh: University of Pittsburgh Press, 1982), pp. 31–55.

[63]The same ambivalence marks the appearance of the ode to Sir William Sidney in the 1616 Folio—as opposed to its probable reception by Sidney himself in manuscript—if, as Hereford and the Simpsons suggest, "Every poem in [*The Forrest*] must have been sent originally to the friends and patrons commemorated in it" (VIII, 8). In the folio, the context of the poem must have been unclear except to those in the court circle who knew Sidney as a profligate. What might have sounded like an inspired exhortation, almost praise, to the uninitiated would have been recognized by those in the know as a reprimand. The poem could only have been properly understood at court. For Jonson's gesture acknowledging his sometime disingenuousness, see "*An*

logical or social genesis of his unease, the result appears to have been Jonson's strong identification with marginality as the location of his moral and poetic activity.

Although Jonson may seem to share the humanist concepts of speech and custom with his sixteenth-century forebears, as some of his statements in *Discoveries* indicate, his poems reveal an author torn between belief in the public institution of speech and doubt that language norms are indeed institutionalized in socially confirmed moral norms. True, the king occupies a prominent position in Jonson's poems, for example, at the beginning of the *Epigrammes* and in the poems on the Sidney and Wroth estates in *The Forrest*. But unlike Ascham (in his *Report*) and Elyot (in *On the knowledg . . .*), Jonson does not distance his concerns by situating the separation of *res* and *verba* in a faraway place such as Germany or the far-off past of Dionysius's Sicily. As a result, for Jonson convention, consensus, "agrement" have become a palpable absence; Jonson is left to write humanist speech without its underlying consensus and consequently must authorize his own words. The dissolution of consensus creates a space that Jonson's poetic, authorial voice rushes in to fill. In a sense, that dissolution creates the very possibility of Jonson's voice. Clearly, then, Jonson has turned the authority of convention on its head. In Jonson's poetry, convention has become the possession of an individual, and of an individual who regards his relationship to his society as oblique.[64] Indeed, the very assertiveness of Jonson's voice thrives on what he presents as the institutional failure of his culture. He thus heralds the decline of the humanist view of language as established by the humanist grammarians. The stance of his poetry, in fact, appears to depend on that decline.

If I am right about Jonson's misgivings concerning the weakness of convention in holding *res* and *verba* together, Jonson shares a surprising intellectual kinship with Francis Bacon. As long as metaphor dominated the study of seventeenth-century poetry, Jonson's poems

---

Epistle to Master IOHN SELDEN" (*Vnder-wood*, XIV): "I confesse (as every Muse hath err'd / And mine not least) I have too oft preferr'd / Men past their termes, and praise'd some names too much" (ll. 18–21). For the topos of *laudando praecipere*, see Summers and Pebworth, *Ben Jonson*, p. 123.

[64]In a different context, see Peterson on Jonson's "proprietary individuality" (*Imitation and Praise*, p. 15).

never figured largely in what was seen as the mainstream of the period. But to see Jonson's poetry in relation to the philosophical context of linguistic reference is to shift the critical focus from the issues defined by the study of metaphysical poetry and to see Jonson responding to the same issues that motivated the most important, the most seminal figure in seventeenth-century English language theory—Bacon. Both Bacon and Jonson were searching for an ideal language in which mind, language, and reality would each mirror the other perfectly in the "congruous" relationship between sign and referent. Given Jonson's deep concern with the breakdown of the proper relationship between *res et verba,* we should not wonder that he admired Bacon and refers to him three times in *Discoveries* (pp. 591–92, 627), specifically as a reformer of language concerned with those "distempers of learning" which involve the relationship of words to things. It is of course ironic that a poet so widely associated with humanism should invoke the authority of the philosopher most associated with the attack on the humanist attitude toward language. But whatever their obvious differences, both Bacon and Jonson were deeply interested in a similar issue. Each in his own way was responding to a cultural and linguistic malaise—what Timothy Murray and others characterize as the crisis of signification—that was to preoccupy linguistic theorists ever more intensely in the seventeenth and eighteenth centuries.[65]

Bacon and some of his followers for the most part gave up believing that a close correspondence between words and things is possible in any spoken language based on convention. Though both Jonson and Bacon saw how language could be imperiled when not institutionalized, Bacon sought transparency of representation in an invented, artificial "philosophical" language of written signs modeled on hieroglyphs and ideograms that circumvent the use of words altogether and thereby avoid the Idols of the Marketplace. Jonson, on the other hand, tried, against what he thought were tremendous odds, to hold words and things together in a poetic language modeled on spoken language. In fact, if one can distinguish in Jonson's poetry between a lexical level of language (the level at which individual words refer to things) and a syntactical level of language carried by the rhythmic pat-

[65]Murray, "From Foul Sheets," p. 650.

terns of speech uttered in a social context, then it is only in the intersection of the two that real language can exist for Jonson. It is the particular (corrupt) social context of Jonson's day that portends the ethical subversion of the referential function of language, and it is the feeling of this threat that gives Jonson's vigorous attempt to hold words and things together its moral urgency.

Jonson could not share the equanimity of La Primaudaye, who, undisturbed by either anxiety or qualification, asserted that words are "the markes and paintings . . . of . . . things . . . and . . . thoughts . . . for if we have no wordes and names to make [things] known by, we must always have the things themselves present, that wee may point at them with the finger, which is impossible."[66] Jonson's anxiety over the dissolution of the bond between words and things brings him closer instead to Democritus Junior, whose solipsistic voice, a voice no longer securely anchored in a sense of moral and social reality, manifests a "roving humour," a "running wit, an unconstant, unsettled mind" that can scarcely name itself. Democritus Junior envisions a world of moral names without referents: "We may peradventure usurp the name, or attribute it to others for favour, as Carolus Sapiens, Philippus Bonus . . . etc., and describe the properties of a wise man, as Tully doth an orator, Xenophon Cyrus. . . . But where shall such a man be found?" In such a world "honesty is accounted folly; knavery, policy . . . : such shifting, lying, cogging, plotting, counterplotting, temporizing, flattering, cozening, dissembling."[67] This distortion of moral truths and their names precisely represents the separation of the Augustinian embrace, a separation that justified Jonson's voice to itself and provided the circumstances of his verse.

[66]La Primaudaye, *Second Part*, p. 98. In the same passage, La Primaudaye rejects any language based on the very hieroglyphic signs that Bacon was to find so necessary a generation later.

[67]Robert Burton, *The Anatomy of Melancholy*, ed. Holbrook Jackson (1932; rpt. New York: Random House, 1977), I, 17, 76, 65.

4/

Space and Textuality: Writing and Speech in the Idea of the Text

THE works of Thomas Elyot, Roger Ascham, and Ben Jonson are all founded on the concept of speech as formulated by the humanist grammar books, but however often these authors appeal to speech as a concept, for the most part they rely on written texts. Indeed, at times the written form of humanist speech comes to the center of attention, especially in Ascham's *Report and Discourse . . . of the Affaires and State of Germany and the Emperour Charles*,[1] where most communication, including the work itself, self-consciously takes place in writing, even though the major historical protagonists are judged according to the moral relation between their heart, speech, and action.

In reading the *Report*, one is struck by all the references to the signing of treaties, writs of executions, and diplomatic emissaries (including Ascham himself) delivering letters. The *Report* itself is written as a letter to John Asteley informing him of events in Germany while Ascham was a diplomat there. Perhaps the most striking example of the emperor's abuse of political power is his distortion of written language to lure the landgrave into his clutches. In a letter he promises that if the landgrave returns to Germany, he will not place him *in einig gefengknes* (in any prison); he later, however, fraudulently changes *einig* to *ewig* "with the least dash of pen so that it shall never

[1] Roger Ascham, *A Report and Discourse . . . of the Affaires and State of Germany and the Emperour Charles his Court . . .* , in *English Works*, ed. William Aldis Wright (Cambridge: Cambridge University Press, 1904).

be perceived"; he thus claims to keep his word by imprisoning the landgrave, though not "perpetually" (*ewig*) (p. 161). The incident most conspicuously literalizes Charles's equivocal, deceitful language, always the vehicle of his immoral actions.

Books themselves figure as important props in the events Ascham records. The two religious cultures of the work create two moral and linguistic cultures at odds with each other, as is apparent in two books, one written by the Catholic Luis de Avila, a member of Charles's party, and the other by the Marches Albert. The books not only seek to represent events; they are themselves causes of events, especially since Luis's book, which "defamed [Albert] to all the world" (p. 144), was a cause of Albert's defection from Charles. (Characteristically, Ascham learns about the book in a conversation with Prince Frederick when Ascham delivers to him some letters from King Edward.) Albert counters with a book of his own which relates his falling out with the emperor because of his double dealing. Writing the history of the events becomes a major component of the narrative of the German reaction against Charles, as Ascham uses the book as a source for his own history and thus recounts events from the point of view of Albert's book. Ascham's belief that the German political struggle was to some extent shaped by a struggle fought in books illustrates the importance humanists ascribed to writing. As devoted patrons and promoters of the printing press, humanists were well aware of the written, or more important, the printed form of their speech; they sagaciously took advantage of print to disseminate their educational and literary program.

The relationship between speech and writing has a long history that culminates in a new dynamic interchange on the newly invented printed page, an interchange integrally related to the Renaissance notion of a text and its ability to authorize its words to mean and to refer. That the word on a page is a different artifact in different cultures has become a familiar idea.[2] The physical condition of the written word has a status of its own, which can vary from one society to another. Even the very idea of a book as a discrete, self-enclosed object does not seem to have been widespread when manuscripts

[2]For an incisive discussion of this issue, see Gerald L. Bruns, *Inventions, Writing, Textuality, Understanding in Literary History* (New Haven: Yale University Press, 1982), chap. 1.

were still the principal means of recording writing: G. S. Ivy has shown that the medieval manuscript book was typically a "leisurely collection of heterogeneous texts" haphazardly thrown together.[3]

Paul Ricoeur has located the very concept of a text in the relationship between speech and writing.[4] He starts from the position that, historically and logically, speech antedates writing, which is a record of speech. Writing becomes a text, however, "when it is not just limited to recording a prior speech, but when it invites directly in written words the meaning of a [spoken] utterance." That is, the "liberation of writing whereby it gets substituted for speech is the birth of a text."[5] Nevertheless, Ricoeur goes on to argue, texts are meaningful insofar as they are returned to the condition of their originating authority in speech, which is the function of interpretative reading. His view more or less accords with the concept of a text among Renaissance humanists, who may in fact have been the originators of the concept. Ricoeur is keenly aware of the far-reaching consequences of basing so much of a culture on texts separated from spoken language, as literate societies do. Though he may be historically correct, his view is itself an example of a particular cultural disposition to regard speech as the pristine, originating condition of language.[6] The notion that the status of a text as text depends on a relationship between speech and writing, however, is useful as a framework in which to situate the different kinds of textuality in the seventeenth century. The inscribed word does not always have the

---

[3]G. S. Ivy, "The Bibliography of the Manuscript Book," *The English Library before 1700*, ed. Francis Wormald and C. E. Wright (London: Athlone Press, 1953), p. 59 and passim.

[4]Paul Ricoeur, "What Is a Text? Explanation and Interpretation," in David M. Rasmussen, *Mythic-Symbolic Language and Philosophical Anthropology: A Constructive Interpretation of the Thought of Paul Ricoeur* (The Hague: Nijhoff, 1971), pp. 135–50. Ricoeur here goes directly against the strain in modern poetry and art which stresses the self-reflexive quality of the work of art, be it in paint or printer's ink. See Gerald L. Bruns on Mallarmé in *Modern Poetry and the Idea of Language: A Critical and Historical Study* (New Haven: Yale University Press, 1974), pp. 101–17. For a view of a text based on speech, see M. M. Bakhtin, "The Problem of the Text in Linguistics, Philology, and the Human Sciences: An Experiment in Philosophical Analysis," in *Speech Genres and Other Late Essays*, tr. Vern W. McGee, ed. Caryl Emerson and Michael Holquist (Austin: University of Texas Press, 1986), pp. 103–31.

[5]Ricoeur, "What Is a Text?" pp. 136–37.

[6]Roman Jakobson and Morris Halle go as far as to contend that even where written forms of language are prevalent, writing is always controlled by speech, not vice versa; see Jakobson and Halle, *Fundamentals of Language* (The Hague: Mouton, 1956), p. 17.

same connection to speech that Ricoeur points to; there are different kinds of texts.

The word impressed onto the printed page is a different thing from a word inscribed on a medieval manuscript or on a Hebrew biblical scroll. Each of these written modes makes different assumptions about just what a text is and how it means. The Renaissance was heir to several modes of textuality, two of which are particularly relevant here: the Latin—or more broadly, classical—concept of language as oral utterance, the written text being a secondary image of the utterance; and the Hebrew concept of a text as written script secondarily oralized. The Latin and Hebrew traditions pass on contrasting ways of relating speech and writing: Latin regards speech as primary; Hebrew (in at least one important strand of the postbiblical textual tradition) regards the written text as primary. This difference between the two traditions accounts for their diverging explanations of the authority of the written word to signify, even when one considers that both Latin and Hebrew were no longer vernaculars, having become dependent primarily on their written forms.

Despite the importance of speech for the humanist, humanist "speech," as Walter J. Ong has pointed out, exists to a great extent in printed texts. Ong has suggestively described the Renaissance retention of an older oral form of expression in the midst of the new developing technology of print. Even in print, however, Renaissance texts reveal the "oral residue" that permeates the literate world of the period.[7] The persistence of learned Latin, Ong observes, is largely responsible for the continuing "oral-aural bent" of both the Middle Ages and the Renaissance. Though learned Latin had been separated from its oral base for centuries, it remained aligned with the classical rhetorical tradition, which conceived of language as oratory, although the tradition persisted long after oratory shifted from oral to written performance.[8] By the Renaissance, the notion that writing follows speech was in fact becoming a conceptual metaphor rather

[7]Walter J. Ong points especially to the oral formulaic nature of such rhetorical devices as the commonplace. See his discussion of Erasmus's *Adages, Apothegms,* and *De Copia* in *Rhetoric, Romance, and Technology: Studies in the Interaction of Expression and Culture* (Ithaca: Cornell University Press, 1971), pp. 23–47.

[8]See Ong, *Rhetoric, Romance, and Technology,* p. 17, and *The Presence of the Word: Some Prolegomena for Cultural and Religious History* (New Haven: Yale University Press, 1967), pp. 76–79.

than an actual description of how a text is composed. However much humanists made their pupils speak Latin in school, they were by and large committed to written rather than oral performance, both in pedagogy and in literary practice. In the end, the Renaissance must be seen as occupying a unique "marginal position" (to use Ong's expression) between oral and manuscript culture on the one side and typographic culture on the other. The Renaissance was "the final upsurge" of oral culture "to which alphabetic typography had given the final blow" by circumventing the spoken word through the printed word.[9] One might add, however, that especially among the humanists some important features of print were anticipated by the spread of writing in the half century or so before the advent of print.[10]

The situation in sixteenth- and seventeenth-century England can be illuminated by Eric Havelock's description of a comparable development in classical Greece when writing and literacy became widespread but without displacing the older oral institutions. The oral and the written word met in a creative, dynamic tension: "language [that was] managed acoustically on echo principles . . . met with competition from language managed visually on architectural [i.e., alphabetic] principles." As Havelock puts it, "ear was continually seduced into collaboration with eye during the high classical period, and . . . the result was a distinctive type of creative composition which straight literacy could never duplicate."[11] The new relationship between speech and writing reinforced by print changed the very perception of what a text in fact is, especially because the written, visual word had acquired a new importance. The change followed an increase in the number of people who read printed (and to some extent manuscript) books and who practiced writing, both developments the result of humanist educational reform.

[9]Ong, *Rhetoric, Romance, and Technology*, p. 38, and *Presence of the Word*, pp. 58–69, 61–63, 87.

[10]For the controversy concerning whether print inaugurated a sudden change in the presentation of language or just intensified already existing trends in late medieval manuscript practice, see Elizabeth Eisenstein, *The Printing Press as an Agent of Change* (Cambridge: Cambridge University Press, 1979), p. 33.

[11]Eric A. Havelock, *The Literate Revolution in Greece and Its Cultural Consequences* (Princeton: Princeton University Press, 1982), pp. 9, 13. For the importance of Plato in Greek habits of thought resulting from literacy, see also his *Preface to Plato* (Cambridge: Harvard University Press, Belknap Press, 1963).

One far-reaching effect of alphabetic script, Ong has argued, was the propulsion of language into the dimension of space, an effect more palpable in the Renaissance printed book than in the medieval manuscript, which was usually meant to be heard rather than read silently by large numbers of individual readers. Print made the presence of the written word pervasive and gave new authority to the word as a visual image retained in visual memory, as opposed to a sound or rhythm retained in acoustic memory, most likely the more dominant mode of memory in medieval scribal culture.[12] The written word of the medieval manuscript did not completely displace an earlier oral culture dependent on acoustic memory, though it modified it in important ways. The great diversity of medieval manuscript practice resists broad generalizations, but some general observations can help us distinguish the late medieval from the Renaissance book (in manuscript and in print), as long as we do not insist on such distinctions with iron-clad rigidity and as long as we acknowledge major exceptions.

Such historians of medieval culture as M. T. Clanchy and Henry John Chaytor hypothesize that the medieval manuscript was for the most part meant to be read aloud rather than examined as writing, and that it was therefore perceived aurally rather than visually. Its crabbed script and extensive use of abbreviations suggest that its writing functions as a reminder of words recalled as oral utterances in the acoustic memory. Unlike the printed grammatical works of the humanists, medieval grammars such as Donatus's *Ars Minor* and Alexander's *Doctrinale* were meant to be heard, not read.[13] Moreover, reading was a skill generally associated with dictating rather than

---

[12]For the written word's lack of authority in the Middle Ages, see M. T. Clanchy, *From Memory to Written Record: England, 1066–1307* (Cambridge: Harvard University Press, 1979), pp. 208–26, 231–57; for the relationship of acoustic and visual memory in reading print as opposed to reading a manuscript, see Henry John Chaytor, *From Script to Print: An Introduction to Medieval Literature* (Cambridge: Cambridge University Press, 1945), pp. 5–21. The interrelation of speech and writing in manuscripts is consistent with Brian Stock's notion of a textual community in the Middle Ages: the oral discourse of a learned community was conditioned by the written texts that had authority in that community; see Stock's *Implications of Literacy: Written Language and Models of Interpretation in the Eleventh and Twelfth Centuries* (Princeton: Princeton University Press, 1983), pp. 88–92.

[13]Chaytor, *From Script to Print*, p. 14; see also Clanchy, *From Memory to Written Record*, pp. 214–26, for the importance of the spoken word in medieval culture.

writing, which was a skill usually consigned to the professional scribe. The author of a document was more likely to have dictated it than actually written it.[14] The scribe himself wrote from his acoustic rather than visual memory, a practice that accounts for the orthographic inconsistency characteristic of medieval manuscripts.[15] From the point of view of both the composer and his audience, the written word of the manuscript was closely associated with the flow of actual speech. If Clanchy is right, many—if not most—medieval manuscripts barely qualify as texts in the way Ricoeur defines the word.

The spatial (as opposed to aural) nature of the printed word is illustrated by a small but telling example from a section titled "The Excellencie of the English Tongue," added by Richard Carew to the 1614 edition of William Camden's *Remaines Concerning Britaine*. Camden plays with the order of letters in a sentence to the extent that he reduces language to sequentially arranged letters only tangentially connected to sound; by reversing the letters of the sentences he discovers that

> some signifie one thing forward, and another backward, as Feeler I was no fo, of on saw I releef. Some signifie one self thing forward and backward, as Ded deemed, I ioi, reviver, and this, Eye did Madam Erre; some carry a contrary sence backward to that they did forward, as I did levell ere veu, veu ere level did I.[16]

Carew's trifling exploration of the properties of English requires that English be thought of as a written language, as a series of letters, rather than sounds, that can be manipulated and rearranged and then converted back to sound, but need not be. The possibility of detaching speech from its originating sounds arises from the pervasiveness of the written word mechanically reproduced in type. The word is reified as a spatial object placed in the abstract geometrical space of the printer's sheet. The boundaries of this space are set by schematic illustrations, word charts, running heads, divisions into chapters, and in general the increasing use of what Ong calls "geometric display." Although the late medieval manuscript did use some of these spatializing devices, and although—as Elizabeth Eisenstein has pointed out—many devices of print were anticipated in scribal

---

[14]Clanchy, *From Memory to Written Record*, p. 88.
[15]Chaytor, *From Script to Print*, pp. 19, 36–37.
[16]William Camden, *Remaines Concerning Britaine* (London, 1614), p. 38.

manuscripts, especially those produced just before the introduction of print, they were used sporadically, they were not standardized, and they were not used extensively until they appeared in the mass-produced printed book.[17]

The transfer of words from sound to the space of a written, typographic text is evident even in Thomas Smith, who, as an initiator of the English orthography debate, insisted that language is primarily vocalized sounds. In laying out the basic principle of the English orthographers—that writing imitates speech and that letters represent sounds—Smith used a spatial metaphor that was to reappear frequently in many orthographic treatises: letters are the pictures of spoken expression (*pictura vocum*), and in this sense writing is related to both speaking and painting (*ars loquendi et pingendi*).[18] It is as if the transliteration of sound into its echo in writing inevitably transfers language to the new dimension of spatiality. The pictorial metaphor reveals a basic ambiguity in the humanist understanding of "speech" as writing represented in space.

For many in the Renaissance who were concerned with the nature of writing and of letters, especially those concerned with the visual presentation of writing, Smith's comparison had more than metaphoric force. Letters also came to receive much attention as physical objects in themselves, as shaped, drawn, carved, or painted artifacts. That is, written letters were by no means completely subordinated to sounded speech. Many treatises on calligraphy and alphabet design were written under the influence of humanism, including the chapter on letters in Dürer's *Unterweysung der Messung* (1525, 1538).[19] One of the most ingenious ways in which words were imaged as things is

[17]Walter J. Ong, *Ramus, Method, and the Decay of Dialogue: From the Art of Discourse to the Art of Reason* (Cambridge: Harvard University Press, 1958), p. 79. The spatialization of the word in print is a major theme in Ong's works; see, e.g., *Orality and Literacy: Technologizing the Word* (London: Methuen, 1982). For the methods of locating places in medieval manuscripts, see C. F. Bühler, *The Fifteenth-Century Book: The Scribes, the Printers, the Decorators* (Philadelphia: University of Pennsylvania Press, 1960), p. 40; Eisenstein, *Printing Press*, pp. 52, 67, 88, 93, 100–7; for opposing views, see Eisenstein, p. 92 n. 154, p. 67 n. 78.

[18]Thomas Smith, *De recta et emendata linguae Anglicae scriptione, dialogus* (Paris, 1568; facs. rpt. Menston: Scolar Press, 1968), sigs. biv–biiv (hereafter cited as Smith, *Dialogus*).

[19]See Emanuele Casamassima, *Trattati di scrittura de cinquecento Italiano* (Milan: Il Polifilo, 1968); and Millard Meiss, "Alphabetical Treatises in the Renaissance," in *The Painter's Choice: Problems in the Interpretation of Renaissance Art* (New York: Harper & Row, 1976), pp. 176–86.

exemplifed in some late-fifteenth-century Italian books, where the printed page is treated as part of a perspective design within a painted ornamental border. For example, the opening page of a fifteenth-century folio edition of Aristotle's works printed in a very readable black letter on vellum is part of an elaborate design in which the entire folio page is treated as a perspective picture (see Figure 1).[20] The major portion of the page is occupied by lettering made to appear as if it were printed on paper (or inscribed on vellum?) that is worn and curled up at the edges. The curling back of this illusionistic page within the folio page reveals a perspectivally conceived border around the page. At a short distance behind the illusionistic page is an architectural setting on the bottom and the sides, and, at the top, a perspective painting of Aristotle instructing Averroes, though the short depth of perspective everywhere on the page suggests a mannerist rather than a Renaissance use of perspective. At any rate, the printed border is not treated as an ornament distributed abstractly around the page; the lettered part of the page is treated as an object with a spatial relationship to the border (though there are a number of apparently deliberate inconsistencies in the perspective design, including an illuminated capital). The page has become an object disposed in space.

To be sure, the practice of painting the borders of a page, even in a printed book and even in perspective space, is derived from the medieval manuscript rather than the printed book. Further, the illusionistically conceived page as thing also appears in late-fifteenth-century Italian manuscript books. The opening page of a folio copy of Augustine's *Explanatio Psalmorum,* written in a humanist hand based on Carolingian miniscules and Roman majuscules of the kind printed books were to imitate, portrays the lettered page as a placard held up by cherubim in front of an architectural setting (see Figure 2).[21] As in the Aristotle volume, the lettered page and border are not set abstractly beside each other but are disposed in space with reference to each other. (Also as in the Aristotle volume, there are some inconsistencies in the perspective design, most notably the inclusion

---

[20]Aristotle, *Opera* (Venice, 1483). The page I refer to is vol. 1, sig. AA2r.

[21]Augustine, *Explanatio Psalmorum* (Naples, 1480). I refer to the recto of the first page of vol. 3.

Figure 1. Aristotle, *Opera.* Venice, 1483. Vol. 1. The Pierpont Morgan Library, PML 21194.

Figure 2. Augustine, *Explanatio Psalmorum*. Naples, 1480. Vol. 3. The British Library, London.

of a miniature painting of Augustine at the top left of the illusionistic page. In this painting Augustine is at his desk with pen and ink before an open book presumably writing the volume itself. The whole pictorial design of the page forms a *mise en abime*, a page within a page [illusionistic "placard" page within the folio page] within yet another page [the pages of Augustine's book within the "placard" page].)[22] Though it may very well be that the concept of the book page as a painting derives from the medieval illuminated manuscript, the treatment of the page as an object is related to peculiarly Renaissance developments. I refer not only to perspective pictorial design but to the very inclination to include words on a page as part of a design that places objects in space (though this phenomenon does not seem to have appeared in the north as it did in Italy).

The Italian painter and theorist Giovanni Lomazzo, known in England through translation, in fact observed that in at least one respect painting had its origin in writing: "If this I say be true, that Characters and the vse of writing were first invented to preserue the memory of the Sciences, it follows inevitably that Painting is an instrument vnder which the treasury of memory is contained, insomuch as writing is nothing else, but a picture of *white* and *black*."[23] That letters are physically constructed objects would have been plain even to the many schoolboys preparing for entrance to grammar schools. As a result of the humanist emphasis on literacy, alphabet charts describing how to form letters with pen and ink were a common feature of school texts, for instance, Francis Clement's *Petie Schole* (London, 1587), and popular guides purporting to teach the advantages and the skill of writing began to appear, among them Martin Billingsley's *Coppie Booke* (London, 1637). The growing awareness of writing as a physical process is manifested similarly, though in a different context,

[22]Both the Aristotle and Augustine volumes appeared in an exhibition at the Pierpont Morgan Library, "Renaissance Painting in Manuscripts: Treasures from the British Library" (20 January–29 April 1984). Noticeably absent at the exhibition were illusionistically designed pages in books produced in the north. These books of course contain many perspective paintings, but they are not integrated with the essentially medieval abstract border designs and crabbed Gothic script. At any rate, these editions of Aristotle and Augustine raise interesting possibilities about the late-fifteenth-century and sixteenth-century book as a mannerist artifact.

[23]Giovanni Lomazzo, *A Tracte Containing the Artes of Curious Paintinge Caruinge & Building*, tr. Richard Haydocke (Oxford, 1598), p. 2.

in Thomas Godwyn's civil and ecclesiastical history of the ancient Hebrews. Godwyn discusses the history of writing, including the various surfaces and the various instruments different nations have used, as well as the influence of a particular writing process on the physical layout of a text in a book, a scroll, or on stone.[24] Doubtless all this interest in the mechanics of writing was related to the spread of literacy, which brought unprecedented numbers of people into contact with both pens and printed books, which in turn must have increased awareness of words and letters as physical objects to be laid out on a page.

The Renaissance spatialization of language is already implied in the humanists' preoccupation with the word order of the elegant period. Ascham's definition of good style as "a true choice and placing of words" had more widespread reverberations than Carew's toying with the word order of eccentric sentences.[25] Ascham's favorite source, Johann Sturm, in fact literally gives spatial values to the members of a period. In his *Ritch Storehouse or Treasurie for Nobilitye and Gentlemen,* he supplies visual representations—lines of varying length—to illustrate the various kinds of periods. Language is thus "figured," to use his word; in a departure from the classical concept of periodic word order grounded on aural effects, combined members of differing lengths are translated into corresponding geometrical shapes.[26]

The more usual form of visualized word order appears in a later work heavily indebted to Ascham, John Brinsley's *Ludus Literarius.* Brinsley too uses double translation to teach "composing, or the right placing of . . . words . . . which . . . is a principal matter in writing pure Latin."[27] Brinsley, however, adds an extra step to Ascham's method: the student first translates an English passage (itself translated from Latin by the master) into Latin in natural, or "gram-

[24]Thomas Godwyn, *Moses and Aaron. Civil and Ecclesiastical Rites, Used by the Ancient Hebrewes* (London, 1634), pp. 276–77.
[25]Roger Ascham, *The Schoolmaster,* ed. Lawrence V. Ryan (Ithaca: Cornell University Press, 1967), p. 14.
[26]John Sturmius [Johann Sturm], *A Ritch Storehouse or Treasurie for Nobilitye and Gentlemen,* tr. T. B. Gent (London, 1570), pp. 25–28.
[27]John Brinsley, *Ludus Literarius: or, The Grammar Schoole* (London, 1612; facs. rpt. Menston: Scolar Press, 1968), p. 152; chaps. 10 and 11 are particularly concerned with word order.

maticall," word order and, when the student is more advanced, into periodic, or "rhetoricall," word order. The process constantly moves back and forth between speech and writing: the master dictates the English, which the students commit to paper; they then read aloud various English words for correct spelling, after which they translate, in writing, the English into naturally ordered Latin; they again read words aloud for spelling, and then, finally, rearrange the unchanged words of the "grammaticall" translation into the suspended periods of elegant written Latin.

Brinsley produces his own visualization of the process in a chart bounded by vertical and horizontal lines and divided into three columns headed "Dictating [the English passage] according to the naturall order," "*Ordo Grammaticus*," and "*Ordo Ciceronianus*," the English column printed in Roman, the Latin in italic typeface (see Figure 3).[28] English words with difficult Latin equivalents are tagged with italic superscripts, and their translations are supplied in the margin. Appropriately, the source of the translation—in the case of Brinsley's example, Cicero—is finally revealed at the end of the third column; thus the circle begun by the master's translation from Latin to English is completed. Unlike Ascham's method of translation, Brinsley's is not just a matter of moving from one language to another. It is a process by which speech is transposed into visual units—words to be rearranged in space. Brinsley's modification of Ascham thus reveals the influence of spatialized print on the teaching of Latin composition.

Brinsley's chart was one outgrowth of the practice of conjoining the teaching of writing with reading. Nevertheless, even while Brinsley assigns the various parts of speech their spatial distribution in the suspended period, he refers to the effect of the "rhetoricall" style on the "eare." That is, he remains mindful of the roots of rhetoric in oratory, supplying precepts for the "sweet sound of letters and words" even as he is aware that most elegant Latin "composed" by the student will never leave the written page.[29] With Brinsley, rhetoric has become visual as well as acoustic, as he acknowledges the reality that the principal medium of rhetorical expression is the written and printed page.

[28]Brinsley, *Ludus*, p. 154.
[29]Ibid., pp. 158, 163.

Dictating 154 *in English,&c.*

THE GRAMMAR SCHOOLE.

Tullies fentences, *De Deo eiufq, natura*, dictating the words
to them plainly, as the children may moft readily make
them in Latine. In their little paper bookes they may write
the Englifh on the firft fide, with the hard Latine wordes in
the Margent, the Latine on the other ouer againft it, in two
columns; the firft plaine after the Grammar order, the later
placed after the order of the Authour: your felfe may make
the wordes or phrafes plaine to them, as they are fet in the
margent.

An Example of Dictating in Englifh, and fetting
downe both Englifh and Latine; and the
Latine both plainly and elegantly.

	Dictating accor-ding to the na-turall order.	Ordo Gramma-ticus.	Ordo Ciceronianus.
a Hath euer bin. *b* At any time (*verb*)infpirati-on fome diuine *c a flatus*, brea-thing into.	No man *a* hath been *b* euer great withcut (*verb*) fome diuine *c* in-fpiration.	*Nemo fuit vn-quam magnus fi-ne afflatu aliquo Diuino.*	*Nemo magnus fine aliquo afflatu diuino vnquam fuit. 2. de Natura Deor.*
d Bring to paffe.	There is no-thing which God cannot *d* effect, and truely with-out any labour.	*Eft nihil quod Deus non pofsit efficere, & qui-dem fine labore vllo.*	*Nihil eft quod De-us efficere non pofsit,& quidem fine labore vl-lo. 3. de Nat. Deor.*
e Ignore. *f* In what mind or with what minde.	GOD cannot *e* be ignorāt *f* of what minde eue-ry one is.	*Deus non po-teft ignorare , qua mēte quifq; fit.*	*Ignorare Deus non poteft, qua quifq; men-te fit. 2. de Diuinati-one.*

In thefe examples all is very plaine ; except that in the
firft

Figure 3. John Brinsley, *Ludus Literarius*. London, 1612.

Brinsley's columns for double translation are heir to the typographic revolution that was largely completed by the 1540s, a revolution ironically most visible in the humanist grammar book purporting to be a rational method of learning Latin *speech*. Early grammar texts such as the anonymous English translation of Donatus's *Accedence* (1495), "Prynted in Caxon's hous by Wynkyn de Word," use solid blocks of Gothic type without any of the devices of geometric display that facilitate easy comprehension and memorability (see Figure 4). Conjugations, declensions, and illustrative examples of phrases and sentences are all printed in run-on lines that use few of the spatial techniques for displaying paradigms we are now accustomed to.[30] Such typesetting is apparently based on the assumption that the printed page is a copy of the uninterrupted flow of speech (the work is cast as a dialogue), the same premise that determined the design of so many medieval manuscripts. (Brinsley's *Ludus* is also in dialogue form, but its speech is spatialized into paragraphs and even some charts. In what sense does one speak a chart?) Like a manuscript, the *Accedence* has a colophon rather than a title page. As C. F. Bühler has argued, from many points of view there was little difference between manuscripts and early printed books; early printers regarded printing as just another form of writing.[31] The vellum Gutenberg Bible, for example, was deliberately made to look like a manuscript.

The changed appearance that Ong describes in the transition from medieval to Renaissance logic books is even more apparent in grammar books. By the time the 1549 edition of the official *Royal Grammar* was published, the appearance of the printed page in grammar texts had drastically changed (though its introductory pages are printed in small, crabbed Gothics). Lily's *Grammar*—whose language norms are based on the "speech" of antiquity—spatializes examples of Latin phrases by placing them one to a line and grouping them together with a single large bracket (see Figure 5). Its other devices include extensive charts and different typefaces with varying historical associations: Gothic letters for English, Roman letters for Latin. Such grammatical paradigms stand apart from whatever potential they

---

[30]Donatus, *Accedence* (Westminster, 1495). Another early printed grammar, John Anwykyll's *Compendium totius grammatice* (printed with his *Uulgaria* [n.p., 1483]) uses two sizes of Gothic letters but even so gives little appearance of spatial display.

[31]Bühler, *Fifteenth-Century Book*, p. 16.

tās verbozumiñ q̃ est? Iñ modis et iñ fozmis
Modi q̃ sunt? Indicatiuus vt lego. Impera
tiuus vt lege. Optatiuus vt vtinam legerem.
Coniunctiuus vt cum legam. Infinitiuus vt
legere. Impersonalis vt legitur. Fozme verbozum quot sunt? quatuoz. q̃? Perfecta vt lego. Meditatiua vt lecturio. Frequentatiua
vt lectito. Inchoatiua vt feruesco calesco Cō
iugationēs verbozum quot sunt? Tres. que?
Prima in a. secunda in e. tercia in i. Primaq̃
est? que in indicatiuo modo tempoze presenti.
numero singulari secunda persona verbo acti
uo et neutrali a productam habet ante nouissimam literam s. Passiuo comuni et deponen
ti ante nouissimam sillabam ris. vt amo amas
amoz amaris. Et futuz tempus eiusdem modi
iñ bo et iñ boz sillabam mittit. vt amo amabo
amoz amabo? Secunda q̃ est? que in indicati
uo modo tpe presenti. numero singulari secda
psona verbo actiuo z neutrali e, punctā habet
ante nouissimā lrām s. Passiuo cōi et deponē-
ti ante nouissimā sillabā ris vt doceo doces.
doceoz doceris: et futuz tpẽ eiusdem modi iñ
bo et iñ boz sillabā mittit. vt doceo docebo doceoz docebo? Tercia q̃ est? que iñ indicatiuo

Figure 4. Donatus, *Ars Minor.* Leipzig, c. 1510? The George Plimpton Collection. Rare Book and Manuscript Library, Columbia University.

EYGHT PARTES OF SPECHE.

	Loue thou	Loue he, or let hym loue,	Loue we, or let vs loue,	Loue ye,	Loue they or let them loue.
Impatiue mode pref. tens sing.	Ama	amet	} Plura. amemus {	amate	ament
	Amato	amato		amatote	amanto.
	Teache thou	Teache he, or let hym teach,e	Teache we, or let vs teache	Teache ye	Teache they or lette theym teache.
	Doce	doceat	} Plur. doceamus {	docete	doceant
	Doceto	doceto		docetote	docento.
	Legi	legat	} Plurali. legamus {	legite	legant
	Legito	legito		legitote	legunto.
	Audi	audiat	} Plural. audiamus {	audite	audiant
	Audito	audito		auditote	audiunto.

God graunt I loue.

Optatiue mode present tens singulat. vtin.
Amem, ames, amet. Pluraliter, amemus, ametis, ament.

God graunt I teache.
Doceam
Legam } as, at. Pluraliter, utinam, amus, atis, ant.
Audiam   reade.
                heare.

Woulde god I loued.
taught
Preterim pfect tens sing. vtin.
Amarem
Docerem } res, ret. Plurali. utinam, remus, retis, rent.
Legerem   read.
Audirem   hearde

I praie god I haue loued.
taughte.
Preterper fecte tens sing. vtin.
Amauerim
Docuerim } ris, rit. Plural. utinam, rimus, ritis, rint
Legerim   read.
Audiuerim   he arde

Would god I had loued.
taughte.
Preterplu perfectes sing. vtin.
Amauissem
Docu issem } ses, set. Plural. utinam, semus, setis, sent.
Legissem   read.
Audiuissem   hearde.

God graunt I loue hereafter.
teache.
Future tese sing. vti n.
Amauero
Docuero } ris, rit. Plural. utinam, rimus, ritis, rint
Legero   reade.
Audiuero   heare.

B.llii.

Figure 5. William Lily and John Colet. *A Shorte Introduction of Grammar.* London, 1549.

have to be spoken; their various verbal elements exist as simultaneously occurring spatial units removed from the linear sequence of
speech. The development of this spatially rationalized page can also
be observed in the successive, alternating Latin and English editions
of Lily's elementary handbook on the eight parts of speech, published
in 1513, 1537, 1540, and 1544.[32]

The visualization of language is particularly apparent in the works
of the fiercest proponent of the spoken nature of language, Joseph
Webbe. Webbe frequently uses spatial metaphors to describe the
period as a series of "clauses" knit together at the proper joint.
Webbe's method involves "vnknitting" the clauses and placing them
into parallel boxes where the Latin clause sits adjacent to its English
translation. The periods having thus been broken into clauses, the
student can then recombine clauses at will to generate his own sentences, a process similar to the disassembling and reassembling implicit in the methods of Brinsley and John Hart. Webbe is explicit
about the visual nature of his method: "clausing" is superior because
it allows "placing," or word order, to be "obseruable not onely by the
eare, but by the eye also" (see Figure 6).[33]

Actually, emphasis on the visible word appears during the half
century or so before the advent of print, in the manuscript hand of

[32]William Lily, *Libellus de Constructione Octo partium orationis* (London, 1513), printed
by Richard Pynson, who introduced Roman type into England. This edition has a high
degree of spatial form, which is lost in the first of the next three editions printed by
Thomas Berthelet, Pynson's successor as the king's printer and perhaps Pynson's
apprentice. By 1544, Berthelet recovers all of Pynson's spatialization; see *Certayne Briefe
Rules of the regiment or construction of the eyght partes of speeche, in englishe and latine*
(London, 1537); *De octo Orationis Partium Constructione Libellus . . . emendata ab Eras.
Roter.* (London, 1540); *An Introduction to the Eyght Partes of Speche and the Construction of
the Same* (London, 1544). For Pynson and Berthelet, see Colin Clair, *A History of Printing
in Britain* (New York: Oxford University Press, 1966), p. 57. There are of course
grammar books whose successive editions show no typographical development at all,
e.g., Lily's *De generibus nominum, Ac verborum* (1520, 1533, 1535, 1539). By the same
token, John Colet's *Aeditio* (1527) already manifests a highly developed sense of spatialized typography, though as late as 1620 Edmund Reeve's *Twelve Rules Introducing to
the Art of Latin* uses barely any spatialization. In general, however, once use of the *Royal
Grammar* became widespread, spatialization became the norm.

[33]Joseph Webbe, *The First Comedy of Pub. Terentius, called Andria* (London, 1629; facs.
rpt. Menston: Scolar Press, 1972), sig. ¶¶1r; see also Webbe's claused translation of
Pueriles Confabulatiunculae, or Childrens Talke (London, 1627; facs. rpt. Menston: Scolar
Press, 1968), sig. *4r. For a summary of the relationship of the acoustic and visual
image in cultures that give primacy to print, see Chaytor, *From Script to Print*, pp. 1–5.

22	ANDRIÆ. ACTVS I. SCENA I.	
hee embraces the wo-man about the middle:	I.I.I.209	*mediam mulierem com-plectitur:*
My *Glycerium,*	I.I.I.210	¶ *Mea* Glycerium,
said he,	I.I.I.211	*inquit,*
What doe you?	I.I.I.212	*Quid agis?*
Why doe you goe [a-bout] to cast your selfe a-way?	I.I.I.213	*Cur te is perditum?*
With that,	I.I.I.214	¶ *Tum,*
she, ——— that you might ea-sily perceiue their ac-customed affection, most famili-arly cast her selfe wee-ping vpon him.	I.I.I.215	*illa,* ——— *vt con-suetum fa-cilè amo-rem cerne-res,* ¶ *reiecit se-in eum, flens quàm famili-ariter.*
What say you?	I.I.I.216	¶ *Quid ais?*
I re-turne: ——— thence ——— ::angry, ——— :—|and|—. ——— ::bearing it ——— :heauily:	I.I.I.217	*Redeò:* ——— *inde* ——— *::iratus,* :— |atque| ::*ægrè ferens:*
Nor [was it] a sufficient cause to chide him.]	I.I.I.218	¶ *Nec satis ad obiurgan-dum cause.*
He might say,	I.I.I.219	¶ *Diceret,*
What haue I done?	I.I.I.220	¶ *Quid feci?*
What haue I ::deserued, ——— :—|or|— ——— :: offended ——— : in,	I.I.I.221	*Quid* —:: *commerui,* —:—|aui:| —— :: *peccaui,*
		Father?

So:
Si:

Figure 6. Joseph Webbe, *The First Comedy of Pub. Terentius, called Andria.* London, 1629.

Italian humanists. This emphasis was probably the result of two developments: the introduction of paper, which allowed the literate man to be his own scribe; and the deliberate break with late medieval hands in favor of the classicizing Carolingian hand.[34] In his later years, Petrarch rejected late medieval script, because, in S. Morison's words, it "delighted the eye at a distance, but fatigued on close inspection." That is, Petrarch's criterion for effective script was easy readability. This standard indicates an important shift in the way a literate humanist regarded the visual status of the written word. Even the small personal devotional manuscript books of the Middle Ages (which indeed continued to be produced well into the sixteenth century), apparently to be read by an individual in private, make virtually no appeal to easy reading; rather, their apparently difficult hand suggests the use of script as a memory aid for the spoken word. Like Petrarch, Salutati favored the *littera antiqua* because, he said, "no other letters are more pleasing to my eyes" (*nullae quidem litterae sunt meis oculis gratiores*). Niccoli expressed the same concern with visual clarity, according to Morison, and Erasmus declared that humanist books required qualities available only in a romanizing script, "an elegant, clear, discretely divided writing, Latin letters representing Latin words" (*scriptura elegans, delucida, distinctaque, Latinis elementis Latina verba representantibus*).[35] The Roman typeface of the printed book originated as an imitation of the humanist hand.

Petrarch, Salutati, and Niccoli, however, used the *littera antiqua* only for Latin classics and their modern imitations, not for legal, ecclesiastic, and vernacular works, and even so the humanist hand did not appear in Latin classics produced in the commercial manuscript book trade till the mid-fifteenth century, on the eve of the introduction of printing.[36] Until then use of the *littera antiqua* was mostly a matter of personal style. And for the printed book, Roman type did not completely replace Gothic till after 1580. By then the Council of Trent had ordered that liturgical books, the last bastion of Gothic type, be printed in Roman. Britain, however, most resisted Roman

[34]For the effects of the introduction of paper, see Eisenstein, *Printing Press*, pp. 11, 47. For the relationship of the humanist to the Carolingian hand, see S. Morison, "Early Humanistic Script and the First Roman Type," *The Library*, 4th ser., 24 (1943), 1–29.

[35]See Morison, "Early Humanistic Script," pp. 3, 4, 7, 24, on the visual concerns of Petrarch, Salutati, Niccoli, and Erasmus.

[36]Ibid., p. 16.

type. The King James Bible was printed in Gothic, and as late as 1637, Archbishop Laud insisted on Gothic for the Book of Common Prayer for Scotland.[37]

If the widespread adoption of easily readable Roman type represents the final break with scribal values, the easily readable written word achieved hegemony only after print had taken deep root. Chaytor suggests that only with the standardization of language made possible by print did European culture shift its confidence from speech to writing as the reliable word. And even with print the process was slow. Early printing attempted to duplicate the manuscript, as is evident in the crabbed, unbroken blocks of Gothic type in the late-fifteenth-century grammars such as that of Donatus.[38] When Mulcaster argued—successfully—that current orthography be retained even when it departed from actual pronunciation, he made a case not just for the importance of custom but also for the primacy of visual memory, which acoustic memory would have to match, rather than the other way round. In so doing, he established a fundamental principle about how words are perceived in print.

Manuscripts of course are not devoid of pictorial elements. Aside from whatever use they make of geometrical display, their most prominent visual aid, the illumination, is more decorative than functional in enhancing the communicative value of their scripts. As Clanchy implies, such visual techniques are vestiges of preliterate pictorialism, and as such they were adopted to lend greater authority to a literate document in a culture still suspicious of the written word.[39] Recognizing such stark differences between the status of writing in the medieval manuscript and that of the typography of the printed book (and to some extent the humanist manuscript) is essential for an understanding of what we mean by a "text" in print culture, the culture of the same humanist grammarians who insisted that writing is a record of speech. The printed page of the humanist Latin grammar handbook implies a notion of textuality based on a dynamic relationship between speech and writing. The morphology of the

[37]In England, Roman typeface may have been associated with both Catholic and Calvinist dissent. Calvin's *Institutes* first appeared in Roman print, and Calvinist printers in many countries promoted Roman type.

[38]Chaytor, *From Script to Print*, pp. 34, 137; see also Clanchy, *From Memory to Written Record*, p. 227. For the interchangeability of manuscripts and incunabula, see Bühler, *Fifteenth-Century Book*, pp. 16, 40, 44–47.

[39]Clanchy, *From Memory to Written Record*, pp. 226–27, 229; see also p. 104.

word is intelligible as a spatialized object, but the authority of the word to signify depends on its origins in the speech of antiquity, a speech passed on in writing. Humanist grammars are not only practical guidebooks on proper Latin usage; they are also, by implication, theoretical explanations of language itself—or at least of the language that, though it presented itself on paper to a silent reader, was still conceived of as originating in speech. The humanist explanation of language, then, failed to integrate its theoretical account of language as speech and its actual transmission of language in writing and print.

The spatialization of language had another motivating force in the Renaissance, the Hebrew notion of a sacred text. This notion was based on a metaphysics of the written word which has no real counterpart in humanistic linguistic thought. Although the influence of this tradition was less pervasive than that of print, it had an equally strong impact on the literary language of seventeenth-century religious poets. Because the relationship between the spoken language and its written record developed quite differently in the Hebrew concept of the sacred biblical text than it did in the Latin grammatical tradition, some strains of the Hebrew linguistic tradition can serve as a useful contrast to the acoustic image in Latin. Further, the Hebrew notion of writing was probably known to anyone familiar with discussions of Bible translation and Christian Cabalism. Though both the Hebrew and the Latin traditions had developed spatialized writing by the time of the Renaissance, Hebrew culture gave to its script a sacred status that had no parallel in the Latin tradition, probably because the Hebrew concept of a sacred text is unlike anything in classical culture. One fundamental difference between the Hebraic and Graeco-Roman traditions is apparent in the identification of the Hebrew sacred text—the Bible—as a written text.

There is ample evidence that the Renaissance understood the primacy of writing over speech in the Hebrew linguistic tradition not only through Christian Cabalism but also in discussions of Hebrew as the original language. John Webster's *Academarium Examen* is a case in point.[40] Though Webster does not specifically mention Hebrew,

---

[40]The following discussion is based on Webster's *Academarium Examen* (London 1653; facs. rpt. in Allen G. Debus, *Science and Education in the Seventeenth Century: The Webster-Ward Debate* [New York: American Elsevier, 1970]), pp. 26–27.

what he says in his discussion of the unnamed, divinely decreed first language was in fact derived from Renaissance notions of Hebrew. Discussing the Creation through the Word, he refers to God's "eternal word" as the "character of his subsistence" which has creative force when it is "out-spoken." Webster consistently identifies God's word—even God's voice—with characters, that is, written letters. Though the Edenic and angelic languages are spoken languages, God speaks in written characters. Sometimes the characters and their vocalization are simultaneous; sometimes the characters precede their utterance. Never does Webster treat the characters as secondary visual marks of God's speech. Creation is an act of "expand[ing] and breath[ing] forth this characteristical word." God coexists with himself as the Word—a series of characters, not sounds—which secondarily "speak[s] out" his wisdom to express itself and which prelapsarian man learned to pronounce as the language that truthfully describes nature. Similarly, God's "expanded" word appears as "true signatures of the divine and characteristical impressions," which in turn express themselves as "so many *Harmonical* and *Symphonical* voices, or tones," which sinful man can no longer easily read and pronounce in his own language. God's characters, that is, issue sounds, not the other way around, as Aristotelian and humanist notions of speech assume. In the order of creation, writing precedes speech. Writing is not the vehicle of human consciousness originally expressed in speech; rather, God's writing produces its own speech and with it the very possibility of human consciousness and human speech.

For the humanists the authority of a written text depends on its origin in speech, at least in theory. However deep their concern with print and written performance, they return to speech as the originator of writing, not just out of nostalgia for classical oratory, but because speech inhabits society, and social consensus gives speech its authority. In the Hebraic tradition, in contrast, the written text receives its authority from the divine ordination of the Hebrew letters. Belief in the divine creation of the Hebrew characters pervades the Hebrew concept of the biblical text.

Whatever the primitive oral origins of the Bible, the supreme importance of the written biblical text is apparent in the strict Masoretic and Talmudic laws that ensure the preservation and transmission of the Bible. Regulations for the actual writing of Bible scrolls to be used in public, ritual reading during the liturgy are strictly decreed for the scribe and specify, among other things, the size and ornamentation of the letters, the exact spacing of the letters, and their arrangement into lines and sections. Yet the inclusion of the punctuation elements necessary for the vocalization of the text (vowel points, endstops, and chanting accents) was proscribed from being included in the scroll, since these elements were believed to be later human inventions rather than divinely decreed like the consonantal letters themselves. Adherence to these precisely defined rules (which apply only to scrolls used in the liturgy, not to texts used for private study) produced an unusual relationship between the written text and its unwritten vocalization. The sacred text, whose main purpose is for public oralization, must be preserved as written unpunctuated consonantal script. The writing is preserved apart from the punctuation necessary for vocalization, even though the meaning of a text ultimately depends on its utterance because so many radically different pronunciations of the same consonantal script are possible.[41] As important as its liturgical utterance is, the written text of the scroll has a status of its own apart from its vocalization.[42]

In fact, the written text requires a separate apparatus for its oralization. That apparatus, known as the Masorah, was itself originally preserved orally by the Masorete, but later was committed to writing in the seventh century, at approximately the same time that Jews first adopted a new textual technology invented by the Romans several centuries earlier,[43] namely, the codex (sheets of vellum sewn in a book instead of a scroll). The Masoretic text is thus the complete transcription of the elements needed for vocalization. The Masoretic

[41] For information in this and the following paragraph, I have drawn on the comprehensive and authoritative article by Aron Dotan, "Masorah," *Encyclopaedia Judaica* (Jerusalem: Macmillan, 1971), vol. 16, cols. 1402–82. Conclusions about the implications of the Masorah for the idea of a written text are my own.

[42] The use of a consonantal alphabet—a syllabary—in written texts suggests that they are deeply tied to their oral roots and are highly dependent on their oral utterance. Writing in this sense is a memory aid for speaking. See Havelock, *Literate Revolution*, pp. 70–71. The problem of variant pronunciation was well known in the ancient Jewish world; see Christian David Ginsburg, *Introduction to the Masoretico-Critical Edition of the Hebrew Bible* (London: Trinitarian Bible Society, 1897; rpt. New York: Ktav, 1966), pp. 450–51.

[43] Dotan, "Masorah," col. 1416.

codex (later the printed book) does not, however, displace the scroll; rather, it exists side by side with the scroll, necessary for teaching and private study but, because it is not authorized for liturgical reading, always secondary to the ritual scroll. (The scroll itself is not used for teaching and study.) That is, the text punctuated with vowels never achieves the same sacred status as the scroll text, and in fact never achieves the highest degree of authoritative status as a text. It remains in the shadow of the scroll, even long after printing made both scroll and codex obsolete for anything but ritual purposes. A new technology of writing—the codex, and later the printed book—created a hierarchy of sacred texts. The unpunctuated consonantal scroll is superior to the punctuated codex or book because, ironically, it alone is authorized to be ritually uttered as speech.[44] The word inscribed on either the Hebrew scroll or codex is a very different thing from the word on medieval vellum. Each form of inscription represents quite different cultural relationships between spoken and written language.

The Masoretic tradition was known in the Renaissance, particularly among Protestants who translated the Bible into the vernacular: they would appeal to the Masoretic vowelization for the proper meaning of a Hebrew word. In England, these translators included John Jewel, William Fulke, and William Whittaker. Luther too had some understanding of the Masorah, though he distrusted it.[45] Nevertheless, it

---

[44]In fact, the Pharisaic—that is to say, the rabbinic—tradition, in opposition to that of the Saducees, kept the methods of transmitting the written and oral law quite separate. Prohibiting the oral law from being definitively committed to writing in the Second Temple period, the Pharisees insisted that whenever a portion of Scripture was recited, either in public worship or private study, it had to be read from a written text, even though knowledge of text from memory was highly valued. Even scribes, who knew the text from memory, had to make copies from another written text while reciting the text aloud. See Birger Gerhardsson, *Memory and Manuscript: Oral Tradition and Written Transmission in Rabbinic Judaism and Early Christianity*, tr. Eric J. Sharpe (Uppsala: Alqvist & Wiksells, 1961), pp. 25–29, 46–47, 63. On pp. 33–70, Gerhardsson discusses rabbinic attitudes toward the written text of the law in the Second Temple period. For a different view of Hebrew biblical textuality, see Bruns, *Inventions*, pp. 17–43.

[45]A major motive of Renaissance familiarity with the Masoretic tradition is accuracy in Bible translation, particularly in arguing against Catholic translation and interpretation. References to Masoretic vowelization can be found in John Jewel, *The Reply to Harding's Answer* [1564], in *The Works of John Jewel* (Cambridge: The University Press, 1847), II, 678; William Fulke, *A Defense of the Sincere and True Translations of the Holy Scriptures* [1583] (Cambridge: The University Press, 1843), p. 79; William Whitaker, *A*

was the Cabalistic tradition that probably had a more direct influence on the Renaissance understanding of the written Hebrew text of the Bible. The primacy of writing appears in a radical, and at times heterodox, form in the esoteric Cabala.[46] Cabalistic speculation about the biblical text proceeds from the assumption that the act of creation and God's expression of himself in Hebrew letters are parallel processes. Both the Bible and the world were emanations from the consonantal tetragrammaton. Consistent with this belief is the Cabalist view of the biblical text as an originally undivided sequence of consonantal letters.[47] Grouped in the customary manner—the Masoretic text—the letters form the commandments and the history of Israel. Grouped mystically, the same letters form all the esoteric names of God. Moses was taught to arrange the letters in both ways. The biblical text is thus regarded as written consonantal letters secondarily vocalized in at least two different ways.

In a different version of this Cabalist interpretation, the vocalization of the text was believed to be contingent on the human spiritual condition in history. After the Fall, God regrouped the letters so that, unlike the original story told by scriptures (now lost), they would spell death and the commandments. An even more radical view holds that the biblical text changes in the various aeons of the cosmic cycle. Since each consonantal letter is a concentration of divine energy, a more intense concentration will materialize in a more spiritually complete age through the creation of a new letter (or in yet another version, a change in an existing letter), which when added to the text will drastically alter its entire meaning. Even as they approach heterodoxy, each of these views depends on, and is a mystical interpretation of, the Talmudic and Masoretic exclusion of vowel punctuation from

---

Disputation on the Holy Scripture Against the Papists [1588] (Cambridge: The University Press, 1849), pp. 55, 159. For Luther, see *Works*, ed. Jaroslav Pelikan and Walter A. Hansen (St. Louis, Mo.: Concordia, 1965), VII, 169 (cf. n. 26). The Bomberg Rabbinic Bible (Venice, 1517–18, 1524–25) and Levitas's *Masoreth ha Masoreth* (Venice, 1538) are also testaments to the Renaissance interest in the Masorah. For Jerome's knowledge of variation in vowelization of the consonantal text, see Ginsburg, *Introduction to the Masoretico-Critical Edition*, pp. 446–49.

[46] For the following material, I am indebted to Gershom G. Scholem, *On the Kaballah and Its Symbolism* (Boston: Schocken, 1965), pp. 32–86.

[47] For the original division of consonantal letters into words and the resulting variations preserved in the Masorah, see Ginsburg, *Introduction to the Masoretico-Critical Edition*, pp. 296–97.

the sacred text, the biblical scroll.[48] They also indicate the letter-centered concept of the sacred text. That is, in the mystical version of the Talmudic and Masoretic tradition, the revealed word is a revealed sequence of unvocalized consonants, secondarily and variously vocalized according to spiritual, historical, and cosmic circumstances.

On the whole, the Christian concept of a sacred text has more in common with the Latin than with the Hebrew tradition, even though the contents of the Christian scriptures are a continuation of their Hebrew predecessor. Clanchy points to a medieval iconographic tradition that distinguishes Hebrew from Christian textuality by portraying the prophets holding a scroll while the evangelists hold a book.[49] And just as innumerable humanist grammars defined Latin, Greek, and English as speech, so a popular Renaissance grammar of Hebrew by Petrus Martinius observes that "*Grammar* is the art of speaking well; as in the Hebrue tonge to speak hebrue." Martinius then describes the components of Hebrew words, letters, and syllables as sounds,[50] and he supplies scriptural passages as examples of Hebrew speech from which grammar rules can be induced. The entire method is a strange adaptation of the methods of Latin grammar, since Martinius's purpose is to teach scriptural analysis rather than Hebrew composition, spoken or written. It is not surprising that in his speech-oriented humanist language program Brinsley recommends Martinius as the best aid for learning Hebrew.[51] Whatever Brinsley's contribution to the spatialization of language, it did not lead to the Masoretic or Cabalistic concept of the written text. But the Hebrew concept of the primacy of writing over speech did make an impact on a group of important Christian Cabalists. This Hebrew

[48]Even in the mainstream Masoretic tradition, the addition of new letters was regarded as divinely ordained and related to events in the history of Israel; see ibid., pp. 289–90, where Ginsburg discusses the replacement of Samaritan characters by Assyrian characters in scriptural writing.

[49]Clanchy, *From Memory to Written Record*, pp. 109–10. For the early adoption of the parchment codex by Christians, in contrast to the ancient Jewish preference for the parchment scroll and Graeco-Roman preference for the papyrus scroll, see T. C. Skeat, "Early Christian Book-Production: Papyri and Manuscripts," in *Cambridge History of the Bible* (Cambridge: Cambridge University Press, 1969), II, 65–75. See also C. H. Roberts, "Books in the Graeco-Roman World and in the New Testament," in *Cambridge History of the Bible*, I, 55–60.

[50]Petrus Martinius, *The Key of the Holy Tongue*, tr. John Udall (Paris, 1567; facs. rpt. Menston: Scolar Press, 1970), p. 5.

[51]Brinsley, *Ludus*, p. 247.

influence, combined with the parallel but distinctive tendency of print toward spatialization, reified certain kinds of sacred literary language in the Renaissance. Although this Hebraic approach never became part of the mainstream of language studies, it is noteworthy because it represents an alternative that ultimately was not chosen in Renaissance culture at large, and thus by contrast it sets in relief the dominant humanist view of the written and printed text.

As letters acquired the status of things in the Renaissance, they also took on a property commonly attributed to natural objects: they were understood to possess symbolic significance. In this chirographic tradition, which made an impact both in England and on the continent, letters came to signify more than just sounds. They became the foundation of a system of alphabetical symbolism in which they assumed the symbolic properties ordinarily associated with hieroglyphs. Renaissance Neoplatonists, for instance, saw in the physical configurations of letters, particularly Roman letters, ideal mathematical proportions that were believed to have symbolic, almost Pythagorean, meaning, much like the mathematical proportions humanist architects used in designing buildings. Similarly, Thomas Smith's metaphorical reference to constructing words from physical, visible letters as an *exaedificare*, a building up, had more than metaphorical significance. And both Lomazzo and, later in the century, Theophilus Gale, thought they demonstrated a connection between letters, hieroglyphs, and in Lomazzo's case, emblems.[52] As Emanuele Casamassima has observed, the Renaissance interest in alphabet design was related to other, broader intellectual concerns of the period.[53]

One of those concerns was the origin of writing. Speculation centered particularly around the mysterious nature of Hebrew and its relationship to Egyptian considered as primeval languages.[54] The issue had a natural connection with orthography, and Smith, like many of his fellow humanists, located the origins of writing in Egyptian hieroglyphs, though he believed that, because hieroglyphs were

---

[52]Smith, *Dialogus*, sig. Civ; Lomazzo, *Tracte*, p. 3; Theophilus Gale, *The Court of Gentiles* (Oxford, 1672), pt. 1, pp. 55–56.

[53]Casamassima, *Trattati di scrittura*, p. 9.

[54]For Hebrew as the original language, see D. C. Allen, "Some Theories of the Growth and Origin of Language in Milton's Age," *Philological Quarterly*, 28 (1949), pp. 5–16.

so cumbersome, they were eventually replaced by more efficient letters that arbitrarily and conventionally represented sounds. This position was characteristic of some humanist orthographers,[55] but Smith was challenged on several of these views. Other Renaissance thinkers, influenced in various degrees by humanism, Neoplatonism, and Christian Cabalism, attributed mystic powers and deep symbolic meaning to the Hebrew alphabet. They viewed its letters as secret hieroglyphs, a quality that in some sense it passed on to its descendants in the modern languages. Johannes Reuchlin, for instance, in his *De Verbo Mirifico* (1494), saw in Hebrew letters the same mystical hieroglyphic meaning that the Renaissance attributed to Egyptian writing, and his view was current in England as well as on the continent.[56] (In the Renaissance, Egyptian hieroglyphs were commonly held to have been derived from Hebrew.) Similarly, the Spanish Renaissance theologian Fray Louis de Leon analyzed the allegorical significance of the letters in the Hebrew word for "word," *dabar,* as the name of Christ, a symbolic significance complemented by the sounded syllables of the word.[57] In *De Occulta Philosophia* (I, lxxiv),

[55]Smith, *Dialogus,* sigs. biv–biiv, civ; John Hart, *A methode or comfortable beginning for all vnlearned, whereby they may bee taught to read English* (London, 1570), sig. A2v; Richard Mulcaster, *The First Part of the Elementarie* (London, 1582; facs. rpt. Menston: Scolar Press, 1970), pp. 56–57. Havelock regards script whose shapes are only incidental to their function as essential to widespread literacy (*Literate Revolution,* p. 53).

[56]For Reuchlin on Hebrew characters, see Edgar Wind, *Pagan Mysteries in the Renaissance,* rev. ed. (New York: Norton, 1968), p. 207, n. 54. For the humanist defense of Reuchlin against his critics, on the one hand, and the fundamental humanist antipathy to Cabalism and magic, on the other, see Werner Gundersheimer, "Erasmus, Humanism, and the Christian Cabala," *Journal of the Warburg and Courtauld Institutes,* 26 (1963), 38–52. Frances Yates agrees that Renaissance magi and humanists were unsympathetic to each other's intellectual presuppositions, but she observes that they found common ground in their concept of and interest in hieroglyphics (*Giordano Bruno and the Hermetic Tradition* [Chicago: University of Chicago Press, 1964], pp. 159–68). Moreover, although the origin of language in the mystic nature of Hebrew was not an issue of great concern to such humanists as Smith and Mulcaster, the merging of characteristically humanist interests in language with interest in the hieroglyphic nature of Hebrew is quite evident in, e.g., Du Bartas's *Deuine Weekes and Workes,* discussed below. Du Bartas, a disciple of the Pléiade and influenced by Cabalism, enjoyed great popularity in England, a fact that challenges Gundersheimer's contention that, after Reuchlin, Cabalism did not have much influence outside Cabalistic circles themselves. In matters concerning language, Cabalism may have been more influential than Gundersheimer suggests.

[57]See Carlos G. Norena, *Studies in Spanish Renaissance Thought* (The Hague: Nijhoff, 1975), pp. 204–9.

Agrippa argued that Hebrew was the first language, calling the Hebrew alphabet the foundation of the world. And evoking a commonplace of Renaissance linguistic speculation, he explained that vestiges of Hebrew letters still survived in the modern languages.[58]

Of the various works that elaborated these views, perhaps the most popular was the section on the tower of Babel in Du Bartas's *Deuine Weekes and Workes,* known in England through translations by Joshua Sylvester (1605) and William L'isle (1637) as well as in the commentary on Du Bartas by Simon Goulart, translated by both L'isle and Thomas Lodge (1621) and based on the authority of Pico, Grotius, Reuchlin, Gesner, and Postel.[59] Du Bartas explains that Hebrew was the first language, and, far from being arbitrary and conventional, its letters and even its Masoretic points (the marks under the letters signifying vowels) have symbolic dimensions. He observes that the very physical configurations of the "holy tongue of God" are "so full of sense and grace, / As not a letter it hath, no not a point so Small, / Without some ornament exceeding mysticall" (L'isle, p. 53); he later remarks that its "Elements [i.e., letters] / Flow with hid sense, [its] points with Sacraments" (Sylvester, p. 425). Du Bartas also compares Hebrew letters to "spirituall pictures" (Sylvester, p. 425) and describes how the symbolic meaning of Hebrew names is revealed in the physical rearrangement of their letters in anagrams, as well as in the elaboration of the meaning of their letters in acrostics, so that the Hebrew characters become an "embleme," superior to Egyptian hieroglyphs (L'isle, p. 61; Sylvester, p. 424; Lodge, pp. 178–79).

In thus connecting Hebrew letters considered as pictures and anagrams to Egyptian hieroglyphs, Du Bartas suggests that the mystic qualities of Hebrew letters are apprehensible by the sense of sight. He

[58]Henricius Cornelius Aggripa ab Nettesheym, *De Occulta Philosophia sive De Magia Libri Tres* (Cologne, 1533), pp. xcv–xcvi; rpt. ed. Karl Nowotny (Graz: Akademische Druck und Verlagsanstalt, 1967), pp. 107–8. For the importance of Aggripa's views on language in general and Hebrew in particular, see Margreta de Grazia, "Language in Elizabethan England: The Divine Model" (diss., Princeton University, 1975), pp. 90–122.

[59]Guillaume Saluste du Bartas, *Deuine Weekes and Workes,* tr. Joshua Sylvester (London, 1605; rpt. Gainesville, Fla.: Scholars' Facsimiles and Reprints, 1965); *Fovre Bookes of du Bartas,* tr. William L'isle (London, 1637); Simon Goulart, *A Learned Summary upon the Famous Poeme of W. of Salustre,* tr. Thomas Lodge (London, 1621). In the text, I quote from both Sylvester's and L'isle's translations, depending on which makes the relevant point more clearly. The importance of Lodge's translation of Goulart is made clear in de Grazia, "Language in Elizabethan England."

explicitly observes, however, that, in its spoken sounds, Hebrew also makes its mysteries apparent to the sense of hearing. Hebrew "with few words expresseth happily / Deepest conceites, and leades the hearing part / Through all the closets of the mazie hart" (Sylvester, p. 423). Accordingly, the etymological meaning of the Hebrew names of creatures, people, and cities inheres in their audible as well as their visible form: "eu'ry ancient name, / By writ, by sound, by sense, from Hebrew language came" (L'isle, p. 61). The symbolic qualities of written Hebrew letters are vocalized in Hebrew as uttered speech, as a language spoken by God, Adam, and the prophets (Sylvester, pp. 424, 425).

Taking a slightly different view, Godwyn proposed that there is lost mystic significance in the discrepancy between the written and pronounced form of some Hebrew words in the Masoretic text of the Bible.[60] This possibility is further developed in Goulart's commentary. On the authority of Jerome and Eusebius, Goulart maintains that each letter of the Hebrew alphabet has an allegorical significance that makes up an articulated sentence: "The doctrine of the Church, which is the House of God, is found in the fulnesse of the Tables; that is, of the diuine bookes" (Lodge, p. 181). For Du Bartas, the idea that letters are physical things with allegorical meaning like other created physical things suggests a variation on the concept of the Book of Nature. Because the Hebrew names of the creatures contain in themselves "Their natures storie," those names are themselves "open Bookes" wherein the spiritual meaning of God's handiwork is explained (Sylvester, p. 425). That is, the names of the creatures, rather than the creatures themselves, make up the Book of Nature. The original word, which is also the originating word that initially generated the words of all other languages, thus constitutes an ideal, meaningful textual space that exists before it is filled with any specific contents by an author and precedes any mental act expressed through speech. The sentence divined by Goulart in the Hebrew alphabet writes its meaning before being spoken; similarly, human language, Webster says, must imitate God's "characteristical word" imprinted in nature. Originary divine writing valorizes subjectivity and speech rather than acting as their instrument and mirror image.

Du Bartas tends to emphasize the loss of these symbolic powers in

---

[60]Godwyn, *Moses and Aaron*, p. 279.

the languages that manifested the confusion of tongues following
Babel, though he does see vestiges of the Hebrew alphabet in the
letters of all languages, since they are derived from Hebrew, "how-
so[ever they may be] disguiz'd" (Sylvester, p. 424). Goulart, however,
stresses the continuity between Hebrew and its modern descendants
(see, for instance, Lodge, pp. 178–79) and insists that the secret
significance of Hebrew words and letters is still recoverable, but not in
its pristine state (Lodge, p. 181). He argues that the basic, "primitiue"
words of languages are derived from the elemental components of
Hebrew, not only from Hebrew words but also from Hebrew letters
and syllables uttered from those letters (Lodge, p. 178). In this way
the God-given capacity of language to signify endures through time
in the history of languages from Hebrew to the modern vernaculars.

Alexander Top's little-known and little-discussed *Oliue Leafe* (1603),
the only native English treatise in this divine chirographic tradition
which is not a translation of a continental work, concisely presents the
Cabalistic view of the primacy of writing.[61] Although Top's Cabalisitic
interests have little in common with humanism, he enunciates his
ideas, strangely, within the context of a humanist concern, the reform
of English spelling. He opens his argument by establishing his position in the Renaissance debate over whether language and alphabets
were divinely ordained or instituted by man. He takes a strong stand
in favor of divine ordination, explaining that "there was but one
[alphabet]; and that one, of God himselfe, the true *Hagiography* or
Hierogly[p]hs of our first Fathers; to wit, the two and twentie severall
vncorrupted Formes or Letters of the *Hebrew* tongue: Which being
graunted the eldest, consequently must be thought the Mother and
very Matrix of all other; so that the Authoritie of all *Abces* ryseth from
hence, as this from God" (sig. A4v). Top elsewhere explains that the
original Hebrew letters were corrupted into modern alphabets not
only as a result of the Flood and the tower of Babel (sigs. C1v–C2v)
but for various other reasons, including political necessity (sigs. B3r–
B3v). As part of his plan to bring English letters back in line with
Hebrew—Top's contribution to the reform of English orthography—
he supplies an extensive chart at the end of the volume showing the
derivation of over twenty-five alphabets from the original Hebrew.

[61]Alexander Top, *The Oliue Leafe: Or, Vniuersall Abce* (London, 1603; facs. rpt.
Menston: Scolar Press, 1971).

Like the Renaissance understanding of Egyptian hieroglyphs, Top's concept of Hebrew letters as hieroglyphs was intimately bound up with an allegorical view of creation. Things of the world are so created that they have hieroglyphic significance; their nature as things is intrinsically related to their nature as signs. Top illustrates this belief by explaining that the sun, moon, and stars were created by God "for signes, for seasons, for dayes, & for yeares" (sig. B2v).[62] He repeats many of the commonplaces of his day, ideas developed more profoundly by Ficino and Valeriano, supported by the Renaissance discovery of the *Hieroglyphica* of Horapollo, and popularized in the emblems of Francis Quarles.

But Top extends this allegorical, hieroglyphic concept of creation from the things—or pictures of things—that language can represent to the very being of language itself. He attributes allegorical significance to the physical elements that constitute written language, namely, letters, particularly "the Mother and very Matrix" of all letters, the Hebrew alphabet. Just as he defines the sun, moon, and stars in their capacity as signs, as *Othoth*—the Hebrew word for both signs and letters of the alphabet—so too he makes a direct connection between letters and created things. Top gleefully observes that God created twenty-two things during the creation week, the same number as there are letters in the Hebrew alphabet, "Wherefore," he says, "I may conclude, that every of these severall *Hebrew* letters, should signifie or import some speciall workmanshyp of the Lordes Creation" (sig. B2r–B2v). Top then carries this reasoning to its extreme, basing his argument on an interpretation of the Hebrew word *eth*. Although in Hebrew *eth* is simply a particle preceding a direct object, Top interprets the word as the singular of *Othoth* and observes that it is used in each verse that describes every act of God's creation, "As, if all things were to be comprehended by this limitation or circumscription *Bara Elohim (Eth) hashamaim*, God created the figure, signe, or letter, of the Heauens, &c. Or the very hieroglyphs of them, this worde

---

[62]Top equivocates between positing, on the one hand, the clarity of the relationship between signs and their spiritual meanings ("by comparing substaunce unto the protrayture") and, on the other hand, the opacity of that relationship and therefore the difficulty of finding spiritual meanings in material things ("the inwarde proprietie *with due recognition*" [emphasis added]). The importance of an enigmatic relationship between the hieroglyphic sign and its meaning distinguishes Top's from Bacon's view of hieroglyphs, as I show below.

[*Eth*] beeing the singular of *Othoth,* which signifieth Figures, Letters, Causes, Signes, or Tokens, of all sortes" (sig. B2v).

Along with everything God created, Top suggests here, he simultaneously created a Hebrew letter as a hieroglyph of that thing. Top thus transfers the allegorical function of Egyptian pictographic hieroglyphs to non-pictographic Hebrew letters.[63] Perhaps even more important, he endows the most fundamental units of the language from which all languages originate with the status of things existing alongside other things. Letters and words share a status similar to that of the very things they signify; letters and words have an ontological weight that humanist concepts of speech and writing lack. Top argues not only for the divine rationale of letters, as opposed to some view of their purely arbitrary nature, but for writing as the foundation of language and knowledge. The true linguistic mark is spatial, not vocal, and its meaning is conveyed by the physical elements of the mark itself. One does not look *through* the mark to see its meaning in its referent; one finds meaning *in* the opaque, physical, divinely created symbol laid out in space and to some extent containing its referent in itself. It is precisely because of the divinely endowed ontological thingness of writing that it is able to signify.

In this Hebraic, biblical version of Plato's *Cratylus,* Top later explains that Adam combined the hieroglyphic letters "to give every speciall thing a proper *Name,*" when "the *species* and *personages* of things grew so abundant and so divers" that the letters themselves were insufficient (sig. C3v).[64] (Just how the species multiplied after creation Top never reveals.) Expressing a thoroughly conventional

---

[63]For the verbal basis of some of Horapollo's hieroglyphs in puns, however, see George Boas, introduction to *The Hieroglyphics of Horapollo* (New York: Phaidon, 1950), p. 30. Moreover, the practice of applying the term hieroglyph to Hebrew letters has a basis in the Renaissance understanding of the relationship between Hebrew and Egyptian writing. In his retrospective summary of patristic and Renaissance views on the subject, Theophilus Gale recounts the invention of Hebrew letters by Moses, from whom the Egyptians learned hieroglyphic writing. Gale identifies Theuth, who according to Plato, invented Egyptian hieroglyphs, as Moses; see *Court of the Gentiles,* pp. 55–56. For Pico's and Reuchlin's attribution to unpointed Hebrew letters of the same sacred and cryptic values as Egyptian hieroglyphs, see Wind, *Pagan Mysteries,* p. 207, n. 54.

[64]For the origin of Egyptian hieroglyphs in the Adamic language, see Ernst Gombrich, "*Icones Symbolicae,* Philosophies of Symbolism and Their Bearing on Art," in *Symbolic Images: Studies in the Art of the Renaissance* (New York: Phaidon, 1972), pp. 149–50; and Gale, *Court of the Gentiles,* p. 56.

idea, Top further argues that this intrinsic connection between word and thing is not only a characteristic of Hebrew but is also the standard by which language in general should be measured: "And this is a current Rule for the *Hebrician,* that no one word in that tongue, ever fayleth of some proper or distinct meaning; as well to instruct the diligent Schollar in some natural reason of things, which is the truth of all Language in deed" (sig. C3v). Hebrew thus becomes a standard for all other languages, for it embodies the principle of perfect correspondence between word (as physical object itself) and thing, a principle Top seems to think can be recovered by all languages. Indeed, he announces that he has recovered the linguistic condition that existed before the Flood, as the "Deluge of the deepe Confusion ebs," so that those who read his book will "upright [their] language, [and] cleare [their] sense" (sig. A3v).

Finally, although Top elevates writing above speech, he connects all he has said about letters as written hieroglyphs to letters as the components of speech. For him as for Du Bartas, language is hieroglyphically significative in the two media through which it is sensibly transmitted—sight (it is visible as letters) and sound (it is audible as speech). Visual hieroglyphs become a means of human communication when pronounced in speech. Words may be spoken by the voice alone without any understanding of the hieroglyphic significance of their component letters, or they may be spoken by the heart through the voice, that is, with an understanding of their hieroglyphic significance. For Top, words as hieroglyphs thus share the same polysemous nature as was attributed in the Renaissance to Egyptian characters.[65] To speak correctly, then, is to utter the occult but intrinsic relationship between words and the essence of things impressed on the physical components of an opaque written, visible language (letters as hieroglyphs) imprinted on the physical apparatus of the spoken voice (letters as sounds) (sig. C3v). Top attempts to base even his suggestions for English spelling reform on the hieroglyphic order of words and things.

Thus, although the Renaissance frequently used the idea of speech as a conceptual model to explain the nature of language, for the most

[65]For the polysemous nature of hieroglyphs, see Boas, *Hieroglyphics of Horapollo,* p. 35, and Gombrich, *"Icones Symbolicae,"* p. 159.

part the speech of the Renaissance appeared in writing. In modifying the idea of speech, those concerned with nature of language drew on two traditions of the written word: that of print and that of Hebrew script. The effect of print in transferring words from an acoustic to a spatial dimension was pervasive. More limited and specific in its impact was the Hebrew word, whose written marks have an iconic significance that is communicated even in their secondary manifestation as uttered speech. The general sensitivity to these three dimensions of language—speech, spatiality, iconicity—produced a unique concept of textuality, a concept that helps explain the Renaissance phenomenon of the hieroglyphic poem. The page becomes a bounded space capable of containing iconically significant letters; the spatial dimension of the word constituted by such letters is the vehicle of its meaning. Herbert's hieroglyphs are situated in this kind of charged textual space.

5/
The Space of the Hieroglyph:
George Herbert and Francis Bacon

I N his life of Herbert, Izaak Walton describes *The Temple* in a way that calls attention to Herbert's collection of poems as a physical object. He records how Edmund Duncon carried the book of handwritten poems from Herbert, who was on his deathbed, to Nicholas Ferrar at Little Gidding and thence to the printer.[1] The sense of Herbert's poems as material things handled, arranged, and set in print is reinforced by Walton's report of the printer's objection to two lines in "The Church Militant," which Ferrar insisted should nevertheless be printed "without the diminution or addition of a syllable, since it was deliver'd into the hands of Mr. *Duncon*."[2] We are also reminded of *The Temple* as a thing being moved about the press room when Walton tells us of Ferrar's preface printed at the front of the book.[3] At the same time, these details chronicling the transformation of manuscript into book emphasize how the poet's

[1]Izaak Walton, *The Lives of John Donne, Sir Henry Wotton, Richard Hooker, George Herbert, and Robert Sanderson* (London: Oxford University Press, 1927), pp. 314–15. J. Max Patrick argues that Walton's story is a fabrication and that, in fact, Herbert planned and oversaw the publication of *The Temple* before his death ("Critical Problems in Editing George Herbert's *The Temple*," in *The Editor as Critic and the Critic as Editor* [Los Angeles: William Clark Memorial Library, 1973], pp. 3–14). Patrick is refuted in Amy M. Charles and Mario A. di Cesare, introduction to *The Bodleian Manuscript of George Herbert's Poems* (Delmar, N.Y.: Scholars' Facsimiles and Reprints, 1984).
[2]Walton, *Lives*, p. 315.
[3]Walton, *Lives*, pp. 314–15. On the reification of the book in the Renaissance, see Walter J. Ong, *Ramus, Method, and the Decay of Dialogue: From the Art of Discourse to the Art of Reason* (Cambridge: Harvard University Press, 1958), pp. 311–12.

voice committed to writing in the manuscript authorizes the accurate transcription of his text (the written record of sounds, i.e., syllables) in the printed book. The printed edition is reliable because it duplicates Herbert's manuscript volume, preserving a direct connection between the printed work and the creator of the poems. Whether or not Herbert originally conceived that his poems would finally be fixed in print, the nature of the textuality emerging in the age of print was at least part of the context of his hieroglyphic poems. Herbert's pattern poems illustrate the spatialization of language that developed in the sixteenth and seventeenth centuries, an age of printed books and the visually perceived word.

Studies of Herbert's hieroglyphic poems have for the most part focused on their relation to Renaissance concepts of metaphor, allegory, and emblems.[4] Joseph Summers's influential discussion of hieroglyphic form in Herbert's poems, for example, examines that form as a function of the allegorical mode of thought encouraged by Herbert's church. Other studies have found prototypes of Herbert's poems in the pattern poems of the Greek Anthology, or have identified the influence of the Renaissance theories of hieroglyphics that stemmed from the discovery of Horapollo's hieroglyphs. Building on these interpretations emphasizing allegorical hieroglyphs, my approach attempts to relate Herbert to a strain of Renaissance thought not often associated with his work: the Renaissance interest in the

---

[4]The principal work on Herbert and Renaissance hieroglyphics is Joseph Summers, *George Herbert: His Religion and Art* (Cambridge: Harvard University Press, 1954), pp. 123–46. John Hollander, *Vision and Resonance: Two Senses of Poetic Form* (New York: Oxford University Press, 1975), pp. 252–68, is also illuminating, especially in calling attention to the importance of George Puttenham's *The Arte of English Poesie* for Herbert's pattern poems. For other views of Herbert's hieroglyphic poems, see Patrick, "Critical Problems," pp. 14–22; and Dick Higgins, *George Herbert's Pattern Poems: In Their Tradition* (West Glover, Vt.: Unpublished Editions, 1977). For Renaissance hieroglyphics in general, see Margaret Church, "The First English Pattern Poems," *PMLA*, 61 (1946), 636–50; George Boas, introduction to *The Hieroglyphics of Horapollo* (New York: Phaidon, 1950), pp. 17–43; Liselotte Dieckmann, "Renaissance Hieroglyphics," *Comparative Literature*, 9 (1957), 308–21; Erik Iversen, *The Myth of Egypt and Its Hieroglyphs in the European Tradition* (Copenhagen: Gec Gad, 1961), pp. 60–100; Peter M. Daly, "Trends and Problems in the Study of Emblematic Literature," *Mosaic* 5, no. 4 (1972), 53–68; Ernst Gombrich, "*Icones Symbolicae:* Philosophies of Symbolism and Their Bearing on Art," in *Symbolic Images: Studies in the Art of the Renaissance* (New York; Phaidon, 1972), pp. 123–91; Rudolph Wittkower, "Hieroglyphics in the Early Renaissance," in *Allegory and the Migration of Symbols* (1972; rpt. Boulder, Colo.: Westview Press, 1977), pp. 114–28.

material underpinnings of language in written letters and spoken sounds. Herbert's pattern poems were written during a time of transition when oral and written approaches to textuality continued to intersect in the written and typographic word. The spread of written and printed language was not the cause of the pattern poem—a genre which long antedates print—but the rise of the visually perceived word created possibilities realized in Herbert's poetry which were not available to ancient and medieval pattern poetry.

The Renaissance ideas that particularly influenced Herbert's poetry involved some aspects of the period's linguistic thought where humanist and Hebraic interests converged. In the Hebraic tradition words were conceived of as material things that belong to the same network of resemblances that endows natural objects with allegorical meaning, a conception of language clearly connected to hieroglyphs and emblem literature. But the combination of the humanist and Hebraic strains of language theory created the possibility of a textual space in which words could be simultaneously icons and significant sounds and thus be both acoustically and visually meaningful. Moreover, where the printed word as visual image combines with the esoteric Cabalist doctrine of the word as symbolic object, the written marks of language take on an ontological status of their own, which to some extent guarantees their power of signification. By ordering the poems' metrical units of spoken sounds into a visual unit, the spatialized text lends its words the authority to signify. Thus, in Herbert's hieroglyphic poems, "The Altar" and "Easter Wings," the letters and words that form the typographical pictogram are also the written marks of the poet's utterance—his prayer, his plea, his spoken word. Herbert's hieroglyphs manifest a particular kind of textuality that draws on the manifold interrelations between uttered and spatialized language inherited from Hebrew and Latin traditions in the age of print. Not only "The Altar" and "Easter Wings" but also such lesser poems as "Iesu," "Love-joy," and "The Sonne" illustrate the way Herbert sees meaning as divinely ordained in the sensible elements of language, both visible and audible.

The hieroglyphic approach to language evident in these poems is interconnected with their use of typological symbols that project the prophecy of Christ across time. In "The Sonne," Herbert praises the English language for the homonymic property (at least in seven-

teenth-century English) of the word "sonne," which of course is the
basis of the popular pun on "sun" and "son." (Unlike the Bodleian
MS, the 1633 edition distinguishes the spelling of the two words as
"sunne" and "sonne," but the poem in either case refers to both as
"one word.") The confluence of the two meanings in one linguistic
unit is the basis of a pun that explains the meaning of a son as both a
"light" to and a "fruit" of his father. On a grander scale, the son/sun is
a "fruitfull flame" whose course from east to west records the procrea-
tive history of mankind from Adam in Eden to the present genera-
tions in Europe. As the pun takes on ever broader significance, the
coincidence of the same sound in the two words reveals the spiritual
nature of Christ:

> So in one word our Lords humilitie
> We turn upon him in a sense most true:
>   For what Christ once in humblenesse began,
>   We him in glorie call, *The Sonne of Man*.[5]
>   [ll. 11–14]

The Word as spoken sound thus becomes for Herbert the sounded
encoding of a series of natural, historical, and spiritual truths. In
effect, in praising the coincidence of the English word's sense and its
sensible, material substance, Herbert praises English for its ability to
name in the manner of Adam. Although a rather slight poem, "The
Sonne" echoes the *The Temple*'s various plays on words and their
sounds, which are not merely the accidents of language but instead
emerge out of the hieratic, sacral, and hieroglyphic properties derived from Hebrew and built into the very physical components of
English as a system of both written and spoken letters, properties
actualized as the sacred pun is vocalized when "we him in glorie *call*
[emphasis added], *The Sonne of Man*."

In "The Flower" Herbert uses a metaphor derived from orthography to describe man's ability to discern the spiritual significance of the
natural world: "Thy word is all, if we could spell" (l. 21). In "Iesu" he
uses the concept of spelling in a more literal way. The speaker's heart,
inscribed with the name Iesu, breaks in pieces, each containing a

[5]All citations of Herbert are from *The Works of George Herbert*, ed. F. E. Hutchinson
(Oxford: Clarendon Press, 1941).

portion of the name. Broken into *I, ES, U,* Christ's name is spatially divided into elements much as sixteenth- and early seventeenth-century spelling handbooks repeatedly break up words to teach reading and writing.[6] (In Herbert's English, *to spell* had not only its present sense, it could also mean *to read.*) When the subdivided written units are translated into sounds, however, the speaker deciphers lexical units, words, which in turn make up a syntactical unit, "*I ease you*" (l. 10). This process is reminiscent of the way Simon Goulart deciphers a sentence in the letters of the Hebrew alphabet. The spatial components of Christ's name sounded as acoustic images take on the status of Alexander Top's and Du Bartas's Hebrew hieroglyphs: the letters of Christ's name "spell" the very essence of the name.

Similarly, the speaker of "Love-joy" (a poem that Stanley Fish refers to as a hieroglyphic riddle)[7] explains the meaning of the letters *J* and *C* "anneal'd" on the picture of grapes in a stained glass window. The letters of course stand for Jesus Christ, but they also stand for the meaning of Christ—joy and charity. They signify that meaning by naming the allegorical and typological significance of the grapes of the vine. The letters contain the spiritual meaning of the name embodied in language, a meaning which is inextricably intertwined with nature and history, insofar as the grapes are a Hebrew type of Christ the vine. The prophecy of Christ transmitted through time by the typological symbol of a natural object is represented by the hieroglyphic capabilities of Hebrew letters transmitted through time in the alphabet out of which English words are made. This hieroglyphic representation of letters is particularly relevant to Herbert's poetry, since both the grapes and the letters appear not in nature but in the sacred art of a stained-glass church window; both the letters and the grapes are physical artifacts. The letters are literally what Giovanni Lomazzo calls "picture[s] of *white* and *black.*" Like the letters in the window, Herbert's language is man-made, and its basic units, letters, also contain in their material being the basis of its spiritual meaning. The poet is a maker in much the same way as the glazier is: each constructs material images that embody spiritual meanings, but the

[6]In discussing "Iesu," Stanley Fish suggests Herbert plays on the orthography of *I* and *J* (*The Living Temple: George Herbert and Catechizing* [Berkeley: University of California Press, 1978], pp. 132–33).
[7]Ibid., p. 28.

glazier's medium is glass while the poet's is his physical, material letters. Herbert's language is a poetic artifact constructed from divinely ordained sensible elements.

A spiritual significance emerging from the physical properties of words is also evident in Herbert's anagram on the name of Mary:

$$Ana\text{-} \left\{ \begin{array}{c} \text{MARY} \\ \text{ARMY} \end{array} \right\} gram$$

> How well her name an *Army* doth present,
> In whom the *Lord of Hosts* did pitch his tent!

In these lines Herbert attributes to English words and names the same capacity for anagramatic and acrostic manipulation which Du Bartas finds in Hebrew. And he subjects the letters of Mary's name to the same search for occult, spiritual significance that he pursues in, for example, the analogies of "The Flower." The letters of Mary's name contain the signature of her importance in the history of redemption as the bearer of the Christ who, as the incarnation of God, was to triumph over sin and Satan on the cross. The military metaphor through which her spiritual and historical significance is expressed is thus embedded in the sequential space of the letters that make up her name. In this sense, the word—here the name—becomes a physical object, the rearrangement of whose letters on the page makes manifest its own meaning. In Herbert's hands the rearranging of letters that for Richard Carew was merely a form of trifling play becomes a serious matter laden with sacred import; the spatial medium of letters holds occult meanings. The anagram is a kind of linguistic hieroglyph, or an *impresa* whose picture is replaced by a word followed by a two-line motto. But whereas an *impresa* contains a picture that represents some thing possessing symbolic significance, in the anagram the very word as printed on the page is the thing that possesses such significance, bearing out Lomazzo's connection between letters, emblem, and picture. Moreover, the word "anagram," split in half and holding within itself the particular anagram that the ensuing couplet explicates, also calls attention to itself as a physical object.

The hieroglyphic significance of the physical properties of language as visible, spatial signs and audible sounds is brought to play in the most conspicuously hieroglyphic of Herbert's poems, "The Altar" and "Easter Wings," which use more elaborate extensions of the linguistic principles underlying the Mary anagram. The typographic arrangement of each of these poems forms in its entirety a single pictographically hieroglyphic unit (thus making both these poems different from those discussed above). These hieroglyphic units also translate into lexical units: altar, wings—that is, the things signified by both the typographic arrangement of the physical materials of written language and by the sense of meaning of the words in the poem. Herbert's pattern poems are like emblems in which poem and picture are combined in the very shape of the poem, inverting the doctrine of signatures: in these poems letters are not imprinted on a thing; a thing is imprinted in an arrangement of letters. The printed letters are the physical stuff of the pictogram, as letters take on the qualities of Lomazzo's "picture[s] of *white* and *black.*"

The hieroglyphic shapes of these poems, however, are not inherent in their physical typography alone. The typographical shapes themselves are formed by the decreases and increases in the number of metrical feet in each line: the typographical patterns are produced by a manipulation of the spaces occupied by the units of spoken poetic language. The poems' spatial arrangement is both seen and heard.[8] The letters out of which the poem's words are built (*exaedificare*), as Thomas Smith describes spelling, become a literal *pictura vocum.* Puttenham too thought of the metrical line as derived from the audible qualities of ordinary speech, and he believed that shaped poems in turn derived from variations of the metrical line. Shaped poems, that is, are made by variations in the length of units of pronounced sounds.[9] That these poems are simulacra of speech is reinforced by their plain-style syntax and diction as well as by their use of meter to imitate the rhythms of speech. "The Altar" and "Easter Wings," then, come close to representing the view that a true spoken language is one that vocalizes the hieroglyphic significance of the components of

[8]Hollander, *Vision and Resonance,* pp. 252–68.
[9]George Puttenham, *The Arte of English Poesie,* in *Elizabethan Critical Essays,* ed. G. Gregory Smith (Oxford: Oxford University Press, 1904), II, 95. For Puttenham, stanza forms in general are visual as well as metrical units. He reprints the shapes of various stanzas as blank lines of varying lengths, commenting: "Likewise it so falleth out most times your ocular proportion doeth declare the nature of the audible; . . . and this is by a naturall *simpathie* betweene the eare and the eye" (II, 89).

written language, written letters. Through the manipulation of meter, and thereby of typographical spaces, the speaker of "The Altar"
and "Easter Wings" literally speaks hieroglyphs. The word is both a
unit of speech and a physical design of ink on the page. Both Richard
Mulcaster and William Bullokar explained that writing involves the
translation of audible sounds into visible signs that merely store the
sounds, as it were, till they are translated back to sounds in reading.
As Bullokar put it, "in true Orthography, both the eye, the voyce, and
the eare consent more perfectly."[10] Herbert draws on this view of
writing in "The Altar" and "Easter Wings," but unlike Mulcaster and
Bullokar, he secures the visible marks of writing and their spatial
medium in a sacred order endowing them with significance of their
own; and (in contrast to the way Paul Ricoeur conceives of a text) he
treats them solely as points of reflection for sound alone. Thus Herbert's language, again, achieves the status of symbolic Hebrew letters.

In both "The Altar" and "Easter Wings" the speaking lines within
the poem's shape explain the spiritual significance of the material
form constituted by those lines, and in both poems the relationship
between material form and spiritual significance is neither simple nor
straightforward. For instance, Summers long ago pointed out that the
stone altars of the kind typographically shaped by "The Altar" were
outlawed in England by the Protestant reformers along with adherence to such doctrines as transubstantiation, the real presence,
and the sacrifice of the Mass, which the reformers called the Lord's
Supper and celebrated at a communion table rather than an altar.
That is, the kind of altar represented by the shape of the poem, with
few exceptions, no longer existed in English churches at the time
Herbert was writing his poems.[11]

---

[10]William Bullokar, *A Booke at large, for the Amendment of Orthographie for English Speech*
(London, 1580), sig. B1r; see also sig. B2v. I quote from the facsimile reprint edited by
J. R. Turner in *The Works of William Bullokar* (Leeds: University of Leeds, 1970), vol. 3.
John Hart appeals to the same aural-visual coordination in his proposal for orthographic reform. In framing a new alphabet so that each sound of English corresponds
to a single letter, he affirms that his alphabet "frame[s] with reason" the connections
between "the eye, the tongue, and the eare" (*A methode or comfortable beginning for all
vnlearned, whereby they may bee taught to read English* [London, 1570], sig. A3r). This work
is a practical application of ideas in Hart's *Orthographie* and actually uses pictures and a
variety of typefaces to demonstrate the aural-visual connections.

[11]Summers, *George Herbert;* pp. 141–42; see also Amy M. Charles, *A Life of George
Herbert* (Ithaca: Cornell University Press, 1977), pp. 228–33.

In addition, because the poem itself identifies the true altar as the heart, the hieroglyphic pictogram shaped by the poem is highly enigmatic. The thing signified by the hieroglyphic shape of the poem (the altar) seems to have little relationship, least of all a pictorial relationship, to the thing signified by the sense of the poem's words (the heart). The spoken lines of the poem explain the enigmatic significance into which the physical, written lines of the poem are shaped: they allude to Hebrew (rather than Catholic) stone altars, as well as to the Psalmic concept of the heart as the true altar. The Psalms were the liturgy of the Hebrew Temple's stone altar, as well as the typological prefiguration, first, of the sacrifice of Christ the Head on the cross and, second, of the spiritual sacrifice of the heart and inward worship of the Body of Christ in the Church. The coincidence of the poem's visual space (altar) and its uttered speech (heart) creates a hieroglyph of the typological organization of historical time whose fulfillment is reached in the Christian worship of the heart solemnized by the outward ceremonial of the Anglican church.

The hieroglyphic signification of the heart by the altar is thus part of a series of resemblances inherent in eucharistic theology, resemblances whose differences are essential in keeping similarity from becoming identity: Hebrew and Christian scriptures; Christ the Head and Christ the Body; body and blood of Christ, and bread and wine; outward ceremony and inward spiritual sacrifice. This polysemous network of things and their resemblances (as well as their differences) is held together in the poem by the coincidence of altar and heart, by the physical shape of the printed letters arranged in the form of a stone altar, which is simultaneously the uttered speech of the poet in the act of understanding those resemblances.[12] The word as thing and the word as speech intersect in the hieratic textual space of the hieroglyphic poem. But in three places in the poem the poet/speaker suggests he plays only a minor role in its composition. The poem's "parts are as thy hand [i.e., God's] did frame" (l. 3). The heart typologically linked to the altar "is such a stone, / As nothing but / Thy pow'r [i.e., God's] doth cut" (ll. 6–8). These lines intimate that the shape of the altar that is the poem is in fact chiseled by a divine hand

---

[12]For the polysemous nature of Renaissance hieroglyphs, see Boas, *Hieroglyphs of Horapollo*, p. 35; and Gombrich, *"Icones Symbolicae,"* p. 159.

rather than a human voice. Finally, the poet/speaker recognizes that
the edifice that is the poem will "sing" God's praise best "if I chance to
hold my peace" (l. 13). The poem's physical contours, shaped by God,
suggest its visual form is a metaphor for divine discourse. The divinely preordained visual text creates the possibilities of the poet's
meaningful speech.

"Easter Wings"—like the Mary anagram, "Love-joy," and "The
Altar"—also plays on the hieroglyphic representation of typological
time in sacred history, but unlike "The Altar," which is a hieroglyph
of a sacred artifact, "Easter Wings" is a hieroglyph of a natural object.
Herbert uses this image drawn from nature to symbolize the rising of
the resurrected Christ as well as the rising of those who participate in
the liturgical reenactment of the Resurrection on Easter, and he
represents this conflation of time emblematically in the "imping" of
one pair of wings (that is, one stanza) onto the other. But again like
the Mary anagram and "The Altar," the hieroglyphic nature of
"Easter Wings" draws on a particular conception of language as much
as it does on an allegorical understanding of creation.

The central image of the poem is man's fall and rise in the historical
scheme of redemption, an image that the poet connects with the act of
composing the poem:

> O let me rise
> As larks, harmoniously,
> And sing this day thy victories.
> [ll. 7–9]

The spatial metaphor of rising and falling is translated into the physical space taken up by the words printed on the page, words which,
again, correspond to the amplification and diminution of the metrical
units of spoken language; rising is translated into filling out the
meter. To rise harmoniously, then, is to modulate the size of the units
of poetic speech. At the same time, the length of the lines also signifies
temporal units. Long lines represent the beginning of either the race
(as in the first stanza) or the individual (as in the second); they also
represent the end of the redemptive process for the individual, specifically the speaker. Similarly, the short middle lines in both stanzas
represent the fallen spiritual state. To "sing . . . thy victories" is to
reify units of speech into a visual lexicon that graphically represents

both the spatial and temporal schemes of redemption. Like "The Altar," "Easter Wings" rests on a polysemous network of analogous things in nature and history—bird, man, human race, Christ—all encompassed in the physical pattern of blocks of letters which correspond to a pattern of uttered speech become meaningful in the hieroglyphic space we call the poem's text.

But as in "The Altar," the poet/speaker again qualifies his own role in the authorship of the poem. Its graphic form may be built out of units of metrical speech, but the prototype of that shape has a divine origin; the wing is not only the "shape" of the poet's voice, it is also a natural type of rising to redemption, and the poet has learned both the shape and its meaning by learning to "imp [his] wing on [God's]." The preceding poem, "Easter," reinforces the subordinate role of the poet's voice by treating it as an imitative voice in a polyphonic counterpoint whose melody is divinely ordained. In "Paradise," another poem whose sense depends on a visual play on words, the shortening of the rhyme word in each triplet is an expression of God's cutting, pruning, and paring of the poet, who is imagined as a tree in God's garden, until he and his word reach their "END." The hieroglyphic act is ultimately performed by God. In both "The Altar" and "Easter Wings," the spatial, hieroglyphic form amounts to the poet's disavowal of the poem as his own. The hieroglyph exists as a local manifestation of a visually conceived divine text prior to the poet's expression of his mental or spiritual state.

Herbert's pattern poems spell God's word by building up letters into pictures in which language, nature, and history intersect with the poet's spoken utterances, recorded in his written words. According to the conception of language implied by these poems, language, especially written language, reveals a divinely instituted connection between the things of creation and their spiritual significance, the same connection that is in turn the very basis of the Renaissance understanding of pictorial hieroglyphs. Such a view holds that language is a thing in the world like other things; its physical properties—spatiality, visibility, audibility—are tied to the spiritual significance of its referents and even possess similar ontological status as other material things. All these characteristics of Herbert's hieroglyphic use of language are of a piece with the merging of humanist views of language as printed, spatialized speech with Hebrew linguistic traditions as adopted to a Christian context by Reuchlin, Agrippa, and in popular form, Du Bartas.

Heather Asals has perceptively observed that Herbert's physical words have a "solidity" to them as "verbal icons," and as such form a "bridge" that establishes a "commerce between Heaven and Earth." "Poetic language," she remarks, "inhabits the ontological distance between the ink, the heart, and Christ himself, joining them as one."[13] In the terms used in this discussion, that ontological distance is the textual space that the poem both creates and occupies. As a manifestation of the divine, the spatial dimension of language lends surety to the power of language to signify. The space of a hieroglyphic text manifests not only the divine, however. It is a location in which elements of language are manipulated by a human hand and voice. As a place co-inhabited by divine and human forces, the hieroglyphic text is potentially the site of discordant discontinuities between heaven and earth which can impede the efficacy of language, erecting a barrier between the Word and the word.

The presence of other such discontinuities in the seventeenth century has, thanks to recent scholarship, become increasingly apparent. The interconnection between visual image, verbal symbol and the allegorical nature of the material world (including words) was often troubled, fragile, and sometimes vulnerable to collapse. S. J. Freedburg has argued that Italian mannerist art of the later sixteenth century often reveals a problematic disparity between sacred iconography and its profane treatment. Ernest Gilman has shown that the best-known example of the hieroglyphic, emblematic mode in English poetry, the emblem poems of Francis Quarles, must overcome "the discord of the confrontation" between text and picture, because the traditional correspondence between the visual "language *in rebus*" and the poetic "language *in verbis*" could no longer be taken for granted.[14]

Some of Herbert's poems exhibit a similar discord and disparity between the intelligible world of spirit and the power of the verbal

---

[13]Heather A. R. Asals, *Equivocal Predication: George Herbert's Way to God* (Toronto: University of Toronto Press, 1981), pp. 26–29, and all of chap. 1.

[14]S. J. Freedberg, *Painting in Italy, 1500–1600* (New York: Penguin, 1975), pp. 210, 219–20; Ernest B. Gilman, "Word and Image in Quarles' *Emblemes*," in *The Language of Images*, ed. W. J. T. Mitchell (Chicago: University of Chicago Press, 1980), p. 61.

icon to embody and express that world. *The Temple* responds to the seventeenth century's sense of discontinuities in the process of symbolization and the problematic nature of allegorical correspondence with a troubled dialectical debate over the issues of correspondence and symbolic language rather than with a unified presentation of a singular attitude. To paraphrase Asals again, for Herbert, language reminds man of both his sin and the possibility of redemption, of Egypt—or, more to the point, Babel—and Canaan.[15] Herbert's language stands suspended between Adamic Hebrew and Babel, often in painful awareness of the gap between the human and divine word.

Although Herbert's redeemed language has received much attention, his awareness of the constant threat of Babel has not. His ambivalence is in fact typical of his age and may thus be illuminated by some of the seventeenth-century discussions of the Adamic language. Renaissance opinion varied on the degree to which the Adamic language could actually shine through its derivative modern vernaculars. Even those such as Top who believed that the disparity between Hebrew and the vernacular could be closed also recognized the magnitude of the gap and the possibility that it could not be bridged. Goulart's commentary on Du Bartas illustrates a typical ambivalence about the properties of language after the linguistic decline that followed Adam's fall and Babel. Du Bartas himself claims that the primordial characteristics of Hebrew remained with the Jews after Babel and are apparent in the coincidence of the utterance of the prophets with sounds recorded by the divine alphabet of scripture. Similarly, Goulart remarks on the concordance of God's speaking and writing the Tables of the Law.[16] But beyond the continuity of the mystical properties of scriptural Hebrew, the nature of language is more problematic for Goulart, who at one time emphasizes the continuities and at another time the discontinuities between Hebrew and its vernacular descendants. This vacillation indicates an insecurity about the reliability of a representational language in human discourse. Adam's sin, for example, "made both his owne discourse, and

---

[15]Asals, *Equivocal Predication*, pp. 23–27; see p. 16 for the constant danger of Babel for the poet. Asals also points to the Puritan derogation of the materiality of even sacred writing.

[16]See Thomas Lodge's translation of Simon Goulart, *A Learned Summary upon the Famous Poeme of W. of Salustre* (London, 1621), p. 182 (hereafter cited as Lodge).

that of his posterities euer since defectiue vnapt, confused, and often-
times false in humane things" (Lodge, p. 186).[17] Nevertheless, Adam
retained the memory of his former eloquence, and that memory is the
foundation of all human knowledge of "the Sciences, the Arts, and
above all, the knowledge of the True God," and since the time of
Adam, "these things have beene more and more discovered" (Lodge,
p. 186). Accordingly, Adam's prelapsarian ability to signify transparently has been to some extent transmitted from Hebrew to Greek
and Latin and thence to the modern vernaculars (Lodge, p. 188). All
these languages in fact are the product of changes in Hebrew which
led to the development of new languages (Lodge, p. 187).

But in another swing in his attitude, Goulart points to inherent
problems in language after Babel, the two most significant of which
are the proliferation of languages and linguistic change, stark contrasts to the singular unity and permanence of Hebrew. As a rule,
Goulart treats human language as speech and asserts the origins of
speech in culture rather than in innate properties of the mind: a
person "should neuer speake or vnderstand any thing distinctly, if
first another spoke not before him" (Lodge, p. 176). Human language, that is, depends on usage. But ultimately usage is the history of
the corruption of Hebrew after Babel. Every language after Babel "is
but a corrupt, effiminate, and inconstant gibridge, . . . which changes
from age to age" (Lodge, p. 175). Adam's transparent language had
no need of usage. As the principle of inexorable change in the rules
that govern human speech, usage always threatens to interpose a
dark screen between knowledge and human understanding. All that
is to be understood must be apprehended through the veil of language, and the ancient repositories of knowledge are cast in a usage
that is not our own:

> in briefe, [man before Babel] might haue had an exact knowledge of
> all things, whereas now hee must spend all his life-time to learne the

[17]See also John Webster, who compares the "Macrocosm to God's book, in which . . .
every creature . . . [is] a capitall letter or character, and all put together make up that
one word or sentence of [God's] immense wisdome, glory, and power," but, he asks,
"alas! who spells them aright, or conjoyns them so together that they may perfectly
read all that is therein contained?" *Academarium Examen*, p. 28 (London 1653; facs. rpt.
in Allen G. Debus, *Science and Education in the Seventeenth Century: The Webster-Ward
Debate* (New York: American Elsevier: 1970).

words of the Hebrew, Greeke, and Latine tongues, that is to say, to learne to babble, and in stead of being excellently perfect in diuine and humane Philosophy, hee now bee now [*sic*] busied in sillables, words, periods, and other such exercises, which maketh vs haue white heads, and gray beards, without hauing any certaine knowledge of Diuinitie, Physicke, or Law, which are the principall Sciences. [Lodge, p. 173]

From one perspective, the grammatical study of languages is a way to overcome the effects of Babel, but from Goulart's perspective here, the study of language is the very sign of Babel and the very token of our mortality. Our study of language never quite enables us to penetrate the opacity of words but instead gives us white hairs that announce our approaching end. And even when we may seem to overcome the barrier of "sillables," all we prove is our attachment to mere mutability; our very proficiency in language draws attention to "the vanitie of humane vnderstanding, which ordinarily gloryeth in those things which are onely constant in vnconstancie" (Lodge, p. 188). Grammar, as the study of a spoken usage continually placed at an ever increasing distance from the transparency of Hebrew letters, is itself a sign of a fall into "linguistic drift" (to use Thomas Greene's term) rather than its remedy.[18] (It must also be said, however, that on other pages Goulart praises the eloquent powers of Greek, Latin, and the vernaculars. He wants to have it both ways.)

While Goulart insists on the connection between primordial Hebrew and the mutable vernaculars, he also points to the difference between an ideal, divinely ordained language and human speech. In one sense, the original language, whose significating powers are divinely guaranteed, transmits itself to all languages; in another sense, Hebrew represents an eternal, unchanging language that the mutable vernaculars based on custom and usage must measure themselves against—inevitably falling short. This kind of duality underlies a characteristic theme in Herbert's poetry: the recognition of a divinely ordained discourse that the poet's utterance must fit, if it can. Such pattern poems as "The Altar" and "Easter Wings" are particularly

---

[18]I am indebted here to the discussion of Dante and humanist philology in Thomas M. Greene, *The Light in Troy: Imitation and Discovery in Renaissance Poetry* (New Haven: Yale University Press, 1982), chap. 2.

conspicuous examples of occasions when the poet's metrical utterance exhibits powers divinely inscribed in the physical material of the written word. But those powers are not always available to the poet.

Herbert's disclaimer about his own authority is evidence of his place in the Renaissance debate, as described by John Guillory, over whether poetry is the product of divine inspiration or the mental powers of the poet.[19] To use the terms of Guillory's analysis, Herbert makes little claim for the self-sustaining validity of his text but instead validates it by association with sacred texts: spiritual events in the speaker's life parallel biblical events or are indeed typological continuations of biblical narrative ("Faith makes me any thing, or all / That I beleeve is in the sacred storie," Herbert's speaker proclaims in "Faith," ll. 17–18). Herbert's formal successes are in fact usually the result, or recognition, of dependence on divine intervention, as in "The Altar," "Easter Wings," "The Collar," "Denial," "A true Hymne," and "Paradise."[20] Herbert's poems follow a middle course between expressing mental acts of the poet and bodying forth an ideal language that logically and really preexists the mind of the poet. Critics who regard Herbert's poems as simply the product of the subjectivity that speaks them do not pay sufficient heed to the model of language and signification described by such writers as Goulart, the model inherent in Renaissance hieroglyphics considered as a theory of language rather than as a theory of pictorial representation (though the two are of course related). The subjectivity expressing itself in language is valorized when it finds itself part of a preexisting, divinely guaranteed text. When the poem cannot locate itself in that text, it is cut loose from the only agency that can validate its meaningfulness. This unmooring is precisely what happens in three separate but related poems in *The Temple*—"Sinnes round," "A Wreath," and "Grief"—which illustrate a fallen, failed strain in Herbert's poetry. Although each of these poems has a successful better-known counterpart in the volume, they themselves manifest the limitations of the hieroglyphic mode. Specifically, they point to the limitations of

[19]John Guillory, *Poetic Authority: Spenser, Milton, and Literary History* (New York: Columbia University Press, 1983), chap. 1.

[20]I have dealt with this issue, from the point of view of the musical metaphor through which Herbert expresses his sense of voice, in "Polyphonic Psalm Settings and the Voice of George Herbert's *The Temple*," *Modern Language Quarterly*, 42 (1981), 422–32.

the representational capacity of the material and spatial dimension of language itself.

"Sinnes round," "A Wreath," and "Grief" all concern the poet's sinful or spiritually deficient condition, and attempt to use the physical elements of language—especially the resources of sound in rhyme—to project some spiritual truth. These attempts, however, are not successful and end in the collapse of the poet's ability to name the spiritual world through the sensible word. At the same time, these poems posit an ideal discourse, but one unattainable by the poet who cannot "spell."

"Sinnes round," for example, explicitly associates its use of language with Babel. On the face of it, the poem has much in common with Herbert's other hieroglyphic poems. It grammatically organizes its words so that the final syntactic member of the last line of each stanza is repeated as the first syntactic member of the first line of each succeeding stanza. The poem thus provides a framework for the reification of those words into a spatial arrangement imitating the links of a chain. The spatial metaphor is further reinforced by the circular pattern formed by the repetition of the poem's first line as its last; and the circular shape is referred to in the "round" of the poem's title, which also refers to the musical round, a form of imitative counterpoint in which the sound patterns of musical motives are successively repeated in a polyphonic musical structure. That is, in accordance with the implications of its title, the poem depends on the material nature of language in its repetition of sounds and syntactic members and in its verbal imitation of the visual properties of a circle.

"Sinnes round" begins by assuming its hieroglyphic circular form is the proper vehicle for offering repentance to God. The word order of the keynote of the poem—"Sorrie I am, my God, sorrie I am"—is circular, with God appropriately at the center. The image of the circle, however, is soon at odds with itself, as the syntax of the first line is completed by the second:

> Sorrie I am, my God, sorrie I am,
> That my offences course it in a ring.
> [ll. 1–2]

In the second line we learn that the circle also represents the shape of the poet's sins for which he is repenting; the poet is sorry that his sins follow a circular, and thus continually repeated, pattern. The rest of the poem describes the three stages that constitute this ring of sin: sinful thoughts give rise to sinful words ("inventions"), which give rise to sinful deeds ("My hands do joyn to finish the inventions" [l. 13]), which in turn issue sinful thoughts, and so on. These three stages of sin Herbert likens to the "three stories" of the Tower of Babel. But in the very process of describing the three levels of sin's round, the poet has created a poetic circle in his concatenated invention that imitates not his repentance but his offenses. He has committed the very offense he laments. His words

> vent the wares, and passe them with their faults,
> And by their breathing ventilate the ill.
>
> [ll. 9–10]

The three-storied Tower of Babel describes not only the poet's sins but also the very language of the poem (made into three stanzas) he writes to purge himself of those sins. Poetic form imitates poetic meaning in a way that the speaker could hardly have intended and could hardly be proud of (though the persistence of the poet's pride is of course the point of the poem).

The result of the poet's loss of control over his own metaphor is a series of disjunctions arising out of the hieroglyph of the circle. At first suggesting the pleasing image of perfection, the circle soon assumes the terrifying shape of sin's trap, from which the poet cannot extricate himself. Moreover, the circle formed by the framing first and last lines, which express the intention to repent, does not coincide with the circle of "offence" which fills the frame. By the last line, "Sorrie I am" has become an apology not only for the poet's general sinfulness but also for the sinfulness of the hieroglyphic language of the very poem that it concludes—a sharp contrast to the successful hieroglyphic closure in "The Altar" and "Easter Wings." In the very act of forming and completing the circle, the last line rejects the circular sinfulness of the poem and erases the hieroglyph of the circle even as it completes it. Try as he might to arrange his repentance spatially in the hieroglyphic form of the poem, the poet succeeds in spatializing only his prideful poetic inventions. In "The Altar" the gap between the poem's spatial form and its meaning is only appar- ent, for the poem's shape is really part of a network of occult resemblances. In "Sinnes round," however, the disparity between the poem's textual space and its meaning is beyond repair. The Augustinian embrace of word, thing, and heart does not hold.

Herbert's successful hieroglyphic poems mesh the Hebrew view of speech and writing—that God's writing is latterly pronounced in human speech—and the humanist view—that human speech is the product of mind, consciousness, or moral perception latterly recorded in writing. In an apparent allusion to humanist linguistic theory, "Sinnes round" hints at Herbert's awareness of the humanist view of language and his failure to build his shaky hieroglyphic edifice upon it. Herbert's description of the progress from "inflamed thoughts" to "ill . . . words" moved by "lewd intentions" to "ill deeds" echoes some of the phrasing of Ascham's well-known passage on the relation between thought, language, and action:

> Ye know not, what hurt ye do to learning that care not for wordes, but for matter, and so make a deuorse betwixt the tong and the hart. For marke all aiges: look upon the whole course of both the Greeke and Latine tonge, and ye shall surelie finde, that, whan apte and good wordes began to be neglected . . . than also began, ill deedes to spring: . . . newe and fond opinions to strike with olde and trewe doctrine, . . . in religion. . . . of ill thoughts commeth peruerse judgement: of ill deeds springeth lewde taulke.[21]

Suffering from a failed spirit, the speaker of "Sinnes round" is unable to marshal the physical materials of language to construct a verbal emblem of anything but that failure.

Many of the spiritual and linguistic problems that beset the speaker of "Sinnes round" also trouble the speaker of "A Wreath." The various devices of rhyme and verbal concatenation that Herbert uses to weave the fabric of a garlanded offering of poetic praise to God are too well known to require description here.[22] The spatial arrangement of words into the intertwined pattern of a wreath reduces the poem's text to its etymological meaning (textus = woven fabric). The inversion of the first four rhyme words in the last four lines of the

---

[21]Roger Ascham, *English Works*, ed. William Aldis Wright (Cambridge: Cambridge University Press, 1904), pp. 265–66.

[22]See Judy Z. Kronenfeld, "Herbert's 'A Wreath' and Devotional Aesthetics: Imperfect Efforts Redeemed by Grace," *ELH*, 48 (1981), 290–309.

poem is similar to a stanza shape visualized by Puttenham as an "ocular example" of spatial poetic form.[23] Yet the poem consistently dismantles the wreathed garland as it constructs it. The first hemistich of many of the lines repeats the second hemistich of the previous line only to negate it; many of the verbs expressing the poet's confident ability to offer praise to God are seriously qualified as they are transformed into subjunctive, conditional, and future forms. The poet comes to envision the achievement and efficacy of his praise somewhere outside the poem, and, as in "Sinnes round," he ends by apologizing for the poem, his "poore wreath." The space of the poem has been emptied of its power to make words signify. What remains in that space is the detritus of a would-be language.

The use of rhyme in "Grief" closely follows that in "A Wreath" and "Sinnes round." Uncharacteristically for Herbert, "Grief" begins in a high style, as the poet summons water springs and rain clouds to supply him with tears. Presumably his grief is that of spiritual dejection, as the poem's last line, "Alas, my God!" suggests. Recognizing his own inability to find a language that measures up to an ideal discourse, the poet finally disclaims his poetry, acknowledging,

> Verses, ye are too fine a thing, too wise
> For my rough sorrows; cease, be dumbe and mute, . . .
> And keep your measures for some lovers lute,
> Whose grief allows him musick and a ryme:
> For mine excludes both measure, tune, and time.
>
> [ll. 13–18]

As in "A Wreath" and "Sinnes round," Herbert here uses rhyme to negate the meaning of rhyme: the poem's final rhymed couplet (ryme-time) has rhyme and meter as its subject only to announce the absence of true rhyme and meter in the poem. The poet finally expresses his grief—as well as the remedy for that grief—in the simple, detached line that is indeed out of "measure, tune, and time" with the rest of the poem: "Alas, my God!"

The title "Grief" presents two separate poetic spaces, two separate printed configurations on the page, one an eighteen-line pentameter poem of four quatrains and a couplet, the other a single line discon-

---

[23]Puttenham, *Arte of English Poesie*, in Smith, *Elizabethan Critical Essays*, II, 89.

tinuous with both the meter and rhyme of the preceeding lines. As it turns out, the space that seems most like a poem—cast in the "measure, tune, and time" of metrical, rhyming lines—is really only a "mutt'ring up and down" (to use a phrase from "A true Hymne") which cannot contain a meaning. On the other hand, meaning is contained in what seems least like a poem, the measureless, tuneless, and timeless detached line outside the "poem." The typographical, spatial arrangement of the poem into two separate units becomes, then, a kind of negative hieroglyph of the poem's inability to use the material resources of language to construct its meaning, except in the final line that is outside all the canons of verse and is in that sense, after all, as inchoate as the first rhymed, metered eighteen lines.

The material basis of language—its audibility and visibility—is thus analogous to the material world as the allegorical shadow of the immaterial world of spirit. In such poems as "The Altar" and "Easter Wings" the written words in the typographical, textual space body forth a richness of spiritual meaning through spoken sounds. And as the poet's ability to see earth as a shadow of heaven depends on his spiritual state, so too the poet's making, his use of the physical components of language to embody the spiritual significance of the created world, reflects his own spiritual condition. Marcia Colish's observation that in his *Confessions* "Augustine interprets his moral and intellectual failings in terms of his misuse of his linguistic faculties"[24] applies with equal validity to the speaker of Herbert's failed hieroglyphic poems. Ultimately, the capacity of the poet to integrate the material basis of language into a sacred order depends on his own place in that order at any given moment, in a relationship that continually fluctuates. Throughout *The Temple*, Herbert self-consciously worries about his ability to make meaning in language; the ups and downs of the state of his soul are finally reflected in the space of his words.

"Sinnes round," "A Wreath," and "Grief" all manifest a concern that informs *The Temple* as a whole: the ability of the human voice to speak God's "characteristical word," as John Webster put it. To the extent that Herbert's poems address the issues that concerned humanist grammarians and Cabalistic Hebraists, they are related to the

---

[24]Marcia L. Colish, *The Mirror of Language: A Study in the Medieval Theory of Knowledge* (New Haven: Yale University Press, 1968), p. 22.

Renaissance controversies about the connection between speech and writing. It is an interesting quirk of literary history that George Herbert should have been one of the scholars to whom his friend Francis Bacon, a prominent promoter of language reform, turned for help in translating *The Advancement of Learning* into Latin. It is tempting to imagine Herbert translating *De Augmentis* VI, i, where Bacon proposes a method of hieroglyphic writing as far removed from Herbert's own pattern poems as can be conceived.[25] We will never know if Herbert did actually translate that portion of the work, but the difference between the two friends' concepts of the hieroglyph represents an historic change in the way the visual linguistic sign was to be understood. A comparison of the vast differences between the views of Herbert and Bacon illuminates the beginnings of a rupture in English linguistic thought of the Renaissance, a rupture that was to be complete by the end of the century and whose repercussions were to be felt in both the scientific and imaginative literature of the period.

Bacon's linguistic ideas have been viewed primarily in relation either to his rejection of humanist language studies of the preceding century or to the linguistic innovations of his followers later in the seventeenth century. Consequently, Bacon scholarship has not paid sufficient attention to the place of Bacon's linguistic thought within the context of the hieroglyphic tradition of Du Bartas and Top, the tradition that underlies Herbert's pattern poems. Indeed, this tradition is particularly relevant to Bacon's ideas since much of his linguistic philosophy is embodied in his comments on hieroglyphic writing.[26]

Like Herbert and others who wrote in the older hieroglyphic tradition, Bacon affirmed the close connection between words and things.

[25]For differences between Bacon and Herbert, see William Sessions, "Bacon and Herbert and an Image of Chalk," in *"Too Rich to Clothe the Sunne": Essays on George Herbert* (Pittsburgh: University of Pittsburgh Press, 1980), pp. 165–78.

[26]My comparison between Bacon and his predecessors has benefited from Michel Foucault's distinction between Renaissance and "classical" discourse in *The Order of Things: An Archaeology of the Human Sciences* (New York: Random House, 1970), pp. 17–78. See also Hans Aarsleff on the Adamic language, "Leibniz on Locke on Language," in *From Locke to Saussure: Essays on the Study of Language and Intellectual History* (Minneapolis: University of Minnesota Press, 1982), esp. pp. 58–63; and Margreta de Grazia, "The Secularization of Language in the Seventeenth Century," *Journal of the History of Ideas*, 41 (1980), 319–29. My own conclusions about Bacon are similar to de Grazia's about seventeenth-century language theory in general.

But Bacon's ideas of hieroglyphic writing and linguistic reference directly oppose those embodied in Herbert's poems. As Sidney War-haft has argued, although Bacon believed in a providential order in the created world and saw a divine plan imprinted on the works of creation as signatures, for Bacon those signatures do not reveal occult resemblances or higher levels of spiritual meaning. Instead they re-veal both the logical and causative arrangement of things in the world. Accordingly, Warhaft suggests, Bacon rejected the idea that things are created analogously to each other as signs of each other, an idea essential to the linguistic underpinnings of Herbert's hiero-glyphic poems.[27]

Bacon's rejection of the analogical structure of reality colored his idea of the relationship between words and things. He maintained the primacy of writing over speech, but he rejected the Hebraist notion that language is a divinely ordained system of signs intrinsically re-lated to the things of the created world; he implied that language is radically separated from the world. Words thus have no existence other than as signs and mean nothing beyond the content of the things to which they refer. As Bacon interprets Echo's relationship to Pan in *The Wisdom of the Ancients*, Echo represents the language of true philosophy, which is "nothing else than the image and reflection" of nature, "to which it adds nothing of its own, but only iterates and

[27]Sidney Warhaft, "The Providential Order in Bacon's New Philosophy," *Studies in the Literary Imagination*, 4 (1971), 49–64. Bacon's objection to the ontological basis of resemblance in nature appears in several forms in the *De Augmentis:* for example, his rejection of the macrocosm-microcosm analogy (IV, 341), especially as formulated by Paracelsus (IV, 379–80), whom Bacon appears to regard as the chief contemporary proponent of this approach to nature. See also his rejection of sympathetic magic (IV, 367). The way in which Bacon transformed the idea of resemblance in nature is suggested by Lisa Jardine's discussion of Bacon's investigation of "forms" (*Francis Bacon: Discovery and the Art of Discourse* [Cambridge: Cambridge University Press, 1974], pp. 128–32. For the importance of analogy in alchemical and Paracelsian thought, see Debus, *Science and Education*, chap. 3. Bacon's rejection of magic, occult philosophies, Hermeticism, and Paracelsianism is discussed by Paolo Rossi, *Francis Bacon: From Magic to Science*, tr. S. Rabinovitch (1968; rpt. Chicago: University of Chicago Press, 1978), pp. 1–35. For, on the other hand, the influence of occult thought on Bacon and his followers, see Rossi, *Francis Bacon*, pp. 56–57; Frances A. Yates, *The Rosicrucian Enlight-enment* (London: Routledge & Kegan Paul, 1972), pp. 118–29, 171–92; Graham Rees, "Francis Bacon's Semi-Paracelsian Cosmology," *Ambix*, 22 (1975), 81–101, and "The Fate of Francis Bacon's Cosmology in the Seventeenth Century," *Ambix*, 24 (1977), 27–38; Vivian Salmon, *The Works of Francis Lodowick: A Study of his Writings in the Intellectual Climate of the Seventeenth Century* (London: Longman, 1972), pp. 95–96.

gives it back" (IV, 327).[28] An ideal language, then, such as one based on written hieroglyphs, would clearly and transparently represent the things it is instituted to signify.[29] The idea that letters and words are hieroglyphs coextensive with creation and possess an ontological status of their own as things would make no sense to Bacon, who helped put the visual linguistic sign on a new footing.

True, Bacon shares with his contemporaries the belief that language was originally able to pair word and thing accurately, that Adam named the animals with names that reveal their essence, as he says in *The Advancement of Learning* (III, 296), and though he believes that the Adamic language was lost after the Flood (III, 297), he sometimes speaks as if his new science would restore Adamic naming. The real goal of scientific knowledge, he observes in *Valerius Terminus*, "is a restitution and reinvesting (in great part) of man to that sovereignty and power (for whensoever he shall be able to call creatures by their true names he shall command them) which he had in his first state of creation" (III, 222). But for Bacon the restoration of the Adamic language has little to do with, say, Top's more traditional Cabalistic view of that language. Bacon's departure from traditional views is clearly illustrated by his analysis of problems of language and by his proposals for curing those problems. Both his analysis and his proposals bear heavily on his understanding of hieroglyphs.

In a well-known passage from Aphorism LX of the *Novum Organon*, Bacon complains about the lack of correspondence between words and things in language as it was used in his time: "[There] are either names of things which do not exist (for as there are things left unnamed through lack of observation, so likewise are there names which result from fantastic suppositions and to which nothing in reality corresponds), or [there] are names of things which exist, but get confused and ill-defined and hastily and irregularly derived from realities" (IV, 61). Here the faults in usage are a consequence of an

---

[28]All references to Bacon, both to the English and the Latin works, are from *The Works of Francis Bacon*, ed. James Spedding, Robert Leslie Ellis, and Douglas Denon Heath, 14 vols. (London: Longman, 1857–74; rpt. New York: Garrett Press, 1968).

[29]The theme of *res et verba* in Bacon, or Bacon's theory of the transparency of scientific language, has been put on a new conceptual footing by Timothy J. Reiss, *The Discourse of Modernism* (Ithaca: Cornell University Press, 1982), pp. 198–225. My own discussion of Bacon's treatment of the visual sign is similar in approach to Reiss's.

imperfect understanding of reality; words cannot properly refer to things because things are not yet sufficiently known. Similarly, Bacon explains in the same aphorism, the same word may have different, even opposed, meanings because a word that refers to the conditions of one phenomenon is abstracted from it and applied to another phenomenon. And unsupported by a view of creation based on analogy and resemblance, such applications can only be misapplications. Bacon's example is the word "humid." "Humid" correctly refers to certain properties of water, but when abstracted from the behavior of water and applied to other subjects—for example, the behavior of fire—the word cannot be accurate even though this usage is common in current speech. Bacon implies that each phenomenon must be studied according to its own natural history, out of which an accurate vocabulary will develop to describe that phenomenon. The inaccurate understanding of nature which arises from the misuse of the word "humid," then, is the result of insufficient empirical investigation, reliance on more similarity in nature than is warranted, and an inadequately differentiated vocabulary to name the discreteness of individual phenomena.[30]

Remedying the inadequate observation and understanding of nature is of course the object of many of Bacon's scientific innovations, especially the inductive method and the compilation of natural histories. The remedy for the linguistic consequence of this same inadequacy appears in *De Augmentis* VI, i, in a passage rarely mentioned in discussions of Bacon's linguistic thought, where Bacon discusses hieroglyphic writing, as well as literary, philosophical, and comparative grammar. Bacon's view of hieroglyphs appears perhaps most clearly in this context in which he recommends the proper applications for the various kinds of grammar and comments on guidelines for spoken language.[31] Bacon explains that literary grammar, "used sim-

---

[30]For a specific example of how the misuse of words has impeded natural history, and for Bacon's attempt at rectification, see his *Historia Ventorum*, V, 140, 145–46, 167, 174.

[31]That the context for the Renaissance interest in hieroglyphics extended beyond the allegorization of Egyptian writing has not been adequately explored. See, however, Madeleine David, *Le Débat sur les écritures et l'hiéroglyphe au XVIIe et XVIIIe siècles* (Paris: Ecole Pratique des Hautes Etudes, 1965), chap. 2; James Knowlson, *Universal Language Schemes in England and France, 1600–1800* (Toronto: University of Toronto Press, 1975), pp. 17–21; and Salmon, *Francis Lodowick*, pp. 128–56.

ply . . . [so] that [languages] may be learned more quickly and spoken more correctly and purely," provides "an antidote against the curse of the confusion of tongues . . . especially as sciences in our age are principally drawn from the learned languages and are not learned in our mother tongue" (IV, 440–41). A philosophical grammar, on the other hand, would remedy those linguistic consequences of the mismatch between words and things in current usage which Bacon complains of in the *Novum Organon*. A philosophical grammar would "diligently inquire, not the analogy of words with one another [that is, literary grammar as an aid to learning a foreign language], but the analogy between words and things, and reason" (IV, 441). Bacon here recommends something like the medieval discipline of *grammatica speculativa*, which elaborates the Aristotelian idea that the grammatical structure of language reflects the metaphysical structure of reality.[32] Bacon is careful to distinguish his projected philosophical grammar from its Platonic counterpart outlined in the *Cratylus* (and by implication, its biblical, Christian version as outlined, for example, by Top). In a statement that severely qualifies his other statements on Adamic naming, Bacon dismisses the view that "the imposition and original etymology of names . . . were not arbitrarily fixed, but derived and deduced by reason according to significance." This idea, he says, is "a subject elegant indeed, and pliant as wax to be shaped and turned, and . . . not without a kind of reverence,—but yet sparingly true and bearing no fruit" (IV, 441). Bacon instead seems to suggest that the ends of philosophical grammar could be best achieved by a comparative grammar, or a survey of existing languages, "showing in what points each excelled, in what it failed. For so . . . the several beauties of each may be combined . . . into a most beautiful image and excellent model of speech [*oratio*] itself, for the right expressing of the meaning of the mind" (IV, 442; Latin: I, 654).

Bacon does not comment extensively on any of his several suggestions for language reform in *De Augmentis* VI, i, nor do his various remarks necessarily amount to a systematic exposition of linguistic

---

[32]Though Bacon consistently identifies Scholastic thought with the hated syllogism, his apparent reference here to medieval speculative grammar suggests some awareness that Scholastic logicians made attempts similar to his own to formulate a scientific connection between words and things. If so, that awareness did not mitigate his hostility to Scholastic logic.

reference. It is therefore often difficult to determine precisely the implications of his linguistic thought. Nevertheless, he seems to suggest here that an ideal language does not depend on an intrinsic relationship between its words and its referents; rather, it would establish a fixed, but arbitrary, connection between words and the mind's correct understanding of nature.[33] Further, the physical marks signifying letters and words in such a language would not occupy a privileged position and would not be inextricably and intrinsically related to their referents. That is, they would not have the same mystical property that Hebrew letters and words have for Top, nor, like Herbert's hieroglyphic pictograms, would they strive to be part of a system of resemblances inherent in the order of creation. Moreover, for Bacon, there is no one language that by its very nature properly matches words and things, as Hebrew did for Top and Latin did for medieval speculative grammarians. Bacon finds that all natural languages have advantages and disadvantages; accordingly, a comparative grammar would make it possible to invent—or, to use Bacon's word, "obtain"—a better, more serviceable language.

Bacon hardly advocates a return to the language of Adam through the recovery of the powers exemplified by Hebrew, which can accurately refer to things because its words were divinely created and coeval with things themselves. The ideal language is not given by God, as the Hebraists would have it. Nor does it arise from the conventions of usage that evolve in a social order, as the humanists believed. And while Bacon's view may appear to rely on the Aristotelian connections among things, mind, and the sounds of speech, Bacon differs from Aristotle in one extremely significant way. Aristotle was explaining how the grammatical structure of an actual language reflects the ontological structure of reality. Even the medieval adapters of Aristotle, the speculative grammarians, though they were not interested in language as speech, assumed that that ontological structure was embodied in a natural language. For Bacon, however, actual existing languages reflect primarily the vulgar misconceptions

---

[33]Bacon vacillates between a view of language in which words refer directly to things (as in his view of hieroglyphs and in his statement in *The Advancement of Learning* that "words are but the images of matter" [III, 284]), and the view in which language refers to things through the mediation of the mind.

of things (the Idols of the Marketplace), stubbornly perpetuated by the linguistic conventions that are the basis of spoken language.

The only type of language that can accurately communicate the structure of reality is one that is artificially designed through philosophical and comparative grammar. Such a language itself has no secure existence as a thing in the world, except insofar as it is composed of fragments of existing languages. As a mental discourse, it exists only in the minds of those who properly understand the nature of things. As an expression of this mental discourse, it exists primarily in written marks recorded on paper rather than in spoken utterance. Bacon may be well aware of the humanist view that, in conventional language, letters represent the sounds that are the constituent forms of words (IV, 360–61), but he does not envision speech as the constituent basis of scientific communication. Although in the allegory of Pan in *The Wisdom of the Ancients,* he does refer to nature as a voice divulging knowledge of itself, his use of "voice" is metaphorical: nature's voice is to be transcribed by the scientist as writing, "for that is the true philosophy which echoes most faithfully the voices of the world itself [*mundi ipsius voces*], and it is written [*conscripta*] as it were at the world's own dictation" (IV, 327; Latin: I, 530). Thus, although Bacon refers to language fashioned from comparative grammar as a form of *sermo,* speech, it is difficult to imagine such a grammar actually being spoken. It would more likely be read in a book.

Indeed, Bacon further removes his language from speech by detaching it from words themselves. To compensate for one of the most serious deficiencies of natural language—its lack of a fixed and univocal relationship between word and referent—he turns to the visual symbols of hieroglyphs and real characters as the most efficient means of liberating language from the obfuscating conventions associated with words.[34] Bacon's views thus signal a major change in the Renaissance understanding of hieroglyphs. This change is implied in Bacon's definition of the hieroglyph and real character: "The Notes

---

[34]Throughout Book III of his *Essay Concerning Human Understanding,* Locke too associates the problems of language with the problems inherent in the way convention shapes speech. John M. Steadman points out that Locke was not alone in proposing the soundless signs of mathematical symbols as a solution for scientific discourse (*The Hill and the Labyrinth: Discourse and Certitude in Milton and His Near-Contemporaries* [Berkeley: University of California Press, 1984], pp. 23–24).

of Things . . . which carry a signification without help or intervention of words, are of two kinds: one *ex congruo,* where the note has some congruity with the notion, and the other *ad placitum,* where it is adopted and agreed upon at pleasure. Of the former kind are Hieroglyphs and Gestures; of the latter the Real Character above mentioned [in his discussion of Chinese characters]" (IV, 439–40). The hieroglyph, that is, has an intrinsic relation to its referent, whereas the real character is conventionally related to its referent.

Even though Bacon saw disadvantages in real characters, it is the nature of conventionally agreed upon real characters which determines his view of hieroglyphs. Hebraists such as Top would have looked at the relationship the other way around. Bacon considers both real characters and hieroglyphs as equally valid methods of signification, barring practical difficulties, and this position suggests he saw nothing in itself superior about a system of signs in which the signs are congruously related to the things they signify. For Bacon, in fact, congruous signification means only that hieroglyphs are pictures of the thing (or idea) to which they refer, not that a sign, thing, and its allegorical meaning are all connected in a divinely ordained correspondence between language and things.

In thus emphasizing the pictorial, visual aspect of the linguistic sign, Bacon dismisses the conceptual foundation of the hieroglyph as definitively formulated for the Renaissance by Valeriano, Ficino, and Horapollo, a foundation based on the belief that hieroglyphs embody the allegorical structure of creation. Unlike the highly symbolic hieroglyph of Renaissance tradition, Bacon's hieroglyph is univocal rather than polysemous, transparent rather than opaque, and it has a clear and singular rather than an enigmatic relation to its meaning.[35] While Herbert's hieroglyphs, for example, frame an inherent tension between divine writing and the human voice that must match it, Bacon's hieroglyphs dissolve that tension and preclude the failure of signification that may arise when the human voice falters. The system of correspondence that can go awry, thereby issuing words that cannot match their referents, is exactly what Bacon was trying to discard.

[35]My view of Bacon's hieroglyphs differs from that of James Stephens, who connects Bacon's view of hieroglyphs to "cryptic pictures" and the didactic use of similitude and parable (*Francis Bacon and the Style of Science* [Chicago: University of Chicago Press, 1975], pp. 71, 124–30).

Whereas failed correspondence may be spiritually instructive to Herbert, it did not suit the needs of Baconian science. Bacon's hieroglyph is, above all, a purely rational rather than hieratic instrument of meaning which all but denies the divine presence of language in the world.[36]

The transparency and univocality that Bacon attributes to the hieroglyph are the particular qualities that in his view make it a useful form of writing. Bacon's view of written letters and their role in constituting words, in fact, follows from his understanding of hieroglyphs. This view, and Bacon's conception of language generally, are illuminated by his comments on orthography. Bacon's brief discussion of spelling in *De Augmentis* VI, i, reflects the humanist debate (which continued well into the seventeenth century) about the proper rationale for English orthography. In the sixteenth century some orthographers, such as Richard Mulcaster, argued that spelling only approximates pronunciation. As pronunciation changes, spelling remains the same, preserved by custom and convention, the only reasonable basis of spelling. Others, John Hart, for example, argued that custom and convention perverted the only rational guide to spelling, the precise correspondence of letters to sounds. They advocated a new system of spelling, including the creation of new letters. Bacon supported neither position. Denigrating the entire humanist quest for a rationale for English spelling, he goes further than Mulcaster in denying that there is any rationale, and he relegates the idea that "spelling should agree with the pronunciation" of words to "the class of unprofitable subtleties" (IV, 444). Bacon seems to imply that letters, the material foundation of writing, have no intrinsic or rational relation to the words they compose.

The diminished status to which Bacon reduces letters by making them arbitrary components of words—a status unthinkable for those

---

[36]It is not surprising that the best-known executor of Bacon's linguistic recommendations, John Wilkins, should brush aside the hieratic writing of Egyptian hieroglyphs that had fascinated Europe for two centuries. He casually observes that "there is reason to doubt whether there be anything in these [Egyptian hieroglyphs] worth the enquiry, the discoveries that have been hitherto made out of them being but very few and insignificant. They seem to be but a slight, imperfect invention, suitable to those first and ruder Ages. . . . And it seems to be questionable, whether the *Egyptians* did not at first use their *Hieroglyphs* . . . for want of *Letters*" (*An Essay Towards a Real Character, and a Philosophical Language* [London, 1668], p. 12).

in the tradition of Du Bartas and Top—is also related to his use of letters in his proposal for a system of ciphers, or secret writing. Bacon himself had more than a passing interest in ciphers and alphabets. He used Greek letters as a cipher in his private notes (see XIV, 3, 48, 389); he refers to a work of his own on alphabets (XI, 134), a work now lost. In *De Augmentis* he proposed a cipher according to which each letter of a word can be translated into an arbitrary though regular "transposition of two letters through five places." *A* is thus disguised as *Aaaaa, B* as *Aaaab, C* as *Aaaba,* and so on. Such a system, Bacon argues, "has the perfection of a cipher, which is to make anything signify anything" (IV, 445). Here Bacon tellingly conceives of letters as arbitrarily signifying other letters, which themselves arbitrarily designate words in writing. In a sense, for Bacon language in general is like this system of ciphers; it parallels the world of things but has no contact with it except insofar as the univocal, arbitrarily assigned words refer to those things. Language, that is, cannot be justified through the order of nature. One word is as good as another; each must simply be established by the consensus of its knowing users.

Bacon's attitude to the place of writing in the order of things may be suggested by his use of the highly charged term, the *abecedarium naturae,* or the alphabet of nature. Though Top, for example, never uses this phrase, he does outline an alphabet of nature in a very concrete sense: letters, he says, were created along with the things to which they are attached through their power of signification. Bacon, however, in the first book of the Latin *De Augmentis,* speaks explicitly of the natural world as an *abecedarium naturae* whose reader—the scientist—ascends from its simple letters to its syllables, "and so by degrees to read in the volume of God's works" (*ad textum et volumen ipsum creaturarum expedite legendum ascendere* [III, 292; Latin: I, 461]). But for Bacon the idea that letters are part of the natural world has become nothing more than an attractive "magistral" metaphor. In a fragment of a work actually titled the *Abecedarium Naturae,* Bacon reveals more specifically his understanding of the relationship between nature and the basic components of language. Bacon lists over seventy proposed subjects of inquiry into natural phenomena, each denoted by letters of the alphabet. He calls the entire list the alphabet of nature. Only a very small part of the list is extant, but it indicates quite clearly that Bacon sees the letters of this *abecedarium naturae* as merely a convenient, provisional means of organizing a series of investigations, the results of which are not yet known:

> The titles [of the subjects of inquiry] by which the order of the alphabet is arranged should by no means have such authority as to be received for true and fixed division of things. For this would be to profess that we know the things which we inquire; since no one can divide things truly who has not a full knowledge of their nature. Let it be enough if the titles are convenient for the course of inquiry, which is our present business.   [V, 210]

Bacon's *abecedarium naturae*, far from being a series of written signs which acts as the foundation and signification of the order of nature (as in Reuchlin, Agrippa, Du Bartas, Lodge, and Top), has become a scientist's methodological instrument. The letters by which the natural alphabet proceeds have no relationship at all to the phenomena to be investigated. In other words, unlike the traditional *abecedarium naturae* of someone such as Top, Bacon's letters are separated from the world they only provisionally signify.[37]

This removal of the visual linguistic mark from the world it represents is Bacon's real innovation. Bacon's role in developing the seventeenth-century view of language based on a correspondence of words and things has long been recognized, but the belief in such a correspondence was in itself nothing new. As we have seen, it ap-

---

[37]Some proponents of alchemical and Paracelsian thought in the mid-seventeenth century saw themselves as followers of Bacon and proposed hieroglyphic writing of the kind I am claiming Bacon rejected. See, for example, Webster, *Academarium Examen*, pp. 27–29, in Debus, *Science and Education*. (Webster, however, also appeals to Aristotelian and humanistic language theory.) Rees believes that Webster responds to a real Paracelsian thread in Bacon, whereas Webster's Baconian opponent, Seth Ward, is what Rees calls a "Royal Society Baconian" of the kind that flourished after the Restoration, a selective Baconian lacking all traces of Bacon's real Paracelsianism ("Fate of Bacon's Cosmology," pp. 31–35). In *Rosicrucian Enlightenment*, pp. 171–92, Yates suggests an interdependence between Bacon's followers (including the founders of the Royal Society) and the Rosicrucians. Salmon also notes an association of early members of the Royal Society with Rosicrucian thought but is cautious about affirming the influence of their mystical views of language on later seventeenth-century linguistic thought (*Francis Lodowick*, pp. 95–96). For the Royal Society's rejection of some of its founding members' association with occult thought, and for Thomas Sprat's repression of such associations in his *History of the Royal Society*, see Aarsleff, *From Locke to Saussure*, p. 231, specifically on Sprat's treatment of Comenius.

peared, in varied forms, in Plato, Aristotle, the Stoics, medieval speculative grammar, and even in the work of some humanists. It was also
prevalent in the linguistic tradition that makes its English appearance
in Top's *Oliue Leafe*. Similarly, Bacon's was not the only system of
artificial writing introduced in the seventeenth century (treatises on
shorthand were popular in Bacon's day). But by combining some
disparate elements from his predecessors in a new synthesis, Bacon
provided a new theoretical grounding for the written linguistic sign
and drastically changed the way we conceive the relationship between
words and things. Although Bacon is commonly held responsible for
unifying word and object, his redefinition of linguistic reference actually divided the word from the same social or ontological substratum
as the thing it signifies. Paradoxically, he did more than any of his
predecessors to sever language from any secure foundation in the
world.[38] Whereas for Top the originary visual symbol guarantees the
bond between word and thing, for Bacon the artificial visual symbol
keeps word and thing apart in a system of transparent signification.
And while for Herbert space is the sacred medium of divinely created
shapes to which his hieroglyphic poems ideally aspire—wallowing in
the linguistic mire when they do not fulfill that aspiration—for Bacon
space is only an efficient medium of the linguistic sign to convey
meaning free of conventions traditionally attached to words.[39] It is
simply the neutral medium in which his hieroglyphs are situated.
Bacon's visual symbols do not share the metaphysics underlying Herbert's poetic pictograms. Because the Baconian visual sign mirrors
the world by fiat, the task of maintaining the correspondence between
word and thing must necessarily be never ending (a task the Royal
Society would later take upon itself), for the artificially devised word
always threatens to split asunder from the thing it represents. G. A.
Padley, in fact, has argued that in the elaboration of Bacon's linguistic
philosophy by Hobbes and Locke, the separation between word and
thing reaches a dangerous extreme: it becomes difficult to know

---

[38]Rossi, *Francis Bacon*, p. 170, seems to make a similar point. For a different view, see
Maurice B. McNamee, "Bacon's Inductive Method and Humanistic Grammar," *Studies
in the Literary Imagination*, 4 (1971), 81–106.
[39]Later universal language schemes included methods of pronouncing the written
universal characters; see Salmon, *Francis Lodowick*, pp. 25–30.

whether the relationships established among the names of things actually correspond to the relationships among things themselves.[40]

In removing the word from the world, Bacon radically alters the idea of authority inherent in Herbert's use of the divine hieroglyph as the prototype of his poetic language. Herbert—especially in the "Jordan" poems and those which play on their own formal construction—may speak self-consciously about poetic vocation, but much of his poetry does not claim an authority of its own. Rather, Herbert deprecates his own poetic ability and frequently leans on some notion of divine intervention in the process of composition. One might say that while Herbert is a poet, he is not an author, in the full sense that word acquires with Jonson. Jonson's works, particularly as they appear in print, stridently call attention to their origins in the intellectual and moral insight of the poet's mind, and this insight authorizes his statements to be considered seriously by a select and specific audience. Jonson is among the most successful in a line of "laureate poets" (to use Helgerson's phrase) that includes Spenser, Drayton, and Daniel. Poetic vocation of this kind—that is, of the full-time author—is comparatively rare in the English Renaissance, and Herbert certainly did not belong to this category, as the facts of his biography attest.

Herbert in fact frequently measures a poem's success by the distance between the poet/speaker and the poem's true Author, or at least by the poet/speaker's recognition of his subsidiary role as the poem's validating originator. In this sense, the poems' attitude toward their own authorship is strikingly different from that implied in Walton's pledge that Herbert's manuscript is faithfully recorded in the printed edition. (A similar claim is made on the title page of Milton's 1645 *Poems*.) For Walton the authenticity of the printed edition lies in its direct connection to the originator of the manuscript and to his final instructions on his death bed. The speaker of the poems, however, seeks to guarantee the poems' authenticity by effacing, or at least subordinating, his role as originator. The printers' notice to the reader echoes Walton, stating that the printed volume offers the word exactly as Herbert composed it in its "naked sim-

[40]G. A. Padley, *Grammatical Theory in Western Europe, 1500–1700* (Cambridge: Cambridge University Press, 1976), pp. 141–42, 150–55.

plicitie, with which [Herbert] left it, without any addition either of support or ornament, more then is included in it self." (Nicholas Ferrar is generally regarded to be the author of the "printers'" remarks.)[41]

But Ferrar goes even further by suggesting he is unveiling the record of a purely private colloquy with God, allowing the reader to look over the poet's shoulder, as it were, in his meditation. Referring to "The Dedication," Ferrar asks, "The dedication of this work having been made by the Authour to the *Divine Majestie* onely, how should we now presume to interest any mortall man in the patronage of it?"[42] Ferrar here plays on the common use of dedications to attract a patron, and he seems to suggest, uncomfortably, that the reader can indeed buy the book of poems even though it recognizes only God as its patron. Ironically, while Ferrar regards the dedication as the very mark of the poet standing behind or within the poem, the poet himself uses the dedication to disconnect himself from their authorship:

> Lord, my first fruits present themselves to thee;
> Yet not mine neither: for from thee they came,
> And must return. Accept of them and me,
> And make us strive, who shall sing best thy name.

Yet even as he detaches himself from the source of the poems, the poet invites potential readers to see him and even themselves in the poems:

> Turn their eyes hither, who shall make a gain:
> Theirs, who shall hurt themselves or me, refrain.

Ferrar's interchange with the text through the dedication thus reveals intriguing ambiguities in both his and Herbert's attitudes toward authorization and publication. Ferrar seeks Herbert's personal spirituality transcribed in the manuscript as validating the poems' authenticity and authority; Herbert eschews authorial validation. Ferrar regards the poems as a private exchange between Her-

---

[41]See Hutchinson, *Works of George Herbert,* pp. 3 and 476.
[42]Ibid., p. 3.

bert and God, almost apologizing for publishing them; Herbert explicitly addresses his readers. (Strangely, the dedication, with the same address and invitation to future readers, appears in the Williams manuscript, which does not seem intended for publication.) Finally, while appearing to apologize for his almost illicit publication, Ferrar was of course responsible for actively pursuing the printing of *The Temple.* Clearly, both publisher and poet are engaging in a complex set of gestures displaying, and displacing, their ambivalence about publication, much as the poet/speaker has reservations about considering himself as an author.

A similar ambivalence is apparent in Herbert's relationship—or lack of one—with an audience. Like the courtly amateur poets, Herbert shunned print, at least in his lifetime. Herbert, however, did not even have an identity as a coterie poet: there is no evidence that any of his poetic manuscripts circulated among friends.[43] This reticence is itself a striking example of a denial, of sorts, of authorial status. Herbert did not use manuscript poetry as a means of maintaining political and social connections or as a means of courtly advancement, as it seems Donne tried to do. (*Musae Responsoriae,* with its triple dedication to James, Charles, and Laud, may be an exception, though it was never printed in Herbert's lifetime.)[44] Nevertheless, his final instructions to Duncon to have his "little Book" published rather than burned if "it may turn to the advantage of any dejected poor Soul"[45] is as much a deliberate if posthumous gesture of authorial self-assertion as it is a gesture of humility. Even more telling is a letter by John Ferrar, Nicholas's brother, who records that "of all his Papers" Herbert singled out his "Divine Poems" for possible publication, if Ferrar "thought good" of them.[46] Moreover, the Williams manuscript, the only surviving manuscript of *The Temple* owned by Herbert himself, shows signs of Herbert's close attention to the details of the collection as a book over a long period of time, even though the manuscript appears to be in the secretary hand of a copyist rather than in Herbert's own recognizable italic hand.[47]

[43]Charles, *Life of George Herbert,* p. 78.
[44]Ibid., p. 91.
[45]Walton, *Lives,* p. 314.
[46]Quoted in Charles, p. 182 n. 11.
[47]Ibid., pp. 79–80. Charles believes the secretary hand is Herbert's own. Nevertheless, as Charles points out, p. 76, Herbert seems to have had a copyist who sometimes even traveled with him.

The ambiguities evident in Herbert's view of himself as an author—in the Jonsonian sense—manifest themselves as well in the interplay between Herbert's successful and failed hieroglyphs, the drama that is at the heart of the problematic of language in *The Temple*. Bacon, however, in designing a written sign that eradicates anything problematic in language, also eliminates the problems of authority which troubled Herbert. By removing the word from divine originary writing, and by depleting language of any ontological substance of its own, Bacon, unlike Herbert, makes the subjectivity that issues words their only authorizing agent.[48] For Bacon the true sign should be a transparent glass between the thing and the mind, as long as the mind's "enchanted glass" is cleared of distorting refraction; the utility of a *signum* depends on the perspicacity of a particular mind. The possessor of such a mind—the scientist equipped with the inductive method—is also the possessor of the authoritative word that qualifies him for authorship. In his transformation of the hieroglyphic tradition, Bacon continues to assert the primacy of the written word but in a way that now calls attention to the importance of writing in transmitting and preserving knowledge, an important theme throughout his scientific works. Elizabeth Eisenstein has argued that the promotion of symbolic writing in Bacon's time—especially in mathematics—is related to the rise of print.[49] Bacon's praise of the printing press, though not a consideration in his theoretical discussions of language, is clearly related to his elevation of the written word for scientific communication. In his remarks on printed publication, his interest in writing shades into his interest in authorship. Authorship and print of course have a social rather than a metaphysical context, and Bacon's emphases on written scientific communication, making scientists into authors, demanded changes in the social identity of the scientist and philosopher. Bacon's concept of authorship, and his practice as an author, must therefore be looked at from a perspective that takes account of his social and political relationship to court life.

[48]For interesting remarks on the emergence of the authoritative subject in Bacon and others, see Don E. Wayne, "Poetry and Power in Ben Jonson's *Epigrammes:* The Naming of 'Facts' or the Figuring of Social Relations?" *Renaissance and Modern Studies,* 23 (1979), esp. 94–100.

[49]Elizabeth Eisenstein, *The Printing Press as an Agent of Change* (Cambridge: Cambridge University Press, 1979), pp. 532–35.

6/

Print and Manuscript: Bacon's Early Career and the Occasions of Writing

IN 1600 Francis Bacon fulfilled his duty to Queen Elizabeth by prosecuting his erstwhile friend and patron, the Earl of Essex, for treason. After Essex was executed, Bacon was instructed by Elizabeth to write for publication *A Declaration of the Practices and Treasons Attempted and Committed by Robert Late Earl of Essex Against Her Majesty and Her Kingdoms*, which was printed in 1601 (IX, 239–321).[1] Sensitive to the charge of opportunism which dogged him as the betrayer of his benefactor, Bacon wrote and in 1604 published *Sir Francis Bacon His Apologie, in Certaine Imputations Concerning the Late Earle of Essex*. James I, who liked Essex, had just acceded to the throne, and Bacon wanted to increase his chances for political success under the new monarch.

Toward the end of the work, Bacon explains that Elizabeth had "commanded" him to write the *Declaration*. After finishing it, he explains, he "propounded it to certain principal councillours, by her majesty's appointment, [after which] it was perused, weighed, censured, altered, and made almost a new writing, according to their Lordships' better consideration" (X, 159). After that, it was "perused by the Queen herself, and some alterations made again by her appointment" (X, 159). Even after it went to print, Elizabeth made

[1] All references to Bacon's works are from *The Works of Francis Bacon*, ed. James Spedding, Robert Leslie Ellis, and Douglas Denon Heath, 14 vols. (London: Longman, 1857–74 rpt. New York: Garrett Press, 1968). All references to Bacon's letters are from the *Life and Letters of Francis Bacon*, ed. James Spedding (London, 1861–74), published as vols. VIII–XIV of *Works*.

further changes. With an obvious design on the sympathy of readers who might condemn his role in trying his former patron, Bacon relates that the queen objected to his calling his old friend "My Lord Essex" and made him change the wording to "Essex, or the late Earl of Essex"; the queen, Bacon records, went so far as to suppress already printed copies with the original epithet and then had the work "printed *ab ovo*" (X, 160). Whatever Bacon's political motives, the passage intimates the working conditions of the court writer and is one more instance of the well-known dilemma of the educated man at court which recurs in the humanist literature of the period. The main intent of the passage is to insist on how little control and authority the hired pen has over its own writing; Bacon's writing at court, he is at pains to suggest, effaces his own authorship. It is really the queen and her councilors who control the writing of the work.

In stark contrast to the attitudes apparent in this work is that expressed in the preface to the *Magna Instauratio*. Although at the time he wrote this preface (in 1620), Bacon was lord chancellor and a close confidant of King James (and thus much higher on the scale of power and position than when he wrote the *Apologie*), the preface was not a product of court life, nor does Bacon present it as such. While the *Apologie*, like Bacon's manuscript works, addresses a specific, immediate audience in order to produce immediate results, the preface to the *Magna Instauratio* is, to a great extent, addressed to an unknown, unseen posterity. In the former work, Bacon's identity is that of a political actor involved in the affairs of his time; in the latter, he transcends the occasional concerns of the court, projecting his authority by portraying himself as an objective seeker of truth for ages yet to come. In the *Apologie*, Bacon is a courtier who also writes; in the preface he is a writer who has chosen to become, and wishes to be remembered as, an *author*. In actual fact, Bacon had always done a great deal of writing, including letters seeking patronage, papers outlining positions on state policy (concerning the Church, royal finances, and war), legal briefs, and notes reminding himself of what to say in conferences with the king and his ministers. But it is primarily in his scientific works that Bacon thinks of himself as an author, transcribing materials that go beyond the ephemeral matters of state and court.

Bacon's claim to a future audience was based on his faith in the endurance of books. Although he disparaged the negative influence of books on the progress of knowledge, his own final scientific achievement (the *Magna Instauratio*) was itself a book, and he believed that one of the primary goals of the scientist was to write an exhaustive natural history, "the book of God's works, a kind of second Scripture," housed in a library he imagines as one of the final products of the investigation and interpretation of nature (IV, 261). Indeed, apart from his contributions to the history of science and philosophy, Bacon was in many ways a pioneer in both the theory and practice of publication as a means of scientific and philosophical communication. His innovativeness is evident in his promotion of an artificial language for science and his support of the printing press as a means to disseminate knowledge. From both the linguistic and the social points of view, Bacon helped establish the authorial scientific identity. The linguistic and social aspects of scientific communications are separate but parallel themes in Bacon's concept of the role of writing in the formulation and preservation of knowledge. On the one hand, that is, Bacon's promotion of an artificial language has a philosophical and linguistic context: as we have seen, Bacon's understanding of the linguistic sign's relationship to reality led him to view properly representative language as primarily writing rather than speech. The linguistic sign is a spatial mark visually apprehended, the instrument of the scientist, who must, as we shall see, transmit the written record of his work. Bacon's exploitation of the printing press, on the other hand, has a social context: Bacon as author seeking publication can be understood in relation to the forces that move the politically active courtier to redefine himself as an intellectual with an ambivalent relationship to the court.

In ultimately stressing the importance of scientific authorship, Bacon takes a relatively unpopular position in the debate among Renaissance scientists regarding printed publication. Whereas Galileo, for example, actively sought publicity through the printing press, Copernicus shunned publication, preferring to circulate his work in manuscript to a chosen few.[2] These two attitudes toward publication were

---

[2]Elizabeth Eisenstein, *The Printing Press as an Agent of Change* (Cambridge: Cambridge University Press, 1979), p. 453. Eisenstein, pp. 3–4, recognizes the importance of Bacon's praise of the printing press. For her exhaustive discussion of Renaissance scientists' attitudes toward printed publication, see pp. 520–74.

typical of literary writing as well, as the careers of Ben Jonson and John Donne illustrate. Donne was primarily interested in advancement at court and wrote poetry as an amateur, circulating his poems in manuscript to an aristocratic coterie. But he tried to keep his social identity separate from his writing. The few occasions on which he did print, or only planned to print, his poems caused him great embarrassment as a violation of an aristocratic code that regarded printed authorship as socially gauche.[3] Authorship—as opposed to amateur writing in manuscript—was antithetical to courtiership. Donne's friend Jonson, on the other hand, though attached to the court as a writer, was not interested in courtiership as such but worked hard at creating a public identity as an author by having his poems and plays printed.[4] By the late sixteenth and early seventeenth centuries, printed publication had become a technological means that provided an opportunity for a new form of social identity, as Jonson was among the first to realize.

Depending on his changing relationship to the court at different times in his life, Bacon alternates between Donne's and Jonson's use of writing for social self-definition. Bacon twice moved from one social identity—and technological medium—to the other, from courtly writing (mostly, though not exclusively, in manuscript)[5] as part of his

---

[3]See J. W. Saunders, "The Stigma of Print: A Note on the Social Bases of Tudor Poetry," *Essays in Criticism*, (1951), 139–64, and "The Social Situation of Seventeenth-Century Poetry," in *Metaphysical Poetry*, ed. Malcolm Bradbury and David Palmer, Stratford-upon-Avon Studies, no. 11 (London: Edward Arnold, 1970), pp. 237–59. See also Phoebe Sheavyn, *The Literary Profession in the Elizabethan Age*, rev. J. W. Saunders (Manchester: Manchester University Press, 1967).

[4]For Jonson's use of print to define himself as an author in print, see Richard Newton, "Jonson and the (Re-)Invention of the Book," in *Classic and Cavalier: Essays on Jonson and the Sons of Ben*, ed. Claude J. Summers and Ted-Larry Pebworth (Pittsburgh: University of Pittsburgh Press, 1982), pp. 31–55; Richard Helgerson, *Self-Crowned Laureates: Spenser, Jonson, Milton, and the Literary System* (Berkeley: University of California Press, 1983), chap. 3; and Timothy Murray, "From Foul Sheets to Legitimate Model: Antitheater, Text, Ben Jonson," *New Literary History*, 14 (1983), 641–64.

[5]Those of Bacon's printed works which are unrelated to his scientific and philosophical interests include: *Essays* (1597), published together with *Meditationes Sacrae* and *Of the Colours of Good and Evil* (which was also included in *De Augmentis* VI, and therefore considered by Bacon as part of his philosophical works); *Essays* (1612, 1625); *Sir Francis Bacon His Apology in Certaine Imputations Concerning the Late Earle of Essex* (1604); *History of the Reign of Henry VII* (1622); *Translation of Certain Psalms into English Verse* (1624). These works amount to a very small proportion indeed of Bacon's writings connected with court life. Another courtly nonscientific work that found its way into print but was initially presented to James in manuscript is *Certain Considerations Touch-*

political career to authorial writing on philosophical and scientific matters (mostly, though not exclusively, in print).[6] Bacon's scientific thought has of course an important and well-documented place in the history of science, but his decision to be a philosophical and scientific author had as much to do with social circumstances as with intellectual interests: it was the product of the same social dynamic that distinguishes Donne from Jonson. Bacon's recourse to scientific authorship took place within a particular courtly context.

Bacon cultivated his identity as a scientific author with sustained intensity during two phases of his life. The first was the period of frustrated political ambition preceding his rise to power in government, that is, the years before 1613. The second was the period following his impeachment and political ruin in 1621. Although Bacon has always been regarded as the textbook example of the Renaissance man precisely because of his ability to balance an active political life with a rich intellectual life, he in fact published only one work, the *Novum Organon,* while enjoying success at court. His first major work, *The Advancement of Learning* (1605), was published when he failed to advance politically. Most of his scientific works, including the *Magna Instauratio,* were written and published after his impeachment. And even the *Magna Instauratio* was conceived during Bacon's early period of disappointment. He articulated its structure and enunciated its final form for the first time in 1607, under conditions quite different from those which defined his social standing when, as Baron Ver-

---

ing the Better Pacification and Edification of the Church of England (1604) (see Spedding's remarks, X, 102). *A Brief Discourse Touching the Happy Union of the Kingdoms of England and Scotland* was also, in 1603, presented in manuscript by Bacon to James, and according to Spedding, "is said to have been printed in 1603." But, he adds, "I never met with a copy" (X, 89). Writings concerning proceedings against Roderigo Lopez (1593–94), Essex (1601), and Sir Walter Ralegh (1618) were produced by Bacon for print but under the direction of Elizabeth and James and as part of Bacon's duties as counsel, and thus they cannot in any real sense be considered works authored by Bacon. For comments on the circumstances of their publication, see, respectively, VIII, 273–74; IX, 240; XIII, 379–83.

[6] According to Spedding, all but three of Bacon's scientific and philosophical manuscript works were either included in the *Magna Instauratio*—or designed to be so—or were superseded by works that were in fact ultimately included (see the tables of contents to vols. I–III of *Works*). The three exceptions are: *Cogitationes de Natura Rerum* (date uncertain, probably before 1605; see III, 14); *De Fluxu et Refluxu Maris* (date uncertain, probably before 1616; see III, 44); *De Principiis atque Originibus, secundum Fabulas Cupidinis et Coeli* (undated).

ulam, chancellor of England, he first published his plan for this work, along with the *Novum Organon*, in 1620. The social context of the *Magna Instauratio*'s genesis was not Bacon's success but his failure at court when he was a younger man. Although Bacon was interested in science and philosophy in all phases of his life, the history of his publications indicates that he tended to give serious attention to his scientific pursuits only when his political life flagged. Only during times of political ill fortune did authorship become his chosen means of self-expression.

In this way Bacon's career conforms to a fairly common Renaissance pattern. Like other eclipsed Renaissance courtiers—Machiavelli, Wyatt, and Sidney, for example—Bacon turned to writing as a response to failure at court; writing was a manifestation of his distance from the center of political life. For Bacon scientific writing thus played much the same psychological role that poetry did for such disappointed courtiers as Wyatt, Gascoigne, and Sidney.[7] As Arthur Marotti has argued, "From the time of Henry VIII . . . up through the later Elizabethan period, writers conventionally used philosophical and religious . . . material to cope with political and social defeat."[8] Frank Whigham describes the same pattern: failure at court was "mystified as a progression away from the grubbing for temporal power and toward some transcendental ideal of pastoral or Neoplatonic society," as in the case of Gabriel Harvey.[9] Thus one of the major tropes of courtly life "was to relieve the strain [of constant struggle for advancement] by postponing, accounting for, or mystify-

[7]In his discussion of Wyatt's discovery of an inward poetic voice, Stephen Greenblatt draws attention to Wyatt's turning to written verse in times of loss of favor at court (*Renaissance Self-Fashioning: From More to Shakespeare* [Chicago: University of Chicago Press, 1980], pp. 115–56). For Sidney, see Arthur F. Marotti, "'Love Is Not Love': Elizabethan Sonnet Sequences and the Social Order," *ELH*, 49 (1982), 396–428. The relationship of politics to Bacon's scientific writing is also discussed by Timothy J. Reiss, *The Discourse of Modernism* (Ithaca: Cornell University Press, 1982), pp. 199–208, though from a different point of view. Reiss is interested in the connection between Bacon's scientific discourse and the modern liberal state.

[8]Arthur F. Marotti, "Donne and Patronage," in *Patronage in the Renaissance,* ed. Guy Fitch Lytle and Stephen Orgel (Princeton: Princeton University Press, 1981), pp. 227–28. See Marotti's remarks on poetry and courtly failure, p. 270. My approach to Bacon owes much to Marotti and to remarks in Frank Whigham, *Ambition and Privilege: The Social Tropes of Elizabethan Courtesy Theory* (Berkeley: University of California Press, 1984).

[9]Whigham, *Ambition and Privilege,* pp. 22–23.

ing the various levels of personal failure."[10] Bacon himself says as much in his letter to Launcelot Andrewes written after his impeachment. He explicitly seeks classical models—Cicero, Demosthenes, and Seneca—who turned to writing after defeat in politics, this at a time when he was writing most of the works in the *Magna Instauratio.*

The correlations between Bacon's political fortunes and his resort to scientific authorship may appear more clearly if we examine Bacon's career in closer chronological detail. Bacon's early adult life is marked by an agonizingly frustrated attempt to rise to a high position in court. His father was Elizabeth's lord keeper, and when Bacon was a child, Elizabeth referred to him as her "young Lord Keeper."[11] This epithet was an emblem, so to speak, of Bacon's sense of his birthright to high political office. But as the youngest son of a father who died before he could settle Bacon's inheritance, Bacon was left with chronic financial problems.[12] He sought both wealth and advancement through two avenues. Having completed his studies at Cambridge, he undertook legal training as an education that would prepare him for public service, and he solicited patronage from his uncle William Cecil, Lord Burghley, and from his cousin, Robert Cecil, Burghley's son. At age thirty-one he writes to Burghley, seeking patronage and complaining that he has not risen as high as he deserves (VIII, 108–9). He asks Burghley to place him at the head of an institution of learning so he can begin his project of reforming science and philoso-

---

[10]Ibid., p. 21. The same issue is dealt with in quite another way in José Ortega y Gasset, "Introduction to Velazquez," in *Velazquez, Goya, and the Dehumanization of Art,* tr. Alexis Brown (New York: Norton, 1972), pp. 84–106. Ortega attributes Velazquez's painterly innovations to his position as a successful courtier. As friend to the king, and as an artist who was not dependent on the king's patronage for his painting, Velazquez had the freedom to create as he pleased. For Ortega, the disinterested nobleman, the aristocratic amateur released from the constraints of political and social pressures, is the one who introduces the modern in art. My own view of Bacon is that his intellectual energies were released precisely as a result of engagement with the constraints of political life, the result of failed political aspirations, but aspirations nonetheless. For various views of the relation between Bacon's political and scientific interests, see Joel J. Epstein, *Francis Bacon: A Political Biography* (Athens: Ohio University Press, 1977), pp. 1–19.

[11]Fulton J. Anderson, *Francis Bacon: His Career and His Thought* (Los Angeles: University of Southern California Press, 1962), p. 3.

[12]Ibid., p. 3.

phy.[13] In this letter we get a glimpse of Bacon's early attitude toward scientific writing: he threatens that if his uncle does not advance him at court, he will run away to an academic life and become "a sorry book-maker." As Benjamin Farrington has pointed out, at this stage in his life, Bacon seeks the renovation of knowledge through administrative rather than literary means.[14] Because of his family and social status, authorship through print was an unlikely prospect. Bacon shows the same gentlemanly disdain of professional authorship as did those of his peers—for example, Donne—who sought courtly advancement. An administrative career would have been more socially acceptable to a member of the governing class who saw his proper place in political activity.

Bacon's perception of full-time authorship contrasts with his attitude toward his political writings during this period, which included a letter of advice to Elizabeth on church government,[15] and a treatise on the same subject, his *Advertisement Touching the Controversies of the Church of England,* circulated in manuscript to influential members of government. These privately circulated manuscripts were a type of court performance intended to gain patronage and win advancement, and as such had limited success. The treatise, according to James Spedding, Bacon's nineteenth-century editor, reflected the views of Burghley and Walsingham, and so Bacon was asked to do more writing of this kind (VIII, 73, 95). Looking back at this period in his *Apologie Concerning Essex* (1604), Bacon recalls that "her Majesty [took] a liking to my pen" (X, 159). Writing became an important part of his political identity, but not the writing of a published author.

---

[13]Spedding (III, 107) takes this remark at face value and holds that throughout his life Bacon aimed to use his political career only as an instrument of his scientific goals. This view is justly questioned in Epstein, *Francis Bacon,* pp. 16–17. Spedding tends to regard Bacon as the very model of the disinterested scientist whose political career was an unfortunate distraction from his true ends.

[14]When I formulated my argument about Bacon's coming to authorship, I did not know it was an elaboration of an idea first presented by Benjamin Farrington; see *The Philosophy of Francis Bacon, An Essay on Its Development from 1603 to 1609 with New Translations of Fundamental Texts* (Chicago: University of Chicago Press, 1964), pp. 11–16.

[15]The letter was originally attributed to another writer, but Spedding (VIII, 47) attributes it to Bacon.

Bacon never received the institutional post he sought from Burghley and after this disappointment only rarely sought political advancement through institutions of learning. In 1593, however, he committed a blunder that all but brought his political career to a halt: he enraged the queen by openly opposing her in Parliament. Soon afterward his patron Essex brazenly attempted to have him appointed attorney general, but Elizabeth passed him over, after keeping him dangling for a year, even for the lesser office of solicitor general. His correspondence at this time is filled with desperate pleas to gain patronly support for the appointment. But while Elizabeth lived, Bacon never rose above a minor legal office and never achieved the political influence he craved so much.

During this period of political frustration, Bacon reevaluated his philosophical aspirations by toying once again with the idea of turning to a contemplative, academic life. In 1594 he writes to Essex that if he is not appointed solicitor general, he will "retire . . . with a couple of men to Cambridge, and there spend [his] life in studies and contemplations, without looking back" (VIII, 291). Even as he wrote for the court, removing himself from the competitive arena of the court was clearly on his mind. He composed, for court masques, two oratorical debates on the philosopher's public duty (VIII, 355, 376–86). And by the time he was turned down for the position of solicitor general, he was expressing regret about his choice of the law as a means of furthering his political aspirations, "because," he observed, "it drinketh too much time, which I could have dedicated to better purposes" (VIII, 372–73)—a reference, presumably, to his scientific and philosophical interests, which did not at this time include authorship. The letter in effect concedes his poor performance in the patronage system. Nevertheless, his attitude toward the contemplative employment of his time can only be described as ambivalent. In the letter to Essex he laconically admits, "If her Majesty command me in any particular, I shall be ready to do her service" (VIII, 372–73; see also VIII, 351, 359, 362). When position did not come to him, he did not in fact carry out his threat to turn to the life of a retired philosopher.

Bacon's irresolute attitude toward intellectual life is apparent in a work he actually did prepare for printed publication, the *Essays* of 1597, written at a time of serious financial problems. (A year later he was arrested for debt.) Bacon presents the *Essays* with a defensive, apologetic stance toward appearing in print, a stance Richard Helgerson describes as characteristic of the gentlemen amateurs set on a court career. In the Epistle Dedicatorie to his brother Anthony, Bacon insists he is publishing the essays only to prevent pirated, unauthorized editions.[16] But if he still looks with one eye toward the court, he sadly expresses his discouragement with politics and court life when he invites his invalid brother Anthony to trade places with him, since he deems Anthony more suitable for the active life than he is, given his own intellectual proclivities: "I sometimes wish," he says, "[my brother's] infirmities translated uppon my selfe, that her Maiestie mought have the seruice of so actiue and able a mind, & I mought be with excuse confined to these contemplations & studies for which I am fittest" (VI, 523–24). Yet with characteristic ambivalence toward a life completely separated from political affairs, the opening essay of the volume, "Of Studies," declares that "to spend too much time in them [i.e., studies] is slouth"; "to make judgement wholly by their rules, is the humour of a Scholler" (VI, 525). In other words, to use studies for anything less than a vehicle of the active life is a form of folly. In his aphorism "Reading maketh a full man, conference a readye man, and writing an exacte man" (VI, 525), writing is treated as a practical instrument for the man of the world, an *aide de memoire*, the kind of writing Bacon himself practiced frequently in preparation for conferences. The *Essays* as a written product of "contemplations & studies" does not acknowledge itself as an authorial presentation of its composer. Moreover, Bacon's bemused condescension toward "the humour of a Scholler," deriving from his exaltation of the active life is at odds with his expressed wish to be "confined" to "contemplations & studies."

The same ambivalence toward the intellectual life reappears in Bacon's letters around the time James acceded to the throne in 1603. His comments here again suggest that for Bacon a purely intellectual enterprise was a crutch to lean on during times of political frustration. In July 1603, Bacon writes to Cecil that he will not continue as a minor legal functionary, and in lamenting tones he adds, "as for an ambi-

---

[16]Richard Helgerson, *The Elizabethan Prodigals* (Berkeley: University of California Press, 1976), chap. 1.

tion, I do assure your Honour mine is quenched." Reminiscing sadly he observes, "In the Queen's, my excellent Mistress's, time the *quorum* was small" (X, 80). Yet he reproaches Cecil: "I thought you might have had more use of me, than now I suppose you are able to have" (X, 81). We also know that when Elizabeth was on her deathbed, Bacon canvassed James's friends, offering his services to the awaited new monarch, "by my head, tongue, pen, means, or friends" (X, 58). Even after James had ascended the throne, Bacon continued to ask Cecil to act as his patron in securing him a post in government (X, 81), and he did in fact continue on as a not very important counsel to the king, in addition to submitting to James manuscript papers on the union with Scotland.

None of Bacon's solicitations produced results, and at the beginning of the Jacobean reign his prospects for an active, influential political career seemed bleak indeed.[17] Even so, Bacon did not remove himself to the life of the mind. Caught between the allurements of the political life and the attractions of the intellectual life, Bacon experienced a crisis of vocation. During this period of psychic turmoil and barren political harvest, Bacon made an extraordinary announcement to Cecil, in the same letter in which he declared his political ambition "quenched": "My ambition now," he wrote, "I shall only put upon my pen, whereby I should be able to maintain memory and merit of times succeeding" (X, 80). Rather than repair to academic calm, Bacon solved his crisis of vocation by resorting to the profession of his pen.

The change was a gesture signaling at least a partial stepping back from the court, though not a total withdrawal from it. The change in fact may have been simply a move from one corner of the patronage system to another, from political patronage for service in government to intellectual patronage for service whose currency was the dedication in the printed book. At any rate, Bacon was as unsuccessful in obtaining remuneration for his scientific and philosophical enterprise as he was in obtaining recognition through a government post. But however little his relationship to the court changed when, regard-

[17]Anderson summarizes Bacon's parliamentary activities in the reign of Elizabeth and in the early reign of James; see *Francis Bacon*, pp. 49–52 and 111–13. Bacon's active engagement in parliamentary affairs did not make up for his failure to rise in court, nor did it fulfill his sense of social identity.

ing his political eclipse as permanent, he professed his pen instead of courtiership, it was enough to allow him to assume a new social stance.

The alteration involved not so much a change in activity—Bacon always wrote—as a change in identity, indicated by, for one thing, an appeal to a new audience, "times succeeding," posterity, rather than the immediately accessible figures of the court. From this point on in Bacon's writings, posterity will appear as a recurrent theme, and as Bacon will observe in other works of this period, posterity can be reached, not through the ordinary means of courtly communication—by letter, court masque, or manuscript treatise—but through books. Writing, the intellectual's distinctive form of activity, which for Bacon had formerly been an expression of his closeness to the court, now represented his distance, for unlike courtly writing, authorial writing is an indication of the writer's detachment from, rather than involvement in, affairs of state, and signals his renunciation of the pursuit of immediate personal fulfillment. Turning to a distant, abstract posterity in scientific works was Bacon's consolation of philosophy, a delayed gratification in response to displacement from his peers. His decision to write as an author rather than a courtier was for him an expression of alienation.

That sense of distance and separation was ultimately embodied in a new mode of communication—the printed word—as Bacon adopted a new technology, movable type, for the presentation of his scientific and philosophical ideas. During Elizabeth's reign, before Bacon decided to place his ambition upon his pen, he committed his scientific ideas to brief mentions in letters; to unrecorded conversations with Essex (who appears to have been sympathetic to Bacon as a thinker as well as a politician); to a lost manuscript work of 1585 titled *Temporis Partus Maximus* (mentioned in a 1625 letter to Fulgentius; see XIV, 532); and to a portion of a court masque of 1592 presented by Essex to the queen (VIII, 123–26). The masque contains in kernel many of the ideas that Bacon was to develop later in his philosophical books: he condemns the lack of utilitarian benefits in traditional science; denounces an uncritical attachment to the ancients; and criticizes the influence of Greek science based on words, disputes, and sects. He praises the three most important modern inventions—as he would twenty-eight years later in the *Novum Organon*—artillery, the compass, and the printing press, the last of which changed "the state of learning" (VIII, 125).

Until Bacon made his decision to cultivate authorship, however, he seems to have benefited from the printing press as a reader rather than as a writer; he himself showed no inclination to appear in print. (Indeed, within the limited context of the court, Essex provided an intra-courtly means of communication far superior to publication, both for Bacon's philosophical ideas and for his political aspirations.) But when Bacon nearly despaired of achieving courtly position and influence, he reconsidered his former condescension about being a "sorry book-maker." The most significant evidence of the change in Bacon's attitude toward publication and authorship was the publication in 1605, some thirteen years after the early letter to Burghley, of *The Advancement of Learning*. This work was important not only in itself but also as Bacon's first work intended for publication, and it was so popular that in later years Bacon was to look back on it as his entree to the intellectual world, though he did not experience that sense of success at the time of the book's publication. Although he continued to write manuscript works,[18] print had become a desirable means of presenting both himself—as in the *Apologie Concerning Essex*—and his ideas, though his actual discussions of publication pertain almost exclusively to scientific writing.

The Advancement is doubtlessly the issue of Bacon's "ambition . . . now put upon my pen" announced in his letter to Cecil two years earlier. In letters accompanying presentation copies of *The Advancement,* Bacon makes it quite clear that the book was the outcome of his thwarted political career, but he rather misleadingly represents his turn to science and publication as a matter of choice, as if he had deliberately removed himself from the corridors of power. "I present your Lordship with a work of my vacant time," he writes to Cecil, sardonically adding, "which if it had been more, the work had been better" (X, 253). He writes more introspectively to Thomas Bodley, expressing regret over having chosen a public career, which has kept him away from his true calling, intellectual inquiry: "Knowing myself

---

[18]These include some scientific works, as well as position papers addressed to individuals. Bacon also published two other works in print which had nothing to do with philosophy, one, his *Apologie* concerning Essex, the other, *Certain Considerations Touching the Better Pacification of the Church of England* (1604).

by inward calling to be fitter to hold a book than play a part, I have led my life in civil causes, for which I was not very fit by nature, and more unfit by the preoccupation of my mind" (X, 253). Not following his true calling he regards as one of his "great [errors] that led the rest" (X, 253). Characteristically, for Bacon the recovery of his true vocation is associated with an appeal to an audience beyond the court, "the world": "Therefore calling myself home [i.e., to philosophical inquiry], I have now for a time enjoyed myself; whereof likewise I desire to make the world partaker" (X, 253). But Bacon's self-portrait as the intellectual alienated from the court because of his philosophical proclivities must be regarded as a fiction that authorizes his projection of himself in his published book; his alienation was more political than intellectual.

Though Bacon turned to print "to make the world partaker" in his joy at having realized his true calling, *The Advancement* is specifically addressed to the king in order to convince him to give financial support to Bacon's new learning in the form of a research or educational institution. This double target is typical of many of Bacon's printed works, which are often addressed to two audiences. On the one hand, the printed author addresses posterity, brought within his reach by the durability of the book. On the other hand, the book, like a manuscript, has a more proximate audience, the dedicatee, from whom the author might hope for some form of reward and so maintain at least indirect contact with the patronage system. In Bacon's oeuvre, his manuscript works usually have only this second intended audience, an individual to whom the work is directly addressed. As artifacts removed from their writers, as objects to be deposited in libraries, manuscript and printed books are usually treated by Bacon as if they were two versions of the same thing (see, for example, VIII, 335). For the writer, though, each form requires a different social identity, a different mode of self-presentation to its respective audience.

Bacon's choice of print to present his views indicated not only his distance from the king; it also indicated his desire to reform the learning of his day. Not surprisingly, Book I of *The Advancement* presents a defense of books and writing as instruments of knowledge. (Book II also comments on the importance of books, but Bacon's emphasis there is on the institutional setting of learning.) Bacon's concern with the role of books in learning, which was awakened by his own assumption of the role of author, produced an extended theoretical discussion of the idea of the book.

This interest in the importance of books is perhaps most evident in Bacon's exaltation of the work of the intellectual above the work of the politician: "We see then how far the monuments of wit and learning are more durable than the monuments of power." And for Bacon the monument of the mind is none other than the book, which outlasts the ravages of time: "the images of men's wits and knowledges remain in books, exempted from the wrong of time and capable of perpetual renovation" (III, 318). Homer is Bacon's example of an author who has outlasted "the monuments of power" he himself described in his epics; Bacon sees authorship in general as a heroic effort not only against the destructive force of time but also, at least in his own case, against the indifference of one's peers.[19]

The Advancement of Learning was written in the midst of a period, 1603–1607, in which Bacon wrote four unpublished works that all share the theme of the transmission of knowledge: *Valerius Terminus* (c. 1603), *The Masculine Birth of Time* (c. 1603), *Thoughts and Conclusions* (c. 1607), and the *Refutation of Philosophies* (c. 1607).[20] The persona of *The Masculine Birth of Time* asks the question that all these works address: "Do you really think it is easy to provide the favourable conditions required for the legitimate passing on of knowledge?" (*MBT*, 62). Although the transmission of knowledge is a Baconian concern usually associated with the later and more complete *Novum Organon*, these works illustrate that Bacon was already formulating his ideas on the subject during the years in which his identity as an author was still evolving.[21]

Taken together, the four unpublished works add up to a coherent

[19]For a very different view of Baconian science and political institutions, see Reiss, *Discourse of Modernism*, pp. 198–225.

[20]I use Farrington's dating, *Philosophy of Francis Bacon*, p. 11, rather than Spedding's. All references to *The Masculine Birth of Time* (hereafter *MBT*), *Thoughts and Conclusions* (hereafter *TC*), and *Refutation of Philosophies* (hereafter *RP*) are from Farrington, *Philosophy of Francis Bacon*.

[21]In his early letter to Burghley seeking an administrative post in an educational institution, Bacon had already drawn a parallel between the deficiencies of Scholasticism and alchemy, on the one hand, and their methods of communication, on the other (VIII, 109). Clearly, the issue interested him from early on, but during this period of his career, he develops the matter at length.

historical sociology of scientific and philosophical knowledge whose thrust is the praise of scientific authorship and the condemnation of traditional scientific organization into warring sects headed by single individuals. "Unity is the hall-mark of truth, and the variety of their [i.e., heads of schools] opinions is proof of error," Bacon proclaims (*MBT*, p. 69). Aristotle, the supreme example of this factionalism, "like the Ottoman Turk, did not think he could reign secure till he had slain his brothers" (*RP*, p. 110). Bacon's primary sociological concern in his history of philosophy is the way the learned organize themselves not only to cultivate knowledge but also to pass it on and maintain its continuity. During most of the history of philosophy, the dominance of sects headed by single individuals made it impossible for their knowledge to last beyond the lifetime of their leader. There was no "succession of wits," and so "the patrimony of knowledge goeth not on husbanded . . . , but wasted and decayed" (III, 226–27; see also 225). As a result, the accumulation of knowledge could not advance beyond the lifetime of a single thinker (III, 226–27).

This problem persisted in antiquity and into the more recent past: "The mistake is to suppose that in the sciences there is a fixed upper-limit of attainment, and that this, as a rule, is reached within the life-span of a single individual, who profiting by the circumstances of the time, becomes the leader of his age, examines and appraises all other writers, and thus brings the sciences to a definitive and absolute perfection" (*RP*, p. 126). Under such circumstances science cannot progress, since "every science grows by the patient observation of many men, one grasping one truth, one another, as different aspects of the subject are seriously handled and essayed" (*RP*, p. 126). The great enemy of this process is the premature formulation of conclusions, which has been fostered by the sectarian organization of traditional science. (Bacon here seems to be calling for what Thomas Kuhn termed "normal" science.)[22]

Bacon discusses the nature of single-authority science extensively in his sociology of Greek philosophy, which presents both the best and the worst of scientific models. On the one hand, Bacon argues, Greek philosophers "opened schools, founded or took over sects with

[22]Thomas Kuhn, *The Structure of Scientific Revolutions*, rev. ed. (Chicago: University of Chicago Press, 1970), pp. 23–34.

a fixed system of beliefs, and had pupils, adherents, and successors" (*RP*, p. 111). Among these philosophers were Aristotle and Plato. In contrast, other Greek thinkers "seriously devoted themselves to the search for truth, and the study of nature" without organizing into groups; "they might either . . . alone . . . philosophize for themselves, or invite a chosen few, who shared their passion, to join in the delights of their converse" (*RP*, p. 111). Such thinkers, whom Bacon imagines as working in near isolation, included the Pre-Socratics Empedocles, Heraclitus, Democritus, Anaxagoras, and Parmenides. Bacon admired not only the Pre-Socratics' aphoristic style (which he adopted for his own purposes) but also the social organization that produced that style.

In Bacon's eyes, the differing social organization of these two types of Greek philosopher determined their different—and not equally valuable—means of transmitting their doctrines. Bacon's animosity toward disputation, discussions (*RP*, p. 115), and oral transmission (*TC*, p. 74) is apparent everywhere in his work, but it is particularly explicit in the distinction between oral and written transmission which he elaborates in his treatment of the Greek philosophers. The philosophers of the sects—Plato and Aristotle—are in fact not very different from orators like the Sophists: both "headed a school, had *hearers,* and founded a sect" (*RP*, p. 112; emphasis added). But whereas sects and schools produced only "the blustering winds of [oral?] disputation," the Pre-Socratics produced *writing:* "You will not find that these men opened schools, but they eventually reduced their speculations and discoveries to writing and so passed them on to posterity" (*RP*, p. 111). The detached seeker after objective truth in nature, the real scientist, works alone or in small groups, attempts to transmit his work beyond his immediate milieu through writing rather than speaking, and is therefore an *author.* (Bacon here appears to be transposing the work habits of the thinker in the age of print back onto antiquity. Moreover, the work habits he ascribes to the Pre-Socratics are strikingly similar to his own after he decided to distance himself from court and become an author who appeals to posterity through the printed book.)

But if the Pre-Socratics addressed posterity through their writing while the oratorical philosophers addressed only their own coterie, how is it, Bacon asks, that Aristotle survived and the Pre-Socratics did not? During "the more civilized age of the Roman Empire," Bacon answers, the written works of the Pre-Socratics did actually survive intact. Only after the invasion of the barbarians did Aristotle gain the upper hand (*RP*, pp. 113–14). The result was the corruption of science that has continued to the present day. What emerges from Bacon's history of philosophy is the sense of the uncertainty of the transmission of philosophic ideas given the inevitable persistence of mediocrity over time. Focusing on a subject he returns to in *The Advancement*, Bacon argues that for knowledge to "stand up against the ravages of time," it must not be of its own time (*MBT*, p. 62). Democritus, for example, "set . . . himself apart from almost all other philosophers, who were prisoners of their times and slaves of fashion" (*MBT*, p. 71). This strategy, he remarks in letters to Toby Matthew, he adopts for himself; indeed, Bacon was convinced of the durability of his own ideas precisely because they did not suit "the present times" (XI, 132, 135).

In elevating the Pre-Socratics above Plato and Aristotle, Bacon was not simply favoring one style of writing over another; he was favoring authentic writing over the oratorically presented ideas of the schools and sects, ideas whose written vestiges happened to survive. Books are "the Shrines where the Saint is," Bacon asserts, appropriately enough, in the letter to Bodley accompanying his presentation copy of *The Advancement of Learning* (X, 253). Though Bacon may warn against attributing too much authority to "the thoughts of one man" (*RP*, p. 114), he implies the entire history of ancient science and the possibility of the renewal of real science in the near future depended on the decision of the solitary scientist to write. Scientists are to build on each others' discoveries, Bacon seems to suggest, not through personal interactions, as in the sects, but through disembodied books, which Bacon at times treats as vehicles of social disengagement. The modern instauration of science is heir to the age of the book. (This view of the way scientists interact differs markedly from the view Bacon presents much later in *The New Atlantis*, where he emphasizes the cooperative nature of scientific inquiry.)

When Bacon discusses the necessity of books for the durability of ideas, he usually makes no explicit distinction between manuscript books and printed books. His prototypal authors after all are the Pre-Socratics. Moreover, throughout most of his writing career, he had serious reservations about the benefits of publishing *everything* in print.[23] At this time in his career, in fact, he stated his proposals most boldly in his manuscript works intended for private circulation (i.e., *Valerius Terminus, The Masculine Birth of Time, Thoughts and Conclusions,* and *The Refutation of Philosophies*), though he was later to see these works as preparatory for the printed publication of the *Magna Instauratio*.[24] Nevertheless, it remains true that Bacon began to develop his explanation of the importance of the printing press at the time when he was formulating his social history of knowledge and scientific authorship, and was seeking to publicize his own scientific ideas in *The Advancement* through print. For Bacon, printing is itself an example of modern learning, as well as an artifact that changed the world of learning and stimulated the pursuit of new knowledge (*TC*, p. 93; *RP*, p. 132).

Bacon is most impressed with the speed with which printing allows the mind to open itself to others. Through print "the discoveries of one man can pass like a flash of lightning and be promptly shared, thus stimulating zeal and effecting an interchange of ideas" (*RP*, p. 132; see also *TC*, p. 95). Print, then, remedies one of the major shortcomings of the pervasive sectarian heritage of Aristotle, for it fosters the progress of knowledge beyond the lifetime and environment of a single thinker at the head of a school that claims all authority for itself. Publication prevents "lay[ing] the foundation . . . of any school" (*TC*, p. 100). It is not enough to observe nature; one must publish one's observations: "the work to be done . . . creates the obligation not only to get the work done, but to share it and pass it on. These are matters of equal concern" (*TC*, p. 100). Most important, however, printing allows the individual to dispense with the approval of his contemporaries who might be incapable of recognizing true merit. Print provides the philosophic author with a medium of communication independent of the coterie—the political coterie of the

---

[23]Spedding (I, 107–13) lists all the passages in which Bacon mentions the relative benefits of printed publication and limited manuscript circulation of scientific materials. Reiss, *Discourse of Modernism,* pp. 188–97, emphasizes Bacon's interest in the secretive nature of scientific discourse.

[24]In his letter to Launcelot Andrewes, Bacon looks back at *The Advancement* as "a mixture of new conceits and old" (XIV, 373), which Farrington, *Philosophy of Francis Bacon,* p. 48, suggests made the work, like *The Wisdom of the Ancients* (1609), suitable for print, as opposed to Bacon's manuscript works circulated among friends.

court and the intellectual coterie of the hated sects. For Bacon, who felt that the court society had not granted him the recognition he deserved, this freedom was a matter of importance not only for the history of philosophy but also for himself personally.

Within a few years of *The Advancement,* Bacon was planning a two-part scientific treatise for publication, though all that he actually wrote was a preface, titled *On the Interpretation of Nature: Proem.* In this preface Bacon unleashes a volley of self-justification unlike anything in his earlier writings; he lets loose his unrestrained intellectual ambition whose ultimate outlet is publication. As a published philosopher, Bacon styles himself the heir of the Pre-Socratics, rising above the sectarianism of schools by posthumously stimulating, through the printed book, an audience yet to be born. Bacon repeats the pattern he followed when he earlier wished to project himself as an author: he represents his dedication to science and scientific writing as the adoption of a profession nobler than that of the politician. Politics he now regards as an accident of his "birth and education," as well as the unfortunate influence of those whose "opinions (so young as I was) would sometimes stagger me" (X, 85). He has left the court because his "zeal was mistaken for ambition," and because he could be most effective working alone, whereas court life demands dependence on others (X, 85).[25] He even claims that the real goal of his political life was to use his position at court for the sake of science: "I hoped that if I rose to any place of honour in the state, I should have a larger command of industry and ability to help me in my [scientific and philosophical] work" (X, 85).

In the Proem, science has become a more effective surrogate for the courtly career it replaces. Bacon can now fulfill his true calling: "I was born for the service of mankind," he says, and to be "the benefactor of the human race" through "the bettering of man's life" (X, 84). Bacon's birthright to public office has been transformed into a birthright to serve through science. Science has in fact become a more heightened form of public service; philosophy raises the fruits of a courtly career to a higher form of disinterested existence. And as in *The Advancement,* Bacon places the scientist above the politician: "the Work of the Inventor [i.e., the discoverer]" outlasts "the good effect

---

[25]Bacon also mentions his poor health as a reason for leaving court politics.

wrought by founders of cities, extirpers of tyrants, and heroes of that class" (X, 84).

Expecting that some will accuse him of being "wise overmuch," Bacon declares that "modesty and civil respect are fit to civil matters; in contemplation nothing is to be respected but Truth" (X, 86). The tropes of self-interested ambition in his letters and behavior are exchanged in the Proem for the trope of the dispassionate, solitary seeker of truth. Thwarted courtly ambition is sublimated into a disinterested intellectual ambition untainted by self-seeking and therefore, Bacon seems to be saying, more legitimate than his political aspirations. We must remember that Bacon turned not so much to scientific experiment as scientific authorship. The ideal intellectual life he imagines is almost another version of Wyatt's "Kent and Christendom," a pastoral of the mind which in Bacon's case still fulfills public obligations, though apart from court life. The Proem exalting the scientist over the politician is of course the preface to a scientific book destined, as Bacon then thought, for publication.

Indeed, Bacon uses the Proem to unveil a "plan of publication" (X, 87). The book he projects will have two parts, one on scientific methodology (the germ of the *Novum Organon*), one on natural history. The first is to be published in print; the second will be circulated among the learned in manuscript. This plan indicates that Bacon had not yet completely broken away from courtly habits, though the assertiveness of the Proem is a far cry from the apologetic tone of the Epistle Dedicatorie of the 1597 *Essays*. (By the time he composed the *Magna Instauratio,* Bacon himself no longer made this distinction between print for methodology and manuscript for natural history; he worked feverishly to include his natural histories in his published masterwork.) So much did he desire publication in fact, he now sought to have *The Advancement* translated into Latin, so that his "bell [could be] heard as far as can be" (X, 301). And by 1607, the approximate date of two of the unpublished works outlining his history of philosophy and philosophic authorship (*Thoughts and Conclusions* and *The Refutation of Philosophies*), Bacon had already formulated his plan to compose and publish the *Magna Instauratio,* and had begun calling it by that name (X, 363), though he did not begin to work on it in earnest till after his impeachment.

In the few years preceding the start of his rise to eminence, Bacon further clarified the nature of his bookish enterprise. In 1609 he wrote a preface to the projected *Magna Instauratio*, which he distinguishes from his manuscript works; these, he says in a 1609 letter to the bishop of Ely, are mere "miscellanies" of tentative preparations for "a just and perfect volume of philosophy, which I go on with though slowly" (XI, 141), an allusion to the *Magna Instauratio*. Bacon's care to produce a polished, perfected, "finished" form of his "great work" (XI, 145)[26] designed to endure beyond "the present times" indicates that he valued this work more highly than his legal, political, and ecclesiastical writing. These occasional writings (and his tentative manuscript works) Bacon regarded as the professional duty of a lawyer, courtier, and would-be statesman, and far removed from the work of the disinterested author unconcerned with the exigencies of the moment.[27] Bacon's plan for a published, enduring book composed from tentative manuscripts is similar to Jonson's consolidation of the "foul sheets" of players' parts into a finished dramatic text— elevated to a volume titled "Workes"—to be presented and preserved in a printed edition.[28]

From Bacon's statements in the prefatory material to the yet to be written *Magna Instauratio* and the never to be written *On the Interpretation of Nature*, it would appear that by 1609 he had given up on his political career and become a true counterexample to the generalization about scientists which he makes in *Thoughts and Conclusions:* one of the reasons for the failure of science in antiquity was that "many of the loftiest intellects took up politics and administration, especially during the period of Roman greatness, when the size of Empire claimed the exertions of many" (*TC*, p. 77). And he decries the fact that "during all those ages up till now no single individual made a profession of Natural Philosophy in the sense of devoting his life to it" (*TC*, p. 77). But if Bacon's expressed commitment to scientific authorship makes him seem like such an individual, he in fact turns out to be one of those who "[takes] to politics and administration." Though he

---

[26]Similarly, in a 1610 letter to Matthew, he comments, "My great work goeth forward; and after my manner, I alter ever when I add. So that nothing is finished till it is finished" (XI, 145).

[27]Bacon did, however, save copies of his letters and preserved manuscript treatises, apparently for *posthumous* publication, as a way of preserving his memory as a statesman rather than as an author.

[28]See Murray, "From Foul Sheets."

pursued some philosophical interests at court, they were minimal compared to his political interests. In typical Baconian manner, he made one more play to become solicitor general during the very time he settled on the plan for the *Magna Instauratio,* a move that suggests that whatever his genuine commitment to science, and however developed his theory of scientific writing, authorship was a compensation for political failure he was ultimately ready to drop should his political fortunes change for the better. In a letter written to Cecil sometime between 1606 and 1607, he petitioned for the position, and in 1607, he received the appointment, though it did not prove to be the springboard to political influence that Bacon yearned for.[29] In his letter to Cecil seeking the position, he insists his main interest in becoming solicitor general is to "amend my estate, and so after fall to my studies and ease where of one is requisite for my body, and the other sorteth well with my mind" (X, 289). Nevertheless, when it looked for a time as if he might not get the appointment, he insisted on his desire to serve, writing to the chancellor: "I think myself born to do my Sovereign service (and therefore in that station I will live and die . . .)" (X, 295–96).

The years between his appointment as solicitor general in 1607 and his appointment as attorney general in 1613, when he began to achieve real influence and position, were a kind of limbo for Bacon. Indeed, his letters from this period present the picture of a man unsure of his direction. To be solicitor general was to have no real importance in government, and so Bacon ambitiously (but unsuccessfully) continued to seek further political advancement—while declaring courtly preferment an expedient means of furthering his *real* interest, scientific studies. And he did continue to pursue his philosophic interests as before, assuming the role of author once again in the *Magna Instauratio,* relishing the prospect of preserving his ideas for posterity, and assuring Toby Matthew that despite his involvement in "civil businesses," his enthusiasm for contemplative pursuits "doth gain . . . upon [his] affection and desire, by years and business" (XI, 136).

At the same time, however, Bacon was also forming plans to associate himself with an institution of learning. Like his letters, his surviv-

[29]See Spedding's remarks (XI, 239).

ing personal memoranda for the period between 25 July and 29 July 1608 give us a glimpse of what was on his mind at the time, and they too demonstrate that his interests were not exclusively authorial. He does note plans for writing and publishing,[30] but refers to projects relating to his older, dormant interest in the institutional and administrative setting of knowledge. He records his desire to establish university stipends for younger scholars in natural history and to find financial backers for experiments (XI, 66). Perhaps most significant, he intends to found a "College for Inventors" or to become the head of an already existing educational institution in order "to command wytts and pennes."[31] (He mentions as possibilities Westminster, Eton, Wynchester, Trinity College, St. John's College, and Magdalene College [XI, 66–67].) From the point of view of science itself, there is of course no inherent contradiction between scientific books and scientific institutions; *The Advancement* calls for both. From the point of view of their practitioners, however, authorship and institutional administration entail markedly different social stances.

It was indeed unusual in the early seventeenth century for a man of Bacon's social background to reconstruct himself as professional author even temporarily. And Bacon himself, though he discerned that even the most efficient social organization of scientists was useless without publication, could not wholeheartedly sustain his identity as an author; he was unwilling to relinquish totally his sense of being born to high public office. As we have seen, he continued to seek courtly advancement even after he defined the role of the scientific author, and he continued his attempt to use writing as a vehicle of courtly advancement. Demonstrating the value of his legal talents, he even offered James a history of England and a digest of English law in exchange for an appointment as attorney general. But perhaps the event that did most to foster his courtly career was the death of Cecil, whom Bacon had correctly suspected of foiling his aspirations. In

---

[30]For example, he mentions plans to translate *The Advancement,* to finish the Aphorisms and the *Clavis Interpretationis* (which he planned to have printed in France), and to circulate *Cogitata et Visa (Thoughts and Conclusions)* to selected readers (XI, 64). He also includes the following brief note: "Qu. [i.e., Query] of the Maner and praescripts touching secrecy, tradition [i.e., transmission]. and publication" (XI, 66).

[31]Farrington, *Philosophy of Francis Bacon,* p. 100 n. 1, interprets a passage in *Thoughts and Conclusions* as indicating "Bacon's willingness to take over a research institute and test the validity of his views."

1613, after Cecil died, Bacon was finally appointed attorney general; by 1618 he was chancellor.

It is impossible to speculate about how much of the *Magna Instauratio* Bacon would have written had he not been impeached. We do know, however, that, after he became attorney general, it took him seven years to write the *Novum Organon*. And this work was separated from his last serious attempt at scientific composition, in the years from 1607 to 1609, by a gap of some ten to thirteen years. In fact, it was not until his political career had failed irretrievably after his impeachment that he once again refashioned himself as an author, measuring all his works by the *Magna Instauratio* (as he does in his letter to Launcelot Andrewes) and measuring his life by the authorial books he wrote (as he does in his 1625 letter to Fulgentius, where his scientific works become the landmarks of his intellectual being). In the end it was his authorial identity that he bequeathed to posterity, but only after his political life was destroyed.

Thus Bacon's interest in both the theory and actuality of the modern scientific book was born of ambivalence. Authorship was an identity he slipped into in the years between the accession of James and his appointment as attorney general, for although he was then about to forsake a political career, the role of author allowed him to occupy a middle ground, detached from the court yet close enough to take advantage of political opportunity when it came. Only when it seemed inescapable that he could not possibly make a political comeback did Bacon accept authorship as a permanent vocation. Bacon thus differed both from authors such as Spenser and Jonson, whose writing careers continued to depend on association with the court, and from intellectuals such as those Puritan ministers whose activities, including writing, were fostered in voluntary association with a political party and who were able to act unconstrained by bonds of kin or courtly patronage.[32] In contrast, Bacon, whenever he could, acted in accordance with a social identity derived from kin, sustained by patronage, and epitomized by Elizabeth's affectionate epithet, her "young Lord Keeper."

[32]The social identity of Puritans as intellectuals engaged in political life is the subject of Michael Waltzer, *The Revolution of the Saints: A Study in the Origins of Radical Politics* (Cambridge: Harvard University Press, 1965).

7 /

The Authority of
Democritus Junior

B ACON found the written word detached from the authority of speech compelling for several reasons, personal,
social, and scientific. But Bacon warned against the
potentially negative effects for science of an excessive dependence on
book learning. He was particularly aware that the written word can
assume undue authority, and at times he cautioned against printed
publication for some scientific materials. Books, he believed, naturally tend to claim for themselves "a blighting authority [that] precludes fruitful research."[1] Bacon most thoroughly tackles the issue of
unwarranted authority in the section of the *Novum Organon* where he
promotes aphorisms over methods, in effect attempting to construct
an unauthorative style in a medium—writing—that by its very nature
projects authority. As a result, Bacon sometimes makes gestures denying any "claim to the sceptre of authority" for himself,[2] though, as
we have seen, at other times he is quite aggressive in projecting his
authority. Although Bacon believed that for the purposes of scientific
advancement it was better to be an author than to be the leader of a
school, he was also alert to the tendency of books to accrue premature
authority that impedes new discovery. Even while forging a personal

---

[1]Francis Bacon, *Thoughts and Conclusions*, in Benjamin Farrington, *The Philosophy of
Francis Bacon: An Essay on Its Development from 1603 to 1609 with New Translations of
Fundamental Texts* (Chicago: University of Chicago Press, 1964), p. 76.

[2]Francis Bacon, *Refutation of Philosophies*, in Farrington, *Philosophy of Francis Bacon*,
p. 110.

identify through authorship, Bacon found the attendent scientific authority a source of anxiety; for him, the relationship between authorship and authority was more ambiguous than it was for Jonson and Spenser.

Bacon returned to scientific writing after his impeachment in 1621, the same year that Robert Burton published the first edition of *The Anatomy of Melancholy;* Bacon's *De Augmentis* was published in 1623, just a year before the second edition of the *Anatomy.* The proximity of dates is purely coincidental, but Bacon and Burton did share similar intellectual preoccupations, specifically an awareness of book culture and the problem of authority. Burton's evaluation of the impact of print, however, is quite different from, even opposite to, that of Bacon. Whereas Bacon feared that print would too easily assume unwarranted authority, Burton stressed that the proliferation of books made possible by print diminished their authority. The sheer volume of printed opinion calls attention to the chaos of conflicting ideas, and so, instead of encouraging truth or even consensus, it creates bewilderment. More specifically, for Burton the sheer volume of conflicting citations regarding melancholy highlights the difficulty of mastering the culture of print.[3] Intellectual incompleteness is an inescapable result of print, Burton appears to suggest, Shandy-like, when he justifies the need for new editions to include citations of newly read books. Just the thought of the quantity of book production and the inability of any one person to keep up with it drives him to a frenzy: "What a catalogue of new books all this year, all this age (I say) have our ... marts brought out ... who can read them? As already, we shall have a vast chaos and confusion of books, we are oppressed with them, our eyes ache with reading, our fingers with turning."[4] It is, ironic, to say the least, that Burton, the librarian of Christ Church and habitué of the Bodleian, should feel threatened by

[3]My comments on Burton parallel the many suggestive remarks about Burton and book culture in Michael O'Connell, *Robert Burton* (Boston: Twayne, 1986), pp. 34–52. See also Jack Goody and Ian Watt, "The Consequences of Literacy," in *Literacy in Traditional Societies,* ed. Jack Goody (Cambridge: Cambridge University Press, 1968), pp. 55–60, on alienation and culture that follows the introduction of writing in previously oral societies.

[4]Robert Burton, *The Anatomy of Melancholy,* ed. Holbrook Jackson (1932; rpt. New York: Random House, 1977), I, 24. All references, unless otherwise noted, are from vol. 1 of this edition.

a surfeit of books. Bacon also believed the overabundance of opinion undermined the authority of science, but at the same time he believed that it would be possible to establish the ultimate authoritative library once the diversity of opinions had been reconciled by a complete natural history, which, when analyzed by the inductive method, would reveal all the laws of nature. For Burton, however, the very availability of books indicates the impossibility of creating such a library. The profusion of books instead creates the setting for a philosophical attitude roundly condemned by Bacon—skepticism.

Burton's most recognizable skeptical tutor is Montaigne, whose presence frequently appears wherever Burton adopts the voice of Democritus Junior. The stance of an observer perched in a tower regarding the world, artlessly writing down the thoughts of his roving eccentric mind, writing not so much to discover truth, but, in Burton's words, to "show myself" in the process of thinking while assimilating the varied thought of others into its own consciousness—all these characteristics point to Montaigne, as does the simple statement of Democritus Junior: "I have assayed" (pp. 26–27). The ever-changing river as a symbol of the mind, the world, and Burton's style (pp. 32, 53) likewise points to his skeptical proclivities, particularly in Burton's self-described extemporaneous style, which, he claims, he adopted to express the free flow of changing thought.[5]

Moreover, for Burton as for Montaigne, the technology of print plays an important role in the enterprise of self-expression. The *Essays* and the *Anatomy* both exhibit the same tension between the extemporaneous flow of thought (which Burton identifies with speech and writing) and the fixed, unalterable quality of the mass-produced printed page, the bounded book (in both senses of the word) represented by the elaborate Ramist scheme at the opening of the *Anatomy*. Frederick Rider has clearly shown the role of print in Montaigne's

[5]For Burton's skepticism, see Herschel Baker, *The Wars of Truth: Studies in the Decay of Christian Humanism in the Earlier Seventeenth Century* (Cambridge: Harvard University Press, 1952), pp. 153–54. On the problem of knowledge in Burton, see Ruth A. Fox, *The Tangled Chain: The Structure of Disorder in The Anatomy of Melancholy* (Berkeley: University of California Press, 1976), pp. 45–121. See also Devon L. Hodges, *Renaissance Fictions of Anatomy* (Amherst: University of Massachusetts Press, 1985), pp. 107–23. J. B. Bamborough argues that Montaigne was of relatively little significance to Burton; "Burton and Cardan," in *English Renaissance Studies Presented to Dame Helen Gardner* (Oxford: Clarendon Press, 1980), pp. 191–92.

self-portrait in the *Essays,* and a brief look at the evolution of Montaigne's *Essays* might illuminate Burton's use of the printed book.[6]

The method of the essays, as is well known, was fully established and articulated in the second edition. The *Essays* as we know it, that is, is the result of Montaigne's becoming a reader of his own book, which the industrial process of printed publication has distanced from him. Struck by the disparity between his past and his present views, he not only added new essays expressing his more current opinions; he also modified existing essays by appending passages that openly contradict the ideas he had already expressed. We are fortunate to know the process by which Montaigne made these changes. (Unfortunately, we have no comparable evidence of Burton's method of revision.) In his own copy of the *Essays,* Montaigne made numerous interpolations in the margins by hand. Rider describes how we may reconstruct the psychological aspect of this process, as follows. The printed volume represents a fixed and objectified self to which a living, continually active subjectivity responds with handwritten marginal notes closer to present, ongoing thought than the printed word could ever be. In other words, Montaigne's annotated page represents a dialectic between thoughts already thought and fixed in print, and thoughts as they arise in the act of thinking and written down by hand as they are conceived. Moreover, the second printed edition incorporates the handwriting into a new, updated objectified self, to which the author/reader can again respond in the same way.

Montaigne's *Essays,* then, suggests an alternative to Bacon's belief that the very nature of the book automatically endows it with the authority of closure, too often taken by critics as an inevitable consequence of print.[7] Like Burton's *Anatomy,* the *Essays* suggests that a book is not permanently fixed; a printed edition can be revised. In Montaigne's case, the process of revising makes print into a technology that can measure psychological change, even growth. Revision is the continuing process of bringing print into line with handwriting, of bringing the objectified self of the past into line with a living self of the present. To revise an essay is itself an essay in personal wholeness,

---

[6]Frederick Rider, *The Dialectic of Selfhood in Montaigne* (Stanford: University of Stanford Press, 1973), pp. 1–31.

[7]See, for example, Walter J. Ong, *Orality and Literacy: The Technologizing of the Word* (London: Methuen, 1982), pp. 132–35.

a way of healing psychological ruptures inevitably produced by the mind in motion in a process that can cease only at death. Response to oneself in print is both the record and instrument of the expansion of consciousness.

Although it is difficult to determine how much Burton knew of Montaigne's revisions, the *Anatomy* is one of the first major works after the *Essays* to exploit the same possibilities of a new communication technology for the development of self-awareness. But Montaigne and Burton differ in one significant way. Montaigne fully exploited the techniques of the skeptic's self-portrait only after his first edition; his inconsistencies are largely the result of revision. Burton's inconsistencies, however, are present in the very first edition of the *Anatomy*. Burton made no dramatic discovery of the possibilities of print while experiencing the process of print; the basic design of the *Anatomy* is established from the beginning.[8] Accordingly, whereas Montaigne's contradictions arising from passages added in subsequent editions reflect mental change over time, Burton's successive editions are only occasionally a record of change, let alone growth. His changes represent not a movement toward elusive wholeness but a continuing affirmation of initial discrepancies and even incoherence.

Burton, unlike Montaigne, left few traces of just how he went about adding to his work.[9] Through Democritus Junior he says a few words about his method, which do seem to be borne out by a comparison of "Democritus Junior to the Reader" in the six editions with which he himself was involved.[10] He apologizes for not having corrected "all those former escapes, yet it was *magni laboris opus*, . . . that as carpenters do find . . . 'tis much better build a new sometimes, than repair an old house; I could as soon write as much more as alter that which is written" (p. 33). And in fact Burton rarely deletes, rarely rewrites; he

[8]For the unchanging structure of the *Anatomy* through the six editions, see Fox, *Tangled Chain*, pp. 6–8; and Lawrence Babb, *Sanity in Bedlam: A Study of Robert Burton's Anatomy of Melancholy* (East Lansing: Michigan State University Press, 1959), pp. 13–29.

[9]For clues about Burton's use of notes and his reliance on memory, see J. B. Bamborough, "Robert Burton's Astrological Notebook," *Review of English Studies*, 32 n.s. (1981), 267–85; and David Renaker, "Robert Burton's Tricks of Memory," *PMLA*, 87 (1972), 391–96.

[10]The six editions were published in 1621, 1624, 1628, 1632, 1638, 1651. The last edition was posthumous and was based on Burton's notes, completed in 1640.

mostly adds. Yet his admission of laziness and his plea of lack of help do not confront the full implications of adding without altering. A hint, perhaps a real trace, of Burton's working method can be gleaned from a collation of select passages in the various versions of Democritus Junior.[11] With few exceptions, almost all the additions are so contrived that the initial phrasing is left in place, either by the simple insertion of words or phrases in existing sentences or by the manipulation of the syntax of added phrases, clauses, and sentences so that they slip right into already existing syntax, even if the result is rather awkward.[12] If this manner of revision held practical advantages for the printer, they are unclear, since the text had to be reset with each new edition anyway. At the very least, this procedure suggests Burton's claim to extemporaneity is disingenuous. Far from following the flow of speech or thought, his pen was circumscribed within the bounds of the already printed text and, if anything, had to follow the flow of the printed word. (How is one to evaluate Burton's claim made in 1628 and repeated in later editions: "But I am now resolved never to put this treatise out again; *Ne quid nimis* [not too much of anything],

---

[11]My conclusions are by no means based on a comprehensive collation of the entire text. I have only collated Democritus Junior's preface, "Love of Learning, or overmuch Study. With a Digression of the Misery of Scholars," and "Air Rectified. With a Digression of the Air." I am grateful to Nicholaus Kiessling and Martin Dodsworth for allowing me to use their computer collation of "Democritus Junior to the Reader."

[12]The following is an example of Burton's additions requiring no change of syntax; I emphasize only added passages. The passage appears in Jackson, I, 20–21. (All translations are Jackson's. Page numbers refer to pages in the original editions.)

1621: I write therefore as P. Aegineta confesseth of himselfe, not that any thing was vnknowen or omitted, but to exercize my selfe.   [p. 6]

1624: I writ therefore, *and busied my selfe in this playing labour, like them, saith Lucian, that recite to trees and declaime to pillers for want of Auditors:* as *Paulus* Aegineta confesseth of himselfe, not that any thing was vnknowne or omitted, but to exercize my selfe.   [p. 4]

1628: I writ therefore, and busied my selfe in this playing labour, *otiosaque diligentia ut vitarem torporem feriandi* [to escape the ennui of idleness by a leisurely kind of employment], *with Vectius in Macrobius, atque otium in vtile veterem negotium* [and so turn leisure to good account].
——*Simul & iucunda & idonea dicere vitae,*
Lectorem delectando simul atque monendo.
[At once to profit and delight mankind, and with the pleasing to have th'instructive joined.]
To this end I write, like them, saith Lucian, that recite to Trees and declaime to Pillers for want of Auditors: as Paulus Aegineta *ingeniously* confesseth ["of himself" deleted], not that any thing was vnknowne or omitted, but to exercize my-self."   [p. 5]

I will not hereafter add, alter, or retract" [p. 34]?) Nevertheless, the additions syntactically manipulated to leave the previous text unchanged do suggest that for Burton revision meant a response to a fixed text, a fixity writ large in type. Thus the precondition of any massive revision in Burton's work is the stability of the printed text, which exists in a state of tension with the extemporaneous impulses of speech and handwriting. (Though we have no evidence, it is tempting to conjecture that Burton made his additions by writing them into his own copy of the *Anatomy*.)[13]

If Burton's additions are thus a response to reading himself distanced in print, then they close the distance between authorial self and reading self to the extent that they repeat statements Burton has already made. This device, a startling departure from Montaigne's method, suggests continuity rather than change in successive editions. Some additions do represent a change of sorts, for example, the revision in which Burton suggests he can no longer claim to have been denied preferment and instead laments not gaining satisfactory preferment: "Preferment I could neuer get" in 1621 becomes in 1628, "Greater preferment as I could neuer get" (p. 18; 1621, p. 4; 1628, p. 3).[14] Some other changes, such as altering words like "the" to "that" seem gratuitous (if they are not printer's changes). Yet others include the occasional alteration of a reference to a citation, presumably for correction. But more often Burton simply provides new examples, new Latin tags, or translations of Latin tags.

Such apparently inconsequential changes, however, indicate the overall impact of the additions, namely, to reinforce what Burton has already said. Toward the end of the 1621 version of Democritus Junior, Burton writes, "I confesse I am as foolish, as mad as any one" (p. 120; 1621, p. 69). In 1624 he left the passage as is, but in 1628 he

---

[13]A copy of the *Anatomy* owned by Burton and deposited in the Bodleian Library shows none of the extensive marginalia Montaigne used for a revised edition.

[14]When comparing the text of the various editions, I quote from the original editions of 1621, 1624, 1628, 1632, 1638, and 1651. I use Jackson's translation of the Latin, unless otherwise noted. For additions reflecting Burton's fortune, and ill-fortune, with patrons, see O'Connell, *Robert Burton*, pp. 20–30. For additions that suggest changed intellectual outlook, see Richard G. Barlow, "Infinite Worlds: Robert Burton's Cosmic Voyage," *Journal of the History of Ideas*, 34 (1973), 291–302; for changes that reflect changed political circumstances, see David Renaker, "Robert Burton's Palinodes," *Studies in Philology*, 76 (1979), pp. 162–81.

added "againe": "I confesse it againe, I am as foolish, as mad as any one" (1628, p. 74). The added word may be understood as emphasizing the repeated confessions of earlier pages, and so Burton may be responding to reading them over once again, or he might be saying that he confesses again in 1628 as he did in 1624 and 1621. If so, rereading the *Anatomy* over three editions has led him to identify emotionally with the argument all over again.

Similarly, a few pages earlier, Burton excoriates the moral madness of dissimulation by typically heaping on phrases and examples for cumulative effect: "To see a man protest friendship, kisse his hand, smile with an intent to doe mischiefe, or cosen him whom hee salutes, magnify his friend vnworthy with hyperbolical elogiums, his enemy albeit a good man to vilifie & disgrace him with the vtmost liuor and malice can inuent" (p. 66; 1621, p. 34). In 1624 he augments this passage with two phrases. To the description of the man who protests friendship by kissing the hand he adds the phrase, *"quem mallet truncatum videre* [whom he would like to see decapitated]" (1624, p. 29); to the words "disgrace him" he adds "and all his actions" (1624, p. 29). Neither addition makes much of a difference; each simply repeats the initial rhetorical technique of adding on parallel details for emotional force. In 1628 Burton reaffirms his initial statement and its slightly expanded 1624 version by once again interpolating a seemingly gratuitous word: he adds "yea" to "all his actions" (1628, p. 36). The effect of this change parallels that of other small changes, among them the revision of one passage in which Burton expresses his fears of the reader's censure. In the 1621 version he laments, " 'Tis the common fate of all writers, and I must endure it" (p. 30; 1621, p. 10). In 1624 this statement becomes, " 'tis the common doone [*sic*] of all Writers, I must (I say) abide it" (1624, p. 9).

What does it mean to add such words as "yea" or "I say"? Like most of Burton's emendations, this kind of addition, it appears to me, intensifies an argument or a sentiment made years before and thus expresses solidarity with a past statement. Even adding a single word establishing direct address with his audience, such as the parenthetical "reader," or as late as 1651, *"o boni"* (p. 122; 1651, p. 78) has the effect of reaffirming an earlier argument. To interpolate what appears to be a gratuitous word or phrase is to participate in a past thought by recreating the conditions of the original statement—

simply by saying, some seven years later, "yea." The vast majority of the expansions of the *Anatomy* require the elaborate process of typographically resetting pages to include repeated assents to a thought already thought. We can never know what went on in Burton's mind when he was moved to reset a text in order to proclaim "I say," but the cumulative force of so many nonemending emendations is that of pressing the same argument, at almost any point in the text, repeatedly over the six editions, so that even so slight an alteration as changing "endure" to "abide," otherwise meaningless, signals Burton's reimmersion in the emotional flow of a thought and illustrates that process of responding to his own text which continued, though with diminished frequency, up to the notes for the 1651 posthumous edition.

In a few instances Burton's additions become a dialogue with himself and his work over typographic time. Directly after a quotation concerning the promise of canonization as a persuasion to fight in a war, Burton parenthetically comments in 1638, "(O diabolical invention)" (p. 61; 1638, p. 33), as if he had just read it for the first time. In his confession to madness quoted above, having added "againe" in 1628, he responds in 1632: *"demens de populo dematur* [let the madman be removed from society]" (p. 120; 1632, p. 76). Moreover, two sentences later, he responds (also in 1632) to this reaffirmed confession, "And though I be not so right or so discreet as I should be, yet not so mad, so bad neither as thou perhaps takest me to be" (p. 120; 1632, p. 76). "Yea" or "I say" is not insignificant when the flow of the mind can change direction on the reset page.

More in character with Burton's changes than the superimpositions of new denials or contradictions is the amplification of a passage in an argument that he has already rejected. In 1621, for example, he asks if the Stoics' claim to tranquility made them an exception to the universality of melancholy, and, following Chrysippus, he rejects Zeno's observation of their imperturbability and quickly answers no. In 1624, just before he dismisses Zeno, he interjects several lines that refer to Plutarch's description of the Stoics' freedom from perturbation, thus adding to the evidence of Stoic tranquility, even though he had rejected this evidence three years earlier and continues to do so now. The passage is further complicated by Plutarch's attitude toward the Stoics: scoffing at their serenity, he makes it that much more credible (p. 118). Burton does not simply add more evidence to dismiss; he in effect atomizes the text so that any portion of it is equally open to augmentation, regardless of its relative importance in the argument as a whole. In 1624 something in this segment of the chain of thought originally recorded in 1621 called forth a momentary reexperience of an idea Burton had introduced to reject in the first place. That the logical conclusion of Burton's argument was to make the addition irrelevant even before it was added does not seem to have mattered. Rereading himself, he becomes able to reidentify emotionally with even the losing side of an argument.

Perhaps the ultimate instance of this obsessive iteration occurs when Burton reassents to both an assertion and its retraction. Declaring his right to speak the truth even if it offends some, he insists in 1621:

> ... & Why may I not then ... speake my mind freely, If you denie me this liberty, vpon these presumptions I will take it; I say againe, I will take it.
> No, I recant, I will not, I confesse my fault and acknowledge a great offence. I have ouershot myselfe, I have spoken foolishly, rashly, vnaduisedly, absurdly, I have anatomized mine owne folly. [p. 122; 1621, p. 71]

In 1624 he added to both sides of this direct address. He continues his assertion that he dares to speak freely: "*Si quis est qui dictum in se inclementius / Existimavit esse, sic exist[i]met.* [If anyone thinks he has been insulted, let him think so.] If any man take exceptions, let him turne the buckle of his girdle, I care not. I owe thee nothing, I looke for no fauour at thine hands, I am independent, I feare not." And in the same year, he adds anew to his earlier recanting: "I care, I feare" (1624, p. 63). In 1624 he experiences the same flow of assertion and denial that he did in 1621.[15] And in later editions, the text acquires additional layers of both assertion and denial. In 1628 Burton in effect reaffirms his liberty of expression when he interpolates "(Reader)"

---

[15]Some lines earlier he contradicts his 1621 assertion that "I writt this" (p. 122; 1621, p. 71) by adding in 1624 that, in Jackson's translation of Burton's Greek, "No one has said it," and continuing, "'tis *neminis nihil* [nothing by nobody]" (1624, p. 63). That is, in addition to the synchronic contradiction of 1621, repeated in 1624, 1628, 1632, and 1651, he adds a rarer diachronic layer of contradiction.

into his assertion (1628, p. 76); but in 1632 he augments his recantation by adding a verse: *"motos praestat componere fluctus* [Let's first assuage the troubled waters]" (1632, p. 78). In 1651 he reaffirms the recantation by interpolating, simply, *"o boni"* in his apology (1651, p. 78). The iterative method, carried out through six editions, reflects what Burton said in the first edition. Situating his work in the context of the proliferation of books in the age of print, he imagines one of his detractors objecting that all he does is repeat "the same again and again in other words" (p. 22)—an objection with which he later agrees.[16] This statement in turn echoes his remarks on the general condition of knowledge in "this scribbling age" (p. 24); "we can say nothing but what hath been said" (p. 25), he observes, quoting Wecker who in turn quotes Terence, as if to prove his point.

Underlying this urge to repeat is a dynamic of fixity and change. Writing a book for print and reading books in print intersect in Burton's text. In 1632 Burton explains that he expands his book to reflect his continued reading (p. 34). For Burton the culture of books leads not closure but to openendedness. As Montaigne discovered in reading the first edition of his *Essays*, a fixed text opens the possibility of changing a fixed text.

Montaigne discovered, as did Burton, in a different way, that the revisable printed book is the ideal medium of the skeptic changing his mind over time; the distanced visible word is the ground of self-essaying. Unlike Bacon, Montaigne realized that the authority of print could easily be subverted; print could thus accommodate his philosophical metamorphosis from stoic to skeptic. He discovered, quite simply, the power of changing his mind in print, and far from objecting, his readers bought even more copies of the record of his inconsistencies. The non-authoritative revisable book, subject to re-writing even after publication, becomes a living thing. How much more did the multiple opportunities for revision in Burton's six editions undercut the authority of print as the location of "showing [him]self."

Fixity and change play off against each other in the two ways

[16]Though I use terms similar to the poststructuralist notion of iterability and repetition, I use them in a very different sense and context. For Derrida on iterability, see Jonathan Culler, *On Deconstruction: Theory and Criticism after Structuralism* (Ithaca: Cornell University Press, 1982), pp. 119–34.

Burton conceives of recording a thought—one that is proximate to the thought and one that is distanced from it. Burton refers to speech and (hand)writing as having an immediate presence to his mind, a presence reflected in his extemporaneous style. Apologizing for the artlessness of his work, he explains that because he had no assistants, he was forced "to publish [the *Anatomy*] as it was first written, *quicquid in buccam venit* [whatever came into my mouth], in an extemporean style, as I do commonly all other exercizes, *effudi quicquid dictavit genius meus* [I poured out whatever my mind spoke],[17] . . . and writ with as small deliberation as I do ordinarily speak, . . . *idem calamo quod in mente* [what my mind thinks my pen writes]" (p. 31).

Here Burton repeatedly stresses the proximity of speaking and writing to thought, and it is that proximity which authorizes his words of voice and pen. The printing press, in contrast, is a force that ineluctably undermines the integrity of personality. Burton contends that the ready outlet of ideas in print has led the ignorant to be "held polymaths and polyhistors." The worthless and the worthy alike have an "itching humour . . . to show [themselves], desirous of [undeserved] fame and honour." The accessibility of print to just about anyone has subverted the proper relationship between the learned and the unlearned: "they that are scarce auditors . . . must be masters and teachers, before they be capable and fit hearers." The lure of print thus encourages the violation of intellectual truth; and the pen itself, the very instrument of integrity of thought and expression, becomes the symbol of that violation: "to the disparagement of their health, and scarce able to hold a pen, they must say something" in order to burst into print. Burton confesses to be no better: "For my part I am one of the number, *nos numerus sumus*" (pp. 22–24). In a different context, he describes the distorting influence of print: he would have published the *Anatomy* in Latin, had he found an obliging printer (p. 30), and so he is forced to write in a language, English, not of his own choice. For obvious technological and commercial reasons the author cannot control print to the degree he can control his voice and pen. The constraints of print are apparent above all in Burton's method of interpolating new passages from one edition to another

---

[17]The translation of both these Latin tags is my own: Jackson's does not reflect the reference to speech.

while leaving the existing syntax stand, no matter how far it was removed from voice and pen at the moment of revision. Speech and writing must find their way into the fixed printed page even if in losing their extemporaneity they also lose their authenticity. The very process of revision is hostage to the fixity of print it is intended to correct.

Richard Regosin observes a similar interplay of speech and print in Montaigne, though Regosin tends to associate writing with print rather than with voice: "Montaigne appears to situate the work at that point where the spoken becomes the written word, as if to seize simultaneously the spontaneous genuineness of the voice and the spatial fixity of the printed page." Although the fixity of the written word violates the "genuineness of the voice," it is necessary for the enterprise of self-essaying: "The acquisition of knowledge . . . of the self depends on speaking through writing: 'Je parle au papier' [writes Montaigne]."[18] As we have seen, the balance between the authenticity of speech and writing and the fixity of print depends on the revisions that are allowed to contradict earlier statements. Speech and writing break into the printed page to remind us that print, separated as it is from the authenticity of speech and writing, lacks authority and is thus open to revision.

Burton's iterations suggest a different dynamic of fixity and change than do Montaigne's alterations. Perhaps his repetition is a way of maintaining continuity of self, even if that self is swept along by the current of mutability, a river that always changes but remains the same, as Democritus' contemporary Heraclitus put it. One key to the role of Burton's repetitions appears in a passage added to the *Anatomy* in 1628 where Burton decries the rush of so many into print: "*Ne feriarentur fortasse typographi, vel ideo scribendum est aliquid ut se vixisse testentur* [they have to write to keep the printers occupied, or even to show that they are alive]" (p. 23). In a sense, to iterate is to use print to show one is alive; a skeptic who accepts mutability can validate himself by keeping up a text parallel to his subjective life through a continuing repetition of the same set of psychological inconsistencies.

---

[18]Richard L. Regosin, *The Matter of My Book: Montaigne's "Essais" as the Book of the Self* (Berkeley: University of California Press, 1977), p. 216. For Burton's spoken voice, see Joan Webber, *The Eloquent "I": Style and Self in Seventeenth-Century Prose* (Madison: University of Wisconsin Press, 1968), pp. 80–114.

The text changes but remains the same. Augmenting the fixed but changeable printed page without changing it is the skeptic's way of maintaining coherence in a philosophy that denies coherence. Print is Burton's aid in a struggle to maintain continuity of consciousness by reacting to his own text, which itself calls into question the continuity of consciousness of a roving humor.

In this context of self-continuity Burton's reference to the story of Zisca's drum is emblematic of the relationship between the book and its writer's self. The reference comes from Montaigne's mention of John Vischa (Zisca), who "willed to be flayed after his death and to have a drum made of his skin to carry into war against his enemies; thinking that this would help continue the advantages he had obtained in the wars . . . against [Bohemia]." Montaigne uses Zisca as an example of the human desire "to extend the concern we have for ourselves beyond this life," in other words, to achieve a kind of immortality.[19] Burton, however, uses Zisca's drum as a figure of writing. In a 1632 addition describing Zisca, Burton concludes: "I doubt not but that these following lines [i.e., his book], when they shall be recited, or hereafter read, will drive away melancholy (though I be gone) as much as Zisca's drum could terrify his foes" (p. 38). After his death Burton will be as if transfigured into his physical book, as Zisca was into a drum. But the beating of the self/drum is a kind of metaphor for the continuing rhythms of periodic repetition to keep oneself extended over time even before one's end.

Burton's book, then, represents a departure from the humanist model of language authorized by speech. As we have seen, the humanist model maintains that the mind's perception of reality is, under the proper circumstances, guaranteed by the participation of the voice in a social or political community sanctioned by convention. Writing is merely the secondary imitation of speech; print makes that imitation more durable. Burton regards his book as authorized by its origins in speech, but, in skeptical fashion, he sees speech, like writing, as referring only to an inconstant mind. And if speech and writing are authentic because they can capture the mind in its fleeting moments, then the attempt to make speech and writing durable

---

[19]*The Complete Essays of Montaigne*, tr. Donald M. Frame (Stanford, Calif.: Stanford University Press, 1958), pp. 10–11.

cannot claim authority. The very authenticity of speech and writing makes it inevitable that, with the passage of time, their authority diminishes, as does the authority of print. Burton accommodates this paradox through repetition: iteration attempts to maintain durability of speech and writing while the necessity to sustain the iteration is an admission that speech and writing are ephemeral.

The paradox may in fact be the expression of a unique historical moment whose occurrence Michael O'Connell attributes to the humanists' cultivation of print and libraries. Burton, that is, writes at a historical juncture when thinkers and writers were poised between two conflicting consequences of print. On the one hand, print stimulated the desire for, and even created the possibility of, universal knowledge. On the other hand, print led to the proliferation of books and thus frustrated any attempt at universal knowledge.[20] In other words, despite the humanists' search for an enduring authority for speech, the technological means they exploited to disseminate speech—print—and its institutional arrangement—libraries—subverted the very authority they sought. Burton's *Anatomy* embodies this tension within humanism not only as a set of ideas but as a means of distributing those ideas. Burton certainly does not end the humanist claim for the authority of language in speech or the Baconian claim for writing, but out of a particular set of techno-cultural circumstances he helps to establish a minority position of some complexity that was to flourish into the next century.

[20]O'Connell, *Robert Burton*, pp. 39–43.

Index

Abecedarium naturae, 177–78
Abelard, Peter, 19–20, 33
Acrostic, 86
Adamic language, 59, 86, 159–62, 170
Aggripa ab Nettesheym, Henricius Cornelius, 140
Alphabet: design of, 117; orthography debate and, 44; symbolism in, 138–41. *See also* Hebrew alphabet; Hieroglyphs
Anagram, 152
Andrewes, Launcelot, 190
Anselm, 25
Anwykyll, John, 46–47, 54, 125*n*
Aquinas, Thomas, 16–19
Aristotle: Bacon and, 173–74, 200–201; *De interpretatione*, 11–12, 25, 30*n*, 57; inner discourse and, 73–74; logic of, 11–16, 37; natural language and, 60; *Opera*, 118, 119; Scholastic theories and, 9, 10; Scholastic vs. humanist approach to, 11–14, 40–41
Artificial language: Bacon and, 174, 186; Scholastic logicians and, 38
Asals, Heather, 158, 159
Ascham, Roger:
classical writing and, 52*n*
linguistic decline and, 92
monarch's influence on language and, 76, 78–81
printed book and, 111
style and, 122
thought, language, and action, 165
two-level view of language and, 65
works: *Report and Discourse . . . of the*

Affaires and State of Germany and the Emperour Charles, 78–81, 107, 110–11; *Schoolmaster*, 53–56, 80–81
Ashworth, E. J., 24
Aubrey, John, 82
Augustine: *De Trinitate*, 30, 71–74; *Explanatio Psalmorum*, 118, 120–21
Authority: of classical authors, 48–49, 50–51, 85; of convention, 14, 31–32, 74–75, 107–9; of custom, 35, 84, 107; of printed book, 209–12, 219; of speech, 35–69, 107, 223
Authorship: Bacon and, 183, 185, 187–89, 191, 192, 195–96, 203, 206, 207, 208; Donne and, 187; Herbert and, 162, 180–83; Jonson and, 6, 101–9, 180, 187, 188

Babel: Herbert and, 159–62, 163–64; study of language and, 59*n*, 160–61
Bacon, Francis:
artificial language and, 7, 174, 186
authority of writing and, 209–10
authorship and, 183, 185, 187–89, 191, 192, 195–96, 203, 206, 207, 208
and the court, 184–85, 188–92, 193–95, 196–97, 203, 206–8
execution of Earl of Essex and, 184–85
Hebraism and, 169, 175
hieroglyphic writing and, 168–80, 183
humanist attitudes and, 10, 56, 69, 107–8

225

Bacon, Francis (*cont.*)
  manuscript circulation and, 186–87,
    191–92, 195, 196
  posterity as theme for, 185–86, 195,
    197
  printing and, 183, 186–87, 195–98,
    203
  on publication, 201–2
  scientific writing and, 185–90, 191,
    203–4, 205–6, 209–10
  sociology of knowledge and, 186,
    197–203
  works: *The Advancement of Learning*,
    168, 170, 188, 196–98, 201, 203–
    4, 207; *Apologie Concerning Essex*,
    184, 185, 192, 196; *De Augmentis
    VI, i*, 168, 171, 172–73, 176, 177;
    Essays, 192–93; *Magna Instauratio*,
    185, 188–89, 190, 204–6, 208; *The
    Masculine Birth of Time*, 198–203;
    The New Atlantis, 201; *Novum
    Organon*, 170–71, 172, 188, 189,
    195, 198, 208, 209; *On the Inter-
    pretation of Nature: Proem*, 203; *Re-
    futation of Philosophies*, 198–203;
    Temporis Partus Maximus, 195;
    Thoughts and Conclusions, 198–203,
    205; *Valerius Terminus*, 170, 198–
    203; *The Wisdom of the Ancients*,
    169–70, 174
Bacon, Roger, 26–27
Baldwin, T. W., 41
Berthelet, Thomas, 128*n*
Bible: Protestant translation of, 135; ty-
  pography of, 130–31; as written text,
  132–37. See also Gutenberg Bible
Billingsley, Martin, 121
Boethius of Dacia, 26
Brathwait, Richard, *The English Gentle-
  man*, 68
Brinsley, John, 63*n*, 128, 137; *Ludus
  Literarius*, 62–63, 122–25
Bühler, C. F., 125
Bullokar, William, 154
Burghley, Lord. See Cecil, William
Bursill-Hall, G. L., 27
Burton, Robert [pseud. Democritus
  Junior]: additions to *Anatomy of Mel-
  ancholy*, 213–19; Montaigne and,
  211–13, 219, 221; printed book and,
  7, 211–12; repetition in *Anatomy of
  Melancholy*, 217–19, 221–23; skepti-
  cism of, 7, 69, 109, 210–12, 221;
  speech and writing vs. print, 220–23
Butler, Charles, *English Grammar*, 44

Cabalism, 132, 136–37, 139*n*, 142
Calligraphy, 117, 128, 130
Camden, William, 84–86; *Remaines
  Concerning Britaine*, 116
Carew, Richard, 116, 122, 152
Caritas, 73–74
Casamassima, Emanuele, 138
Causae, of language, 25–26, 64
Causa inventionis, theory of, 23–24
Cave, Terence, 3
Cecil, William (Lord Burghley), 190,
  192, 194, 196, 206
Chaytor, Henry John, 115, 131
Chomsky, Noam, 9*n*
Cicero, 9, 48, 50, 54, 55, 57, 67
Ciphers, 177
Clanchy, M. T., 115–16, 131, 137
Classical authors: authority of, 48–49,
  50–51; Latin speech and, 52
Classical values, and Jonson, 86–87, 89,
  92–94, 95, 97–100, 102
Clausing, 128
Clement, Francis, 121; *Petie Schole with
  an English Orthographie*, 60
Codex, 134–35, 137
Cohen, Murray, 4, 5
Colet, John, *Aeditio*, 42–43, 47–48, 49,
  61, 128*n*. See also *Shorte Introduction
  of Grammar* (Lily's *Grammar*)
Colish, Marcia, 167
Consensus, 88–100, 101, 107
Consent, 75
Convention: as authority for language,
  14, 31–32, 74–75, 107–9; reality
  and, 21–24. See also Consensus;
  Custom
Copernicus, 186
Court: Bacon and, 184–85, 188–92,
  193–95, 196–97, 203, 206–8; hu-
  manist language program and, 81*n*–
  82*n*; Jonson and, 86–92, 93, 96,
  106–7. See also Monarch
Creation, hieroglyphic concept of, 143–
  44, 175
Croll, Morris, 56*n*
Culture, 5, 38, 51, 114. See also Conven-
  tion; Custom
Custom: as authority for language, 35,
  84, 107; English spelling and, 44–46;
  Jonson and, 84, 100, 101, 107; language norms and, 74–75, 91–92

Deconstruction, 1–3
Democritus, 200, 201

Library of Congress Cataloging-in-Publication Data

Elsky, Martin.
  Authorizing words : speech, writing, and print in the English
Renaissance/Martin Elsky.
    p. cm.
  Includes index.
  ISBN 0–8014–2173–X (alk. paper)
    1. English language—Early modern, 1500–1700—History. 2. Languages—
Philosophy—History—17th century. 3. English literature—Early modern, 1500–
1700—History and criticism. 4. Written communication—England—History—
17th century. 5. Oral communication—England—History—17th century.
6. England—Intellectual life—17th century. 7. Printing—England—History—
17th century. 8. Humanists—England. 9. Renaissance. I. Title
PE1081.E45 1989
420'.9'031—dc20   89–42875